Access Your Brain's Joy Center

OTHER BOOKS BY PETE A. SANDERS JR.

The Dynamics of Being a Free Soul
(Textbook and Cassettes)

Scientific Vortex Information

You Are Psychic!

Access Your Brain's Joy Center

The Free Soul Method

Pete A. Sanders Jr.

An M.I.T. - Trained Scientist's Mind/Body Discovery for Greater Success and Happiness

Free Soul • Sedona, Arizona

Free Soul
P.O. Box 1762
Sedona, AZ 86339

ISBN 0-9641911-2-1

Cover Art and interior Illustrations by Katie Bechtel, Phoenix, AZ (except Figs. 8 & 9 by Moises Ramirez, Sedona, AZ)

20 19 18 17 16 15 14 13 12 11

10 9 8 7 6 5 4 3 2 1

Printed in the United States
by Mission Possible Printing, Sedona, Arizona

Dedicated to Humanity's Right to Full Freedom:

freedom to create your own happiness,

freedom from the pain of emotional distress,

freedom from chemical dependency and overeating.

• Acknowledgments •

First and foremost to all the Free Soul instructors and students who contributed to the work with their stories and/or involvement in the research and development of this new method of mood-elevation.

To my wife, Debbie, and my sons, Brain and Michael, for their forbearance, as I went through both the life crisises which led to this discovery and the subsequent stresses of getting it to the public. Those trials helped me refine and improve the techniques contained in the book, but not without some turmoil. The pressures of pioneering a new field gave me an abundance of opportunities to transform difficulties, from problems into research material, for advanced versions of the Joy Touch. During those refinements, life was not always as harmonious as I would have liked. Once, early on, I took Michael (then eight) to a newspaper interview with me. When I told the reporter that I used the Joy Touch to lessen my irritability and anger when the kids got into mischief, he asked, "Michael, is that true?" Michael responded, "Yep, but he needs to do it more." It humorously reminded me of my humanity and ongoing personal growth.

On a more serious note, this edition of the book would not have been possible without the editing assistance of Joyce McNelly and Wray Plunkett. Their help has been invaluable in polishing my thoughts and lecture material into written form.

Thanks also to Katie Bechtel of Phoenix, Arizona for her inspired work on the cover art and her professionalism with the interior illustrations, all accomplished in addition to her being a full-time teacher and mother of three. Special thanks to Moises Ramirez of Sedona, Arizona for his assistance with two last minute illustration requirements (Figs. 8 & 9).

My gratitude to O'Ryin Swanson, of Mission Possible Printing, for making what often seemed the impossible happen on time in meeting the publishing deadlines and quality needs of this book.

Many thanks to my mother, Aurora for raising me to believe both in myself and that, with hard work, anything can be achieved. Those cornerstones were essential for not giving up. Countless times it would have been easier to listen to those who didn't believe in the work and quit.

Finally, my appreciation to you, the reader, for wanting a better way of life. Serving your interest, need, and desire have been the primary motivation for my getting this book out. Together, we can make a difference in humanity's quality of life.

• Contents •

Preface - Inner Technology: Key to Greater Success and
Happiness in the 21st Century 1
The Millennium of the Mind..1
Rise Above the Dinosaur Brain..2
The Drugging of America 4
A Revolutionary Discovery 6
Slipping the Shackles of Your Struggle Reflexes 7
Become a Pioneer of the Mental Frontier 9

Chapter 1 - The Joy Touch: How to Trigger the Brain's Natural
Mood-Elevation Mechanisms 11
The Septum Pellucidum Area 12
Locating Your Brain's Joy Center 14
Triggering the Body's Natural High 20
Command and Control of Your State of Mind............................23
Additional Options For a Stronger Initial Effect........................26

Chapter 2 - Breakthroughs for Defeating Limbic Stress
and Depression..35
The Tyrannosuarus of Stress: Limbic Stress...............................36
Black Hole of the Brain: Destructive Cycle of Limbic Stress 38
How to Rapidly Clear Emotional Turmoil...................................40
Keys for Self-Healing Inner Hurt and Secret Pain......................46
    Dealing with Rejection...46
    The Pain of Betrayal...48
    The Emptiness of Loss & Loneliness...................................51
    Loss of Job or Opportunity..54
The Shadow of Secret Pain 57
Defusing Your Inner Explosives..59
    Anger at Not Feeling Heard...61
    Anger at Feeling Helpless and/or Unfairly Controlled............65
    Anger at Not Being Valued..66
    Irritation Anger..67
    Anger at Getting Angry...67

How to Silence Your "Worry Machine"..69
   Getting It Right...71
   The Burden of Responsibility..73
   Security Issues (Worries about Job, Health, and Money) 75
   Worry about Family 76
Skills for Dealing with Fears..78
   Fear of the Unknown...78
   Fear of Being Helpless or Being All Alone............................79
   For Phobias, Panic Attacks, and Obsessive Compulsive........81
Keys For Defeating Mild Depression 82
Skills For Countering Prolonged Depressiveness.......................84
   Using the Joy Touch in Motion...85
   Joy Touch from Above and Other Alternate Directions........88
   Specifically Countering Negative Thoughts........................90
   Recharging Your Brain Chemistry 93
Preventive Maintenance and Self-Nurturing..............................95

Chapter 3 - Enhancing the Love in Your Life..............................97
Neutralizing the Acid of Put-Downs..98
Not Feeling Fully Loved...101
Seize the Put-Upable Moment 104
Easing the Irritation that Undermines Love 105
Self-Solving Relationship Issues with the Medicine Wheel 109
Having More Enjoyable Time Together 112
Joy Touch For Enhanced Sexual Experience............................113
Tapping the Soul For Greater Oneness.....................................115
The Search For the Location of the Soul 116
Making the Soul-shift..117
Being a Soul: Key to Universal Love 120
Blending with the Universe...123
Other Keys for Spiritually Enhancing the Love in Life...............125
   Blending with the Love Dimension...................................125
   Doing the Joy Touch from Above.....................................126
   Seeing the Soul in Others 128

Chapter 4 - Success without the Achievement Addiction............131
The Biology of the Achievement Addiction 131
Your Periodicity of Perceived Success 133
Value Analysis...135

The Trap of Desire 136
Dealing with Financial Pressure / Success Issues 140
Wants Versus Needs 141
Creating Happiness While You Work..142
Working Three Jobs, Getting Paid For Only One........................144
Play at It, Don't Work at It 147
Feeling Behind 150
You Are Unique..154

Chapter 5 - Weight Control: Five Steps For In-Joying
Your Diet 156
Feel Good About What You Eat..156
Wait Control..159
Care about Your Diet, Not Worry about What You Eat 161
Value Yourself, Not Your Size 163
You Control Your Weight, Don't Let It Control You 165

Chapter 6 - Joy Touch Keys For Reducing - Pain, Smoking,
Alcohol Consumption, and Substance Abuse 168
Pain Control 168
    Headaches...168
    Migraines and Throbbing Pain 169
    Dental Discomfort 170
    Joy Touch Before, After, and During Surgery [and PMS].......171
    Back Pain..172
    Severe and Chronic Pain 172
    Mind over Matter...174
Keys For Reducing Smoking 174
    Specifics For Joy Touch Substitution....................................174
    Learning Your Triggers...175
    Incorporating Nicotine Gum or Patches 177
Joy Touch Specifics For Reducing Alcohol Consumption 178
    You Are the Key...178
    Not Just Cold Turkey or Wild Turkey...................................179
    Strategies For Reduction and Relapse Prevention...................180
    Let the Joy Touch Assist Other Professional Options 181
Dealing with Drug Abuse and Other Chemical Addictions........182
    Joy Touch Keys to Add to Professional Help.........................183
    Soul Over Substance 184

Chapter 7 - Honestly and Nobly Bearing Life's Difficulties 185

Chapter 8 - Quick Reference Guides 189

Septal Area Location and Self-Touch Triangulation 190
Ways to Trigger and Types of Sensation 191
Joy Touch from Alternate Directions...192
Joy Touch For Enhanced Intimacy 193

Limbic Stress Definition & the Two Questions for Clearing.......194
Comforting Connections For Hurts...195
Comforting Connections For Angers...196
Comforting Connections For Worries..197
Comforting Connections For Fears..198
Keys For Clearing Secret Pain 199

Four Steps of the Peaks and Valleys Concept...............................200

Lifeskills and Countering Put-Downs...201

Approaches For Countering Depression 202

Gender Strengths for Solving Relationship Issues........................203

Basics of the Soul-Shift...204
Soul-Blending Options...205

Secrets For Feeling Successful All the Time 206

Five Simple Steps For Weight Control 207

Joy Touch Variations For Pain Control 208
Joy Touch Specifics For Reducing Smoking.................................209
Joy Touch Keys Lessening Alcohol Consumption 210
Joy Touch Assistance For Drug Abuse..211

Keys For Nobly Bearing Life's Difficulties..................................212

How to Reach Free Soul 213
Additional Free Soul Training Options..214

• Preface •

"Inner Technology"
Key to Greater Success and
Happiness in the 21st Century

Imagine being able to feel better whenever you want. Imagine being able to control physical and mental/emotional pain. Think how your life would be different if you were unperturbed by hassles and always felt happy and in command of your destiny. These abilities can be yours. All you have to do is learn to self-trigger your brain's natural mood-elevation mechanisms. This frontier is the herald of the 21st century and its promise belongs to you. This book will give you the keys to live that future potential today!

The Millennium of the Mind

I frequently ask business people, "What is your most important piece of equipment?" Some say it's their FAX or phone system. Some are positive it's their computer or their copy machine. Then I ask, "How many of you would be satisfied with your most vital equipment working at only ten to forty percent of its potential?" That is the percentage of our brain power that scientists estimate we currently use.

Do you want to settle for only ten to forty percent of your ability to love? Are you willing to accept life with only ten to forty percent of your potential for happiness? Regardless of your sex, age, or occupation, the mind is the most important item you use every day. It is time to tap more than a fraction of it. No wonder life is a struggle. What isn't, when you cut your abilities and options by more than half? The future of humanity is to break free from the muck of suffering and struggle, to soar to new horizons of joy and fulfillment. Learning to tap the full power of your brain is the gateway to that freedom.

In the eighties, Dr. Howard Gardner's *Frames of Mind* revolutionized the brain science and education communities with his theory of multiple intelligences. Closely following was research that showed that the brain can continue to make new neurosynaptic connections throughout your life. The implication was that at any age you can boost your learning potential and IQ. Recently, Daniel Goleman, Ph.D. through his book, *Emotional Intelligence*, has made the public aware of the importance of EQ as much as IQ, for success and happiness in life. The foremost pioneer of the field of emotional intelligence, Dr. Goleman points out that EQ too can be learned, that you can increase yours and your children's with focused effort.

What if in one step you could boost both your mental and emotional abilities. Imagine the power of a physiological discovery that allows your rational mind to consciously increase your emotional well-being in seconds. Think of the quantum leap that could bring to your life. The frontier of mind research is not what we can learn *about* the brain, but rather what you can do with yours.

The PBS series, *The Brain*, states that there are more possible pathways in the brain than there are atoms in the entire known universe. The enhanced joy and improved performance possible with such an unlimited network, is incalculable! The key is learning to access the marvel of inner technology that you already are.

For centuries science has given us primarily *outer* technology, improved machinery and new energy sources. This industrial revolution has provided greater control of our environment and dramatically increased our leisure time, but at a cost to our mental well-being. Science and technology have created a culture shock that pressures everyone. The result has actually been a decrease in our quality of life. We don't feel like we have more leisure time, because it takes twice as long to unwind from our increased stresses. All to often, to relax we need that extra drink or cigarette, or to vegetate in front of a television. Even then, many people still experience disrupted sleep from the turmoil of life's pressures. We have mastered controlling our outer environment at the expense of our inner harmony and happiness. That loss not only robs you of joy, it decreases your ability to function at your full potential.

It is time to make struggle and unhappiness extinct. They are relics from your evolutionary past. Your future is to use Inner Technology to replace them with joy and contentment. Feelings of helplessness are the result of your dinosaur brain. Your birthright is to rise above them.

Rise Above the Dinosaur Brain

Until recently researchers described the brain's parts and functions more by physical location (i.e., forebrain, midbrain, and hindbrain). Lately, led by neuroscientist Paul MacLean, Ph.D., of the

National Institute of Health, science has begun a new view of the brain based on its three stages of evolution.

This "triune brain" concept is radically different. It describes what most people think of as *the brain* (the outer cerebral cortex) as just its most recent evolutionary addition. This neomammalian brain (the cortex) has been added atop two previously existing brain structures. Those "lower" brains are the limbic system (the old mammalian brain, found in almost the same form in all mammals) and the brain stem (also called the reptilian brain, found in all vertebrates from reptiles to man).

These lower evolutionary portions of the brain comprise what could be called our "dinosaur brain." Their functions date back to humanity's early struggles for *physical* survival. Together they can suck the joy out of life. This is particularly true of the limbic system, described by Dr. MacLean as having the raw stuff of negative emotion built into its circuitry. By perpetuating feelings of worry, anger, hurt, and fear, the limbic brain can keep you in misery.

In ages past, the limbic system was crucial for staying alive. It was far better to worry about being eaten by a saber-tooth tiger, than to be its lunch. It was preferable to obsessively remember the hurt a tribe over the hill did to you, than to forget, and be killed by them the next time. Most of those survival pressures from our evolutionary past are now extinct, but the limbic system remains basically the same. This disparity may be the primary reason that our enjoyment of life has not advanced as rapidly as has our technology. Our science has made quantum leaps, but our physiology has barely crawled a few steps out of the cave. An out of control limbic system still has the power to make us feel like a threatened species.

Alcohol and drugs mask or suppress the distress that can be caused by the limbic brain, but with harmful side effects. Overeating and food bingeing creates a full sensation that also dulls limbic pain. This too, however, has side effects (like on the hips and thighs).

It may seem bad news that there is a part of the brain specifically designed to create the negative emotions and unhappiness. The good news is that these repetitive cycles of worry, hurt, anger, or fear are not your fault. They are the undesirable byproducts of your limbic brain and can be eliminated. The management and integration of intense emotions is a large part of the EQ abilities identified by Dr. Goleman. You can learn to corral out-of-control limbic reactions.

Even better, there are specific parts of your higher brain that can aid in the process. This book will show you how to access and control those areas. It is your key to naturally creating inner peace and happiness without alcohol, nicotine, drugs, or overeating.

The Drugging of America

For too long our society has been manipulated into the ravages of substance abuse, as the answer to life's stresses. It's not just the pushers and cocaine cartels that are to blame. The alcohol, tobacco, and pharmaceutical companies have for decades been getting rich off the miseries of society. They would deserve every dollar of profit if their products provided safe relief. But they don't. Alcohol, nicotine, Prozac, and lithium etc. are all drugs. Ultimately drugs hurt more than they help, and not just because they are addictive. A 1995 University of Manitoba study found that even normal dosages of common medications (such as pain killers, antihistamines, and antidepressants) caused more rapid growth rates of tumors in animals.

America is being drugged to death. In 1994, the *Journal of the American Medical Association* stated that the number one causal factor of senior citizen admissions to hospitals is alcoholism or alcohol related effects. Despite the wonderful efforts of MADD, every year drunk drivers still kill thousands of innocent pedestrians and drivers. Recent studies indicate that one in ten Americans may suffer from alcohol abuse. Although men are smoking less, cigarette use among teenagers and women is on the rise. It is estimated that close to half a million people die annually from the hazards and complications of smoking. While rampant cocaine use may be slowly declining, heroin abuse is rapidly making a comeback. According to the Department of Health and Human Services, drug use among teenagers has doubled in the last five years. If these numbers and trends were related to AIDS or some other disease, it would be considered intolerable.

How is the medical establishment responding? Their answer seems to be more drugs, just new ones masquerading as medicines. Prozac has become the Valium of the nineties. Each month close to a million prescriptions for Prozac are written in the United States alone (in most cases by non-mental-health physicians). Billions are being spent by the public on pills that take two weeks to two months to work, are effective for only 75% of patients at best, and that can have a wide range of side effects (from irritability and insomnia to sexual dysfunction for both men and women).

In our search for greater happiness, food has also been abused. Overeating and other eating disorders are becoming chronic. Americans spend billions on diet plans and products that have been scientifically shown to be useless, and sometimes even harmful, in the long run.

Taken individually every current option is personally and financially ruinous. The sum total is insane. *The price is just too high.* So why does our society continue to pay it? There are several reasons.

First, we *do* need relief from life's stresses. Everyone, regardless of race, gender, economic status or age, wants to feel better. That desire is so strong that we will use whatever helps to ease the pressures and tensions. The sex drive is frequently thought to be one of our most powerful urges. The need to feel better is even stronger. Each day, far more people smoke, drink, take drugs, or overeat than have sex. The need for relief and greater happiness is universal and unrelenting.

Second, alcohol, nicotine and drugs are addictive, both physically and psychologically. The cravings created by chemical dependency are hard to ignore. They are the biological equivalent of a ringing phone that demands to be answered. Equally potent is the compulsion created by psychological addiction. The mind subconsciously associates relief with not only the substance, but also with the rituals of the habit pattern.

Added to all this is brainwashing. Tens of billions of dollars are spent annually on advertising by alcohol, tobacco, and pharmaceutical companies. Infinitely more dollars have been spent on advertising market research than on the search for a natural alternative. More is known about how to best motivate people to buy pills, beer, and cigarettes than about the *physiology* of happiness. This alone has prolonged society's substance abuse. Take, as an example, the 47 billion dollars spent each year by the public on tobacco products, despite decades of health advisories.

The paramount reason for the drugging of America, however, is that there hasn't been a natural alternative that is quick, simple, and effective. Now, at last, there is! A new form of biofeedback I call *"Inner Technology"*® shows you how to self-trigger the brain's natural mood-elevation mechanisms. Chief among its discoveries is a way to stimulate the part of the brain that clears the emotional distress generated by the limbic system, and also triggers a feeling of well-being. That magical area is the septum pellucidum. It can figuratively become your brain's "Joy Center." Chapter 1 teaches methods for mentally activating the septum pellucidum area. I call the process the "Joy Touch" technique. Chapters 3 and 4 give you specific variations of the technique for enhancing the love in your life and having success without the achievement addiction. Chapter 5 has keys for using the Joy Touch to assist with weight control. Chapter 6 contains the specific adaptations of the technique for reducing pain, smoking, alcohol abuse, and substance dependence.

A Revolutionary Discovery

Why hasn't this discovery been made sooner? Why haven't the medical and scientific communities more vigorously explored how to mentally trigger the brain's mood-elevation mechanisms? One doctor listening to me speak in Denver responded, "That's simple. There's no money in it. If you teach this to people, they don't have to keep buying your pill or product." It's sad but true. That lack of profitability alone has probably dissuaded many scientists and commercial laboratories from pursuing research in this area.

Why have researchers not motivated by profit alone also missed this discovery? Two reasons: First, most brain scientists traditionally have been educated only to use chemicals and electrode stimulation to effect brain function. Most have no experience with biofeedback or mind/body techniques. Further, electrical voltages and drug dosages are much more measurable and analytically satisfying than the vagueness of asking, "What did you feel?" Second, even if there had been earlier efforts at mind/body mood elevation, researchers may have failed by attempting to stimulate the wrong area.

The hypothalamus is generally thought to contain the brain's most powerful mood-elevation or pleasure centers. Unfortunately, however, it is located very close to many of the limbic brain structures responsible for negative emotional effects (anger, rage, and irritability or anxiety). Consequently, any earlier attempts to trigger mood elevation by mentally stimulating the hypothalamus may have yielded null results (negative emotions canceling positive sensations) or possibly even adverse reactions.

A 1995 pilot study I conducted jointly with psychology professor Larry Stevens, Ph.D. of Northern Arizona University, showed just that. Not only did all of the study's trends show the benefits of mentally stimulating the septum pellucidum area , it also documented the negative effects when focus areas were too close to the limbic system.

Although the brain's mood-elevation mechanisms and centers may be diverse and complex, the key to successful biofeedback is simplicity. An easy and specific way to focus is essential. It must also produce clear and palpable results. The septum pellucidum is the solution to both those requirements. For the layman its location is easier to describe than the hypothalamus. Further, it lies above and away from the limbic mine field, but has direct neurosynaptic connections to the area in the hypothalamus that opium affects. Knowing how to trigger the septal area gives you the ability to stimulate a mood-elevation portion of the hypothalamus without also setting off the negative-emotion centers of the rest of the limbic brain..

Imagine being able to elevate your mood in seconds *without* alcohol, nicotine, drugs, or overeating. Imagine being able to create happiness without *dependency* on constant success in achievements or relationships. Knowing how to trigger the septum pellucidum will give you these abilities. Further, triggering the septal area can temporarily halt the emotional distress of worries, hurts, angers, or fears.

It is a direct physiological relief mechanism you can self-initiate. You are no longer limited to psychological platitudes to soothe yourself (try to calm down, look for the silver lining, try to think of positive thoughts, etc.). You have something specific and biological that you can *do*. Even better, it doesn't take hours of meditation, addictive chemicals, or changing your faith. It is quick, natural, and best of all, it's free. Once you learn the technique, it costs you nothing for the rest of your life. It is the first half of gaining freedom from domination by your dinosaur brain.

Think of the life changes that will be yours from this one skill alone. No longer need you be an adrenalin yo-yo. Instead of being held prisoner by the fight or flight reflex and depression, you will know how to activate your brain's natural mood-elevation mechanisms at will. Rather than reacting to life with tension and anxiety, you will know how to give yourself a mellow energizer, whenever you need it.

Slipping the Shackles of Your Struggle Reflexes

For too long we have been living in the grip of our evolutionary past. Without specific countermeasures, *perceived* survival struggles can still dominate our everyday lives. Even when you do not have physical survival issues (adequate food, shelter, etc.), it is still easy to slip into the struggle reflexes created by emotional pressures. Concerns about achievements and relationships can also trigger your limbic brain into a repetitive loop of negative emotions.

These limbic negative emotions are intensely destructive. Like a broken record, they keep repeating over and over. When events trigger your limbic brain to short-circuit, you can feel stuck in a cycle of emotional anxiety that overrides your higher mental functions. That override is what I call *limbic stress*. It is another way of succumbing to your dinosaur brain. Not only are you pulled out of your higher mind's reasoning and problem-solving abilities, limbic stress also robs you of the positive emotions of love and joy. You are sucked into the struggle reflexes of your animal past. You can even feel cut off from the higher power of your faith.

I specifically prefer the term limbic stress rather than emotional stress, because the latter might imply that all emotions are bad. That would be a gross misrepresentation. Life without emotion would be bland and passionless. Also, for too long many men have disparaged women for being "too emotional." I do not want my strong statements about the hazards of limbic stress to be mistakenly viewed as just another male put down of women. Emotion is the spice that gives life flavor. Without it we would be surviving, but on gruel. Out-of-control negative emotional cycles, however, are slavery to our evolutionary past. Our destiny in the 21st Century is to counter them with the brain centers designed to provide relief.

To be fully happy and free, you must know how to clear limbic brain dysfunction more than just temporarily. You must be able to break free from the black-hole grip of negative emotions that lead to long-term foul moods and depression. Chapter 2 shows you how. You will learn a clear and simple approach that works in minutes for clearing the source of your limbic stresses. Instead of needing something, or someone, to make you feel good again, you will know how to shut off the cause of repetitive limbic brain irritations. This "Comforting Connection" method is adaptable to *all* circumstances, even those you have yet to experience.

Imagine being able to instantly ease the pain of rejections and hurts. Think how your life would be more peaceful if you could defuse frustrations and angers quickly. How much happier would you be if you could reduce the repetitive cycles of worry and fear? These are the skills that Chapter 2 will give you.

In a brain science course at Massachusetts Institute of Technology, I had the opportunity to take part in a fascinating experiment dealing with taste buds. We were given tablets that when chewed, blocked the sensation of sour taste. I was amazed as I savored lemons and other naturally sour foods without the least bit of discomfort. With the sour taste buds blocked, I was able to experience the sweetness that also existed in the lemon. I could more fully appreciate many foods I would normally have avoided.

The skills you will learn from this book provide an analogous effect on your quality of life. You will be able to focus on life's joys and pleasures, rather than be controlled by its sour notes. You will be able to savor the sweetness of emotion, not be stuck in the bitter prison of being *passion's slave*.

The rigors of living will always present you with challenges. Additional keys for handling that reality are contained in Chapter 7.

They, and knowing the Joy Touch and the Comforting Connection, can prevent pressures from dominating and controlling your happiness. You will be less vulnerable to the bumps and bruises of life's turmoils. You will be able to rise above mere survival to create joyous living.

I still have a mortgage, the complexities of running a national organization, and the challenges presented by my two sons (who frequently seem like composites of Tom Sawyer, Huck Finn, and Dennis the Menace). What I no longer have is the feeling of being a helpless victim struggling with problems. Knowing how to control the brain's natural mood-elevation mechanisms and clear limbic stress has given me the freedom to savor the beauty of life. That gift can be yours as well. With the Quick Reference Guides contained in Chapter 8 you can rapidly find and utilize the key Comforting Connections or Joy Touch variations that your life may require.

Learning to tap the unlimited powers of your mind and spirit is your most valuable resource. Even after years of microcircuitry and superconductor technology, no computer on Earth can approach the human mind. No machine can feel love or joy. Each day you handle millions of new situations, interactions, and problems. Think how your life can be improved once you have an owner's manual giving you full control of this, your ultimate personal computer. Advances in mind power are the cornerstones of a fast-approaching new era.

Become a Pioneer of the Mental Frontier

There are three great frontiers in our world today: space, the oceans, and inner human potential. We can't all be an astronaut or a Jacques Cousteau. But each of you can be a pioneer expanding the boundaries of the human potential. Your desire to learn is the only qualification you need to begin your exploration.

My own personal explorations started with the physiological psychology and brain science courses I took at Massachusetts Institute of Technology. They opened the door for me to look within. The more I learned about the brain and nervous system, the more I realized how much was still unknown. One of my professors, Dr. Jerome Letvin, summed it up best when, after describing the myriad branches and connections of each nerve cell, he said, "The wiring exists within the brain for each nerve cell to talk with any other nerve cell." In my own mind I added, "and with that type of unlimitedness, anything must be possible *once you learn how!*"

After graduating with honors from M.I.T., I was accepted to Harvard Medical School. I chose, however, not to pursue a career in orthodox medicine. I wanted to develop methods that all people could use to enhance their inner abilities and happiness. I loved medicine, but being just one more caring physician was not enough. I felt I could accomplish more for humanity by teaching responsibly in the human potentials field.

In my twenties I pioneered breakthroughs for instant stress reduction, effective mind/body self-healing, and practical understandings of psychic sensitivity. In my thirties and early forties I experienced the adventures of raising a family and going through a mid-life crisis. This turned my attention to brain science keys for easing the pressures of emotional and family issues.

People interested in exploring such issues are often presented with only two options: either becoming a devotee of some guru or cult, or paying outrageous fees for seminars that are frequently long on hype and short on substance. Both have always seemed wrong to me. I feel the public deserves better. Scientifically based training in your higher mental potentials should be reasonably priced and available to everyone. Further, it should not require the sacrifice of your independence or your existing faith.

Toward that end in 1980 I founded Free Soul, a mind/body education program, in Sedona, Arizona and began training others in the scientific secrets and techniques I had developed. Free Soul now has hundreds of instructors and its *Discover "Inner Technology"*® and *Accessing Your Brain's Joy Center* workshops are helping people and businesses worldwide to live their unlimited potentials. For more information about them and other training options, write to Free Soul, P.O. Box 1762, Sedona, AZ 86339 or check our web site at http://freesoul.net on the internet.

I have never regretted the decision to devote my life to discoveries in the field of human potentials. It has provided me with riches of mind, body, and spirit beyond calculation. These methods and techniques will do the same for you. You will learn secrets for going beyond mere mental health to creating mental wealth. More important, you will learn the ultimate aspect of inner technology—how to become *your own* teacher. You don't have to be an intellectual giant or a lab scientist. All you have to be is willing to explore. It is your attitude, not your IQ, that is the determining factor.

Explore with the spirit of adventure, and page by page you will find yourself breaching old limitations. You will experience the joy of taking new command of your happiness and success. Welcome to the millennium of the mind, fellow pioneer. Let's begin.

• 1 •

The Joy Touch:
How to Trigger the Brain's
Natural Mood-Elevation Mechanisms

I stood in awe looking at the raging flood. Submerged below the churning, brown water was my only way out to civilization. The bridges upstream and downstream had been washed away during the night. I could not tell if our bridge had survived below the still-rising torrent.

The strange weather patterns of 1993, which later that summer would cause devastating floods in the Midwest, hit Arizona earlier in the year. Areas that were usually high and dry saw the reality of the "hundred year flood plain." Along Oak Creek trailers washed away, homes were damaged, huge ponderosa pines were uprooted, and whole communities were stranded.

As I watched the liquid destruction, I slowly moved the fingers on my writing hand. They were still a bit numb from a scorpion's sting the night before. Wandering into my house to escape the rains, it had felt my bed was a good place to get cozy. My self-healing discoveries were working to ease the pain and swelling, but my mind conjured up more troublesome fears. All the possible emergencies that could befall my young children paraded before my eyes. I envisioned life-threatening consequences of being cut off from the road.

Our normally peaceful environment was in chaos. For days we had been cut off from food, and if the bridge was actually gone, we would be living for months in a nightmare. Yet through it all, I had felt amazingly calm. I was at peace, even happy. That was not my usual pattern.

I had never been a person who took kindly to the unexpected. "A bull in a china shop" described my usual response to feeling trapped. Situations like this usually found me reverting to the colorful language of my military days, what my wife disgustedly called inventing new Navy adjectives. This time, however, even though circumstances were far worse, *I* was infinitely better.

I had learned to mentally stimulate my brain's "joy center." I could stay calm and feel happy, even in the midst of turmoil. Life's events no longer held a tyrannical rule over my happiness. I had learned to mentally access the septum pellucidum area and self-trigger the body's natural mood-elevation mechanisms.

The Septum Pellucidum Area

Nestled above the main part of the limbic system (the area within the lower shaded loop) lies the septum pellucidum (see Fig. 1.), the gateway to triggering your brain's joy center. Although it is mainly a fluid filled sac, the septal nuclei at the front of this special area has direct connections to the hypothalamus, the limbic brain's control center. When the septal area is triggered, it creates a mellow, energized feeling that is best described as an inner smile. Activating it also clears the repetitive cycles of worry, hurt, anger, and fear that can be created by the limbic brain.

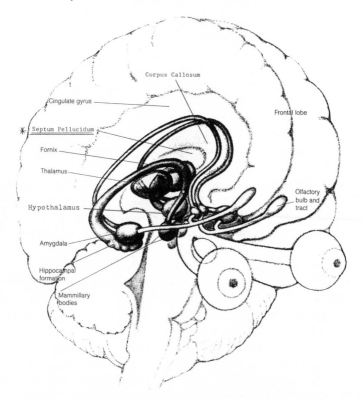

Fig. 1. Brain with limbic system highlighted

This area of the brain is so vital that it is surrounded on three sides by ventricles, the fluid-filled cavities that are the brain's inner shock absorbers. Further, the roof of the septum pellucidum is formed by the corpus callosum, the huge bundle of fibers that connect the brain's right and left hemispheres. The anatomy of its location alone tells you that the septum pellucidum is vital to your well-being.

The scientific discovery of this septal link to mood elevation was made by Dr. Robert Heath, a neurologist and psychiatrist at Tulane University School of Medicine in the 1950's. When Dr. Heath electrically stimulated the septum pellucidum area in a patient suffering from severe depression, the patient instantly felt cheerful. Cancer victims received pain relief from electrical septal stimulation. Heath also found that this area of the brain shows increased activity during sexual arousal. Further, Heath believed that damage to the septum area may account for anhedonia, an emotional disturbance that renders an individual incapable of experiencing pleasure. His book *The Role of Pleasure in Behavior* chronicles case after case of the remarkable effects of septal area electrode stimulation.

So striking was the effect of these experiments that Timothy Leary, when asked about concerns that his LSD research and advocacy might have negative future implications, responded, "This is nothing. In a few years kids are going to be demanding septal electrodes." Obviously that didn't happen. Instead we got cocaine and prozac.

Nothing evolved from Dr. Heath's research for several reasons. First, there were technical problems. The electrodes were so thin that all too often they broke after too short a time. There was also an adverse public reaction to electrode implantation. It was viewed almost as monstrous, or thought of as the "Brave New World" of creating zombielike mind control. Most important, however, neither the skill nor the interest in mind/body methods was available at the time. Research efforts turned to pharmacology as the answer to mood problems. Valium and the modern spate of antidepressants are the legacy of that chemical fork in the road.

It is time to return to the path that was visible, but due to the lack of inner technology, was never discovered, much less taken. The mind/body knowledge is now available and its effectiveness is proven for controlling blood pressure and improving heart health. Now, you can learn to use this readily available and natural inner medication to improve your mental well-being. Why pay someone else (alcohol, tobacco, and pharmaceutical companies) for something you can do yourself for free? Why suffer chemical side effects and health risks when a safer option is available?

Mentally triggering the septal area is not mind control or emotional manipulation. It is *mood* control. The Joy Touch technique gives you a physiological method for consciously controlling your feeling of well-being. It is inner technology that allows you to boost your emotional intelligence and quantum-leap beyond society's current evolutionary level of mental health, to creating mental wealth.

For your whole life this natural inducer of joy and suppressor of pain has been there. It has been waiting for you to discover it. Knowing how to self-trigger the septum pellucidum is the key to accessing the brain's natural mood-elevation mechanisms at will. Learning how to mentally activate it has changed my life.

The technique is simple and rapid. It has worked for thousands, including people with no previous exposure to Free Soul techniques or other forms of meditation. It will work for you as well.

Locating Your Brain's Joy Center

Before experiencing where to focus to stimulate your joy center, it is essential that you know how to focus. The first step is knowing *what not to do*. Do not try, force, or overconcentrate. A lighter form of attention is required. Gently focus your awareness, as opposed to forcing concentration. A good analogy is the difference between staring tightly and the subtlety of attending to your peripheral vision.

Stare at something in front of you and notice the constricted, forced feeling you experience. Contrast that sensation with the feeling of merely noticing something in your periphery. Without turning your head, see if you can enhance your awareness of the color or shape of some object off to the side. Guide your attention to the object. Experience being aware of it, but without straining. If you find yourself scrunching up your forehead, it's a good bet you have slipped into overexerting. Squinting your eyes is also a sign that you may be trying too hard, rather than gently focusing your attention.

Whenever you force or overconcentrate, your brain shifts to its more accustomed circuits, to what is called your voluntary nervous system. This keeps your awareness stuck in your muscles and your physical senses, the parts of the body normally under conscious control. Now you want to experience guiding your mind to a new area of the brain and its associated autonomic (involuntary) nerve networks. For the best success, remember this key: *focus--don't force*.

A second important tip is to lighten up! Don't worry about getting it perfectly the first time. As with all things, the more you experience stimulating your joy center, the easier it gets. Overworrying about performance has an automatic deadening effect on the involuntary nervous system (as many men know). Approach locating and triggering the septum pellucidum as an adventure, rather than a test of your ability. Allow yourself the freedom, to be learning rather than the pressure of "getting it right."

You *have* experienced that natural mood-elevation boost many times in your life. Think of how you felt when you received a piece of good news or some information that gave you a ray of hope. The inner joy you feel when your team (or someone you care about) wins is also similar.

Reexperience these sensations.

- **Remember how you felt when you received good news.**
- **Sense the uplift you felt when someone or something gave you a ray of hope.**
- **Recall how it felt when someone you were rooting for won.**

You have experienced these positive sensations many times. You are not having to learn something completely new. The difference is now you will to be able to trigger that uplift at will, rather than it being dependent on external events. All that said, let's start learning the *where* of triggering the body's natural high.

Measuring from both front to back and side to side, the septum pellucidum is located near the center of your head. Gauging from top to bottom, its level is approximately one and a half inches above your eyebrows (see Fig. 2.). The key is to make sure you focus well above the level of your eyes.

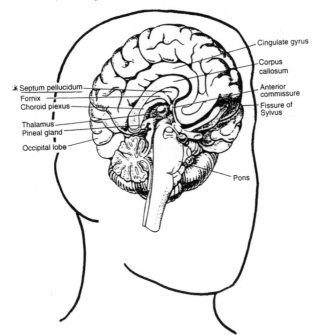

Fig. 2. Head showing level of septum pellucidum

Letting your attention slip down to eyebrow level causes you to attend to your physical vision rather than reach the septum pellucidum. Also if you focus too low, you travel inward at the level of the limbic system. Focusing there can actually create irritability and discomfort rather than relaxation. If at any time in the exercises that follow, you are not getting the desired effect, it is probably because you are focusing too low. Try a little higher.

Many people find that when they mentally visualize, their attention shifts up to the middle of their forehead. For them, locating their joy center is as simple as going up to that "mind's eye," and then thinking inward. Instead of focusing outward at an image, they go inward with their awareness.

Here is a simple technique to help you pinpoint the location of the septum pellucidum within your head. Some of you may feel a gentle "ah!" as you focus on that area. At this point, however, remember you are just warming up. Focus, don't force. Allow yourself to be exploring--not pressuring. Merely practice how to guide your mental awareness to the region described. You may have your eyes open or closed; but eyes closed is recommended, because it helps reduce distractions.

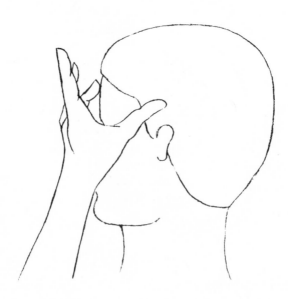

Fig. 3. Head showing touch points for septal area locating

Note: Do not skip this warm-up. It is crucial for the succeeding exercises to be maximally successful.

- Place your middle finger at mid-forehead (between eyes, 1&1/2" above eyebrows). (See Fig. 3.)
- At the same time touch the center of the side of your head with your thumb. (See Fig. 3.)
- Mentally extend a line inward from each finger.
- Feel where the lines would intersect inside your head.
- Try also middle finger on forehead and thumb at top center of the head. (See Fig. 4.)
- Alternate thumb on top center and thumb on side center several times.
- Note how you can feel or visualize the spot where the three lines would intersect.

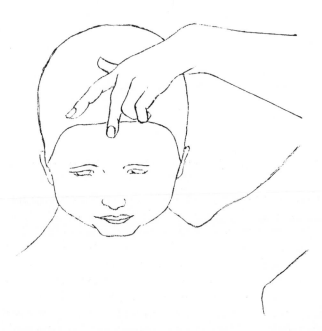

Fig. 4. Head showing touch points for septal area locating

One of my California students, Charlene, experienced a major calming effect just from practicing locating the septum pellucidum. Not only did it soothe her, she felt it also gave her a sense of inner command. Charlene's work in a high-stress real estate office kept her constantly on edge. She felt buffeted by the never-ending ringing of phones, the overload of details, and the constant pull of work versus family issues. Once she learned about the septum pellucidum, she found a way to tune out the external frenzy. Just mentally turning inward to her joy center helped her feel more in control. She described the inward focus as a calming mental breath that restored her composure. She received an even stronger effect when I showed her how to use her hand to guide that inward mental focus. If visualizing is not your strong suit, you may find that this second warm-up exercise helps.

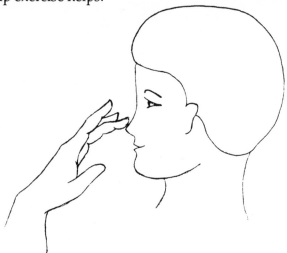

Fig. 5. Head showing step 1 of second warm-up exercise

Using whichever hand you wish, place one fingertip at the bridge of your nose (Fig. 5). Lightly touching your skin, slowly draw your finger up to the middle of your forehead (Figs. 6 & 7). Then gently press. At that press, let your thoughts go inward. Do not be distracted by your finger's contact with your skin. Use the touch only to pull your attention above eye level. When you press lightly at the center of your forehead, let it trigger going inward with your awareness. Do not focus on where your finger is touching. Instead, use the gentle pressure as a catalyst for sensing inward to the septal area.

At first, just go in and explore the feeling of focusing your awareness in the septum pellucidum. Then experiment with what gives you the most relaxing effect. Try going in a bit higher or right or left. Also explore adjusting the depth of your inward focus. Relax and enjoy refining your awareness of the exact location of your joy center. Try five or six repetitions of this version before reading further.

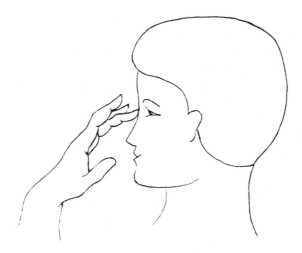

Fig. 6. Head showing step 2 of second warm-up exercise

- Gently place a finger on the bridge of your nose.
- Raise your focus above the eyes by slowly stroking upward.
- Press lightly when you reach the center of your forehead and travel inward with your awareness.
- Feel for the location that gives you the greatest "ah!"

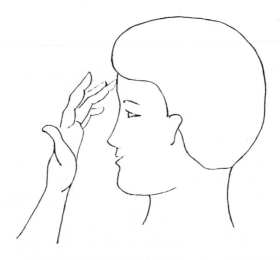

Fig. 7. Head showing step 3 of second warm-up exercise

Note: Even if you are right-handed, you may wish to also try this exercise with your left hand. Recent research indicates that the area of the brain just behind the left side of the forehead (called the left prefrontal cortex) helps to decrease the intensity of negative emotions. When you use your left hand, you may also gently stimulate this area with the biomagnetic field of your hand, thus lessening tense or anxious feelings that may mask subtle mood-elevation sensations. In contrast, the right prefrontal cortex increases the intensity of negative emotions. Remember also, eyes closed is recommended.

This hand-assisted version is the best way to begin triggering the septum pellucidum to naturally elevate your mood. You frequently see people rubbing their forehead in an effort to relieve tension. It is almost as if they are trying to get their hand through the skull to caress the septum pellucidum area. The hand can't get there, but your mind can.

Further, many religious rituals also anoint this area as part of their ceremonies. Subconsciously, we have been trying to reach into that joy center for centuries. Now you know a more exact pathway.

Triggering the Body's Natural High

Once you know how to get there, the next step is to *fully* activate the septum pellucidum's mellow, energizing effect. The technique is called the Joy Touch and, in fact, you have already begun. Merely guiding your awareness to the correct area begins the triggering process. Projecting a thought to stimulate the septum pellucidum completes it. That thought can be a feeling, an image, a word, or even just a knowing.

For me, I find that the image of a gentle caress works best. I picture going inward and brushing by the septum pellucidum area. The feeling is similar to lovingly stroking a pet or gently touching a sensitive area. The key to unleashing that "natural high" reflex is doing it with a light, caressing hand rather than a heavy one.

Some people prefer picturing a pulse of light bathing the area, or feeling a wave of energy flowing by it. One student successfully visualizes using an artist's paintbrush to tickle and trigger the septum pellucidum. You are not so much pushing a button. Instead, you are brushing by the nerve fibers that connect to the hypothalamus (almost like strumming a harp). Actually, this is more akin to the way nerves really function. They fire in pulses, as opposed to staying on all the time.

People have also had success with thinking a word that epitomizes peace and happiness to them, or just knowing that the septum pellucidum can create that inner relief. Each approach is just as effective. Experiment and choose whichever one is easiest and most comfortable to you.

If you choose a visual approach, remember that you don't have to "see" anything specific. Holding the image you want in mind is sufficient. Further, think about the effect you want to create as you caress. It will enhance your results. You *have* experienced the body's natural high before. As you caress, remember the time you received good news (that you reviewed earlier), or think of the relief that getting a ray of hope brings, or how you feel when your team wins. Use those memories to assist in triggering that same feeling at will.

Exactly what should you feel as you trigger the septum pellucidum area? Some students have described it as the feeling of an inner "ah," or a mellow, energized sensation. Others say it gives them the feeling of a weight being lifted off their shoulders, or just a sense of inner relief. Initially, all you are looking for is an increased feeling of well-being. The more experienced you become with the technique, the stronger the sensation will be.

Now let's go a step further. Instead of stroking your fingers up from the bridge of your nose, simply raise one hand and gently touch yourself in the center of your forehead. Use raising your hand to guide your awareness up above eye level. When you lightly touch your forehead, let that be your trigger for going inward. As you go in, specifically focus on stimulating the septum pellucidum. See how your mental caress causes that "ah!" sensation and the feeling of an inner smile.

Many people find the effect is stronger if they *do not* touch themselves. Instead they merely bring their hand up and toward their forehead. As they do, they picture or feel a wave of energy pulsing inward from their hand, activating the joy center. I recommend starting with the version where you touch lightly as a warm-up, but try both. In each case do at least four or five repetitions to get the full effect. For optimum results do the touch rhythmically. Generally once every five seconds works best. Some people get stronger results with once every ten seconds. Experiment to find the pace that is most comfortable for you.

It is also helpful to make sure that your jaw is not tight. Biting down holds tension and prevents the relaxation you need for an effective inner touch. If the sensation is not as strong as you would like, try letting your mouth fall gently open during the technique. As an interesting side note, whenever people are in deep relaxation their mouths naturally open slightly.

Now put the book down. Don't read any further until you've experienced at least one or both of the versions four or five times. **Treat yourself to the experience of fully self-triggering your own joy center**.

- **Raise your focus above your eyes by bringing one hand slowly up.**
- **Touch your forehead lightly or pulse energy there.**
- **Travel inward to the septum pellucidum area and caress it.**
- **See and/or feel your Joy Center activating.**

Note: As mentioned earlier, you may want to try this exercise with your left hand even if you are right-handed. See if your hand's biomagnetic field over the left prefrontal cortex helps to give you a stronger sensation (by stimulating that area's negative emotion suppression ability, thus making mood-elevation sensations more noticeable).

For many people this touch technique works even better if they slightly chill their finger tips (either by touching an ice cube or holding a cold can of soda). Interestingly, for centuries we have soothed people in distress by placing a cold compress on the forehead. This is not so much for cooling (placing it at the neck and the carotid arteries would be better for that) as to to provide a feeling of relaxation and relief. By the way, it generally does not work to press the ice cube to the forehead. The temperature difference is too great and your attention just goes to your freezing skin. Slightly chilled fingertips work best.

If you are having trouble getting as strong a sensation as you would like in the exercises thus far, remember you are learning. There is nothing you have learned in you life that you perfected to mastery in one day. How long did it take you to learn to walk or to read. This technique will not take that long, but it is new to you. As with all biofeedback, your ability will improve steadily with practice. The two key reminders are: not to over try, and to make sure you are focusing well above eye level. The sensation is a bit harder to get from reading alone (as opposed to learning from a video or a live presentation). Reading tends to pull your focus down to eye level. Remember when you are doing the exercises to specifically focus on getting out of reading mode. Pause a moment to relax your eyes and then caress well above them at that mid-forehead level.

If you want a stronger experience before going on, go back and redo the preceeding exercises with these reminders **or try this other warm-up**.

- Place the finger tips of your two hands on your mid-forehead (at the septum level.)
- Separate your hands, gently stroking simultaneously across your forehead.
- Stop when you reach the side of your head just above the ears and repeat the process
- Keep stroking and picture caressing beneath the skull.
- Eventually feel imaginary hands caressing straight back and brushing by the septum

Command and Control of Your State of Mind

Jan, one of my students in Virginia, uses an interesting modification of the hand-assisted Joy Touch. It helps her with the stress of rearing two young sons. A working mother, Jan confesses to guilt at not being with her children as much as she would like. She feels even worse when their short time together is marred by being angry. As boys will be boys, they give her plenty of opportunity for frustration and upset. One day after she had learned the Joy Touch, Jan found a way to break her cycle of irritation—anger—explosion—guilt.

The boys had found a particularly creative way to push her over her limit. This time they were bickering about "who had just peed the most on the toilet seat." As she adopted her normal finger-pointing posture for scolding them, Jan had a flashback and an insight. She remembered the old saying, "when you point one finger at someone, three are pointing back at you." Instantly she knew that the negativity of her anger was affecting herself as well. Jan further realized that she could use those three backward pointing fingers as a reminder to use the Joy Touch. Instead of exploding into anger, she could activate her septum pellucidum.

"I've known for years that to young children, words can hurt just as much as blows," Jan explained, "but I didn't know how to keep my frustration from boiling over. Now I can do the Joy Touch before I explode. I find it mellows me and makes it easier to discipline without hostility or verbal abusiveness. Not only are my children better off for the change, but I have benefited even more. Dealing with the stresses of being a parent no longer erodes my happiness. Also, by preventing my outbursts, the Joy Touch has reduced my bouts of guilt. I can activate the septum pellucidum and feel at peace despite their shenanigans. When I do have to discipline, I can do it fairly, without negative emotions. The technique has made my life easier and happier."

By using the Joy Touch regularly Jan gives herself a daily EQ boost. She is better able to process the intense emotional challenges that parenting produces. Better still, she demonstrates for her children the emotional intelligence skill of how to effectively soothe herself. That modeling has made it possible for her to also teach her children the technique and help them better manage their own behavior.

Try using the Joy Touch for yourself to diffuse a circumstance that makes you irritable or frustrated. Bring to mind a situation or person with whom you have conflict. Then, activate your joy center. See if doing the Joy Touch eases any upset feelings and helps you think more clearly. Even if you don't get new insights, notice how stimulating your septal area helps you to detach from the problem.

You can't control everything in life. Not even the wealthy or powerful can always make things go their way. Ivan Boesky, Leona Helmsley and Donald Trump can attest to that. There is, however, one thing you can always control—your state of mind. You are in command of how you perceive life's trials and tribulations. You can feel burdened, or you can feel challenged. You can feel helpless, or you can seek to learn. Knowing how to activate the septum pellucidum makes it possible to physiologically trigger the more positive perspective. That always puts you more in command. At a minimum, you can be in command of your state of mind. Being able to do the Joy Touch anywhere and at any time is the key.

That is your next step. Once you know the feel of triggering that natural mood-elevation, you can do the Joy Touch without using your hand. You can mentally activate the septum pellucidum without anyone even noticing it. Just think inward from that mid-forehead level. Let your thought be the touch that stimulates the caress of your joy center.

Again, pause in your reading and treat yourself to four or five pulses of self-generated relief. Let the mellow, energized feeling build with each pulse. Just go to the area of the septum pellucidum and self-trigger your body's natural creator of peacefulness.

- **Bring to mind a tense situation or conflict.**
- **Close your eyes.**
- **Mentally bring your awareness up above eye level.**
- **Think inward from the center of your forehead.**
- **Caress the septum pellucidum to trigger a feeling of well-being.**
- **Notice how you feel less distressed or tense about the situation.**

Once you can stimulate the septum pellucidum mentally, you can use the Joy Touch anywhere. This gives you an advantage in anything you do. You can create a feeling of calmness in any circumstance. I have even used the technique while on television, without anyone being the wiser. During a San Diego TV evening news interview I had a real need for that natural tranquilizer.

I have done television interviews with everyone from NBC's Lucky Severson to CNN's Larry King. Despite years of experience, however, news interviews are always challenging. First, because they are "live." Second, because they are so short. And third, because you rarely get to meet your interviewers before you go on. The pressure is tremendous. You have to get it right the first time. You have to be clear with only minutes to get your message across. And you have virtually no chance to establish a rapport with your interviewer.

Usually I've countered those negatives by getting myself as calm and prepared as possible ahead of time. I meditate and tune in before driving to the station. I arrive fifteen or more minutes before the time they ask me to be there. With the extra time, I get a feel for the interviewer and the set where we will be. This normal routine helps me to be as clear-headed and quick-thinking as possible. In San Diego I was denied that luxury.

I was preparing for the interview when my staff discovered that the 2000 handouts I would need for the next morning's presentations had been left in Arizona. Worse, it was very near closing time for most printing facilities. Needless to say, my meditation went out the window. Actually the scene was comical. While hurriedly dressing, I was getting the originals faxed out from Arizona, briefing the local personnel on the reprinting effort, and coordinating getting the right handouts delivered in time for the right programs. I was living the antiperspirant commercial that states, "When life turns up the pressure, your body turns up the heat." To stay physically cool, I stood under an air conditioning vent, but then struggled to keep my hair combed.

Knowing how to activate the septum pellucidum helped me to keep my *mental* cool. I did it under the vent. I kept it up on the last-minute drive to the station. I even used the technique during the interview. It worked wonderfully. I stayed calm and unperturbed by the turmoil. I even had fun giving what turned out to be an excellent interview.

I had no preparation time. The luxury of arriving early for an important evening news program was lost. Despite it all, I was at my best, thanks to the Joy Touch. I was able to guide the interview. I quickly and clearly made the promotional points I wanted to communicate. I even enjoyed myself. Learning how to trigger the body's natural tranquilizer has made media interviews fun rather than stressful for me. Instead of viewing them as nerve-wracking tests, they have become pleasant opportunities to reach out and share with the public. Knowing this form of inner technology has made my life both more successful and happier.

Try for yourself using the Joy Touch to facilitate difficult portions of your day. Today or tomorrow pick something that you know will be challenging. Then remember to activate your septum pellucidum before, during or even after it. Doing the Joy Touch ahead of time will help you to be more at peace and in command. Giving yourself mood-elevation boosts during the situation can prevent you from reacting poorly or losing your cool. The technique works, even if you forget to use it before or during a stressful situation. You can still do it afterward to relieve your residual tension and clear any feelings of unpleasantness.

Knowing the Joy Touch by itself will not solve all of your problems. It also won't make you a Pollyanna or a grinning idiot. What it does is give you new methods for coping with the rigors of life. Even better, its positive benefits come without negative side effects. You don't have the expense of getaways for unwinding, or the time loss of longer meditations. There are no external devices you need to buy or hook up. You avoid the risks of chemical dependency and hangovers. If anything, you get a bonus benefit: the more you activate the brain's joy center, the higher your everyday mood becomes. All of life seems brighter and more enjoyable.

If you feel you have the basics of the Joy Touch, you can proceed to the next chapter and learn the second facet of Free Soul's mood-enhancement system, the Comforting Connection. If not, here are some additional exercises for helping you get off to a better start.

Additional Options For a Stronger Initial Effect

If you are not yet feeling as strong a mood-elevation triggering as you would like, you may wish to try several options with a partner. This also has the benefit of giving you less to think about as you endeavor to locate and stimulate the septal area. For each of these exercises one person should be sitting in a chair experiencing and the other standing, assisting. Then switch positions.

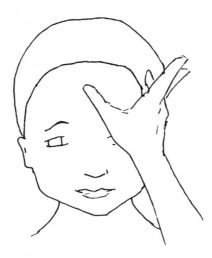

Fig. 8. Head showing touch points for helping locate septal area

First repeat the simple warm-up exercise for locating the septal area within your head. The one difference is that the standing partner will reverse the position of the thumb and middle finger to make it easier when touching another person (see Figs. 8 & 9).

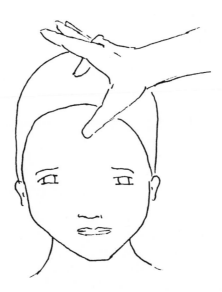

Fig. 9. Head showing touch points for helping locate septal area

The instructions for the standing (assisting) partner would thus read as follows:

- **Place your thumb at mid-forehead (between eyes , 1&1/2" above eyebrows). (See Fig. 8.)**
- **At the same time touch the center of the side of your partner's head with your thumb.**
- **(Sitting Partner) Mentally extend a line inward from each finger.**
- **(Sitting Partner) Feel where the lines would intersect inside your head.**
- **Try also thumb on forehead and middle finger at top center of the head. (See Fig. 9.)**
- **Alternate middle finger on top center and then on side center several times.**
- **(Sitting Partner) Feel or visualize the spot where the three lines would intersect.**

Note: For the next two exercises it is recommended that the assisting individual stand on the sitting participant's left side and use the left hand (for the reasons stated earlier concerning the left prefrontal cortex of the brain).

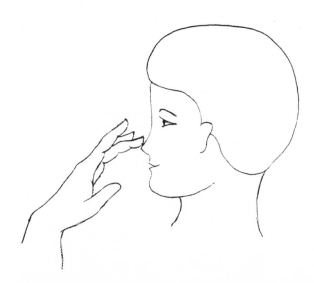

Fig. 10. Head showing step 1 of partner-assisted Joy Touch

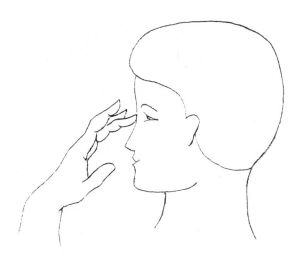

Fig. 11. Head showing step 2 of partner-assisted Joy Touch

Next, do the second warm-up exercise with your partner (described on pages 18-19). Stand on the side of the sitting partner so that your finger is gently brushing up the nose (see Figs. 5 thru 8) not pushing on it from the front. Be sure, however, to stand enough toward the front that you can clearly see the middle of the sitting participant's forehead. Here are the instructions for the standing (assisting) partner:

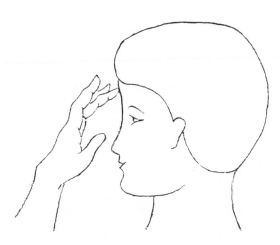

Fig. 12. Head showing step 3 of partner-assisted Joy Touch

- Gently place a finger on the bridge of sitting partner's nose.
- Help him or her raise their focus above the eyes by slowly stroking upward. (See Fig. 11 & 12.)
- Press lightly when you reach the center of his/her forehead.
- (Sitting Partner) At that pressure, travel inward with your awareness.
- (Sitting Partner) Mentally caress your septal area.
- Gently move your hand away and start again at the bridge of the nose. (Fig. 13 then back to Fig. 10.)

(For the Sitting Partner, eyes closed is recommended.)
(Standing Partner, definitely have your eyes open.)

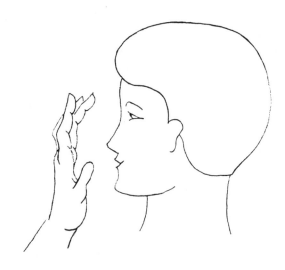

Fig. 13. Head showing step 4 of partner-assisted Joy Touch

Do this at least four or five times allowing the sitting individual to practice traveling inward and caressing his or her septal area with each light pressure on the forehead.

One additional option is a variation where, instead of touching the sitting partner, you stroke through his or her biomagnetic field as seen in Figures 14-16.

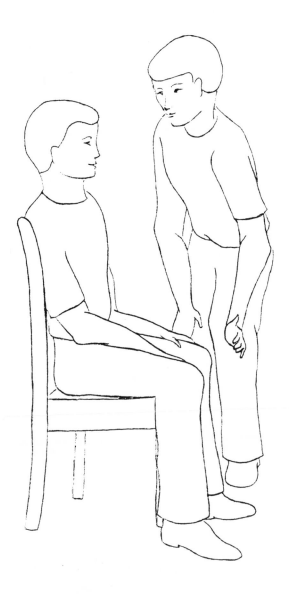

Fig. 14. Step 1 of biomagnetic field partner-assisted version

Many people prefer this approach, where they are not distracted by having their skin touched. They are able to feel the heat of the hand and use the gentle air movement to help them pulse a triggering of the septal area.

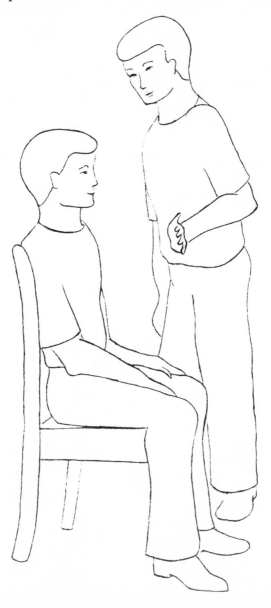

Fig. 15. Step 2 of biomagnetic field partner-assisted version

Repeat the steps four or five times so that the sitting individual has the opportunity to give himself or herself several triggering attempts (each timed to the pulse of the standing partner's hand toward the sitting individual's forehead).

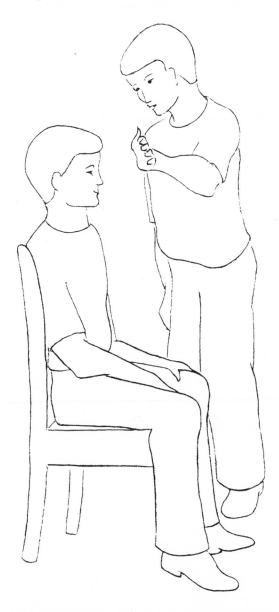

Fig. 16. Step 3 of biomagnetic field partner-assisted version

The instructions for the standing (assisting) partner are as follows:

- **Stand to the side and start with your hand at about knee level. (See Fig. 14.)**
- **Help him or her raise their focus above the eyes by slowly stroking upward. (See Fig. 15.)**
- **Keep your hand one to two feet away from the body until forehead level.**
- **Then pulse your hand lightly toward the center of his or her forehead. (See Fig. 16.)**
- **(Sitting Partner) At that pulse, travel inward with your awareness.**
- **(Sitting Partner) Mentally caress your septum pellucidum area.**
- **Gently bring your hand away and start the cycle again at the knees.**

(For the Sitting Partner, eyes closed is recommended.)
(Standing Partner, definitely have your eyes open.)

At this point you should be ready to proceed individually with the exercises on pages 20-26 of this chapter (using your own hand and mental activation only). Remember, for most people the initial sensation is light. The more you practice, the stronger it will get.

If you feel you want further assistance, instructors near you offer workshops or are available for one-on-one instruction. Contact Free Soul for their numbers by writing to Free Soul, P.O. Box 1762, Sedona, AZ 86339 or checking our web site at http://freesoul.net on the internet.

• 2 •

Breakthroughs for Defeating
Limbic Stress and Depression

Author's Preparatory Note:

This chapter has sections that, by their very subject matter, may be difficult to read. They will take you into the depths of how worry, hurt, anger, and fear can make life painful and unpleasant. Why write such a chapter? Because it also holds the keys for relief. Within it lies your gateway to freedom from the unhappiness caused by negative emotional turmoil.

As you read about the various limbic stresses, don't allow yourself to be pulled into out-of-control distress. Use the Joy Touch technique you learned in the previous chapter to stay mellow, despite the intensity of the topics. Feel the emotion of the angers, worries, hurt, and fears, but don't let them control you. Don't let them drag your mood down.

Think of this chapter as a journey that illuminates a pathway to your future. As you read each section, your awareness will shine a light on your future potential to handle life's emotional challenges, with a minimum of trauma and discomfort. You are quite literally a pioneer exploring a better way of living, one where you free yourself from the pain caused by the dinosaur brain. Free to live more happily.

As you do the exercises, focus on the joy of releasing old baggage. Feel yourself learning new methods for doing it better next time. Know that you are uncovering secrets for greater happiness in your future. If at any time you find yourself slipping out of that frame of mind, simply pause and do the Joy Touch. Do it repeatedly until you can return to that perspective of pioneering new insight and wisdom.

Know also that everything you learn in this chapter will directly boost your EQ (emotional quotient). One of the key measures of emotional intelligence is how you process intense emotion. EQ reflects your ability to integrate your analytical mind to appropriately manage your anxieties, frustrations, and sadnesses. Each limbic stress section will show you how to identify your *specific* mental soother for that particular distress.

That comforting connection gives you a second powerful tool for emotional mastery. With the Joy Touch you can physiologically soothe yourself. With the Comforting Connection you can mentally heal the root cause of the anger, worry, hurt, or fear.

You may find it best to read only a few sections of the chapter at a time. Even the most hardy of explorers can become fatigued and fatigue makes everyone more vulnerable to negative emotions. This chapter is not meant to test your emotional endurance. Rather, it is a resource. The various sections give you keys for freedom from the pain of each of the different types of limbic stress.

Once you have learned the Comforting Connection technique, you can skip ahead to whatever sections or later chapters you wish. The next time you pick up the book, you can read the next limbic stress in order, or leave them until you encounter that particular trauma (rejection, worry, anger, betrayal, etc.) in your life. Before you even begin to read, however, know that you have already won for your courage and your desire to explore.

The Tyrannosaurus of Stress: Limbic Stress

No matter how much you think you know about stress and its hazardous effects, you haven't even scratched the surface until you understand the negative effects of limbic stress. Limbic stress is the greatest enemy of performance and quality of life in our world today. Without the ability to clear it, you will consistently function at only a small fraction of your potential. Further, you will resign yourself to a life that is unduly frought with anxiety and unhappiness.

Relieving limbic stress requires techniques beyond traditional stress management, because it is a totally different physiological and psychological phenomenon. Most stress-reduction efforts deal only with the negative effects of adrenal and cardiovascular stress. These are the fight-or-flight stresses on the body (primarily heart and circulatory system) caused by adrenalin and other related hormones.

What I call limbic stress is the mental short-circuit created by the limbic system of the brain. It is what you feel when out-of-control, negative emotions degrade your happiness and ability to function. Physiologically it can be described as what occurs when the limbic brain overrides and dominates the higher cortex. In practical terms, it is the dysfunction that occurs when you get stuck in the turmoil of negative emotional issues (hurts, worries, angers, and fears).

As stated earlier, it is not emotion and having feelings that is the problem. Emotions add great meaning and texture to life. Knowing your feelings is also a key indicator of what Howard Gardner, Ph.D., of Harvard University calls Intrapersonal Intelligence. The problem occurs when unhealthy feelings get blown out of proportion. Think of all the times you have felt overwhelmed by a sadness, anxiety, frustration, or apprehension. That is the cycle of limbic stress. It is the mental broken record of *negative* emotions that the limbic brain can create.

The limbic system is one of the oldest and deepest parts of the human brain. It is frequently called the early mammalian brain because it dates back to humanity's earliest evolution. It is found in all mammals but not in reptiles or other lower species. While the limbic system is still far from fully understood, we do know that it deals with the processing of emotions. For years scientists have marveled at the variety of negative emotions elicited by electrical stimulation or injury in this area.

One of the classic stories about the limbic system I remember from my brain science studies at Massachusetts Institute of Technology was that of Joe, a wounded World War II veteran. Joe had been shot in the head and survived with a bullet fragment lodged in one of the ventricles of his brain. He suffered no ill effects from the fragment unless he moved his head too rapidly. That would cause the fragment to slide within the ventricle and scrape against portions of his limbic brain. He could be perfectly happy moments before, but in an instant tears might start running down his cheeks. When asked, "What's wrong, Joe?" he would reply, "It feels like I'm crying inside."

The limbic brain also houses what is frequently termed the "rage center." This part of the brain, when stimulated, causes extreme and irrational flashes of anger. Nobel Prize-winning physiologist Walter Hess experimented with placing electrodes in this part of a cat's brain. A docile, purring animal was instantly transformed into a hissing, spitting beast that tried to claw and bite at the least provocation.

This extreme sensitivity and power are what makes the limbic brain such a potentially lethal enemy. When events or thoughts trigger this part of your brain, you are in for a roller-coaster ride of negative emotions that is all but unstoppable. Short-circuits in the limbic brain (whether caused by electrodes, bullet fragments, or everyday events) can dominate the conscious thinking mind. Limbic stress can, in an instant, degrade both your abilities and your happiness.

Knowing the Joy Touch helps to provide temporary relief. It can momentarily ease the discomfort of worries, hurts, angers, or fears. Alone, however, it is not always sufficient to defeat limbic stress. The intensity of negative emotions that the limbic brain generates can overwhelm or cut short the relief provided by the Joy Touch.

That domination is why it is crucial to fully understand and separately deal with limbic stress. Once you learn to recognize and clear it, you can achieve the ultimate control of your inner environment. Gaining mastery over limbic stress gives you the skill to free yourself, for life, from prolonged negative emotions and the darkness of depression.

Black Hole of the Brain: The Limbic Cycle

There are several reasons why limbic stress is far worse than its adrenal cousin. The first is its longer duration. The negative effects of adrenal stress usually subside when the events causing the stress end. When you are out of the stressful situation you stop producing adrenalin, so your heart rate, blood pressure and other physiological functions begin to return to normal. With limbic stress (hurts, worries, angers, and fears), the mental short-circuit can continue long after the actual event that triggered the upset. How long have you seen hurts or worries linger in your life? Frequently the distress actually gets worse over time, rather than better. As we rehash the triggering event mentally, the dysfunction may actually deepen. That process frequently includes memories of previous hurts, doubling or tripling the inner turmoil.

Second, because of its prolonged duration, limbic stress touches multiple facets of our lives. How can you be at your best with others, if you are in pain or trying to deal with emotional unrest? The degradation of your performance is not confined just to work situations; it also affects your personal life. Even more important, limbic stress directly damages your relationship with yourself. Negative limbic stimulus has been shown to physiologically suppress and override the brain's normal mood-elevation cycles. How can you experience maximum happiness when you are caught in a recycling hurt, worry, anger, or fear? Limbic dysfunction is the stress that causes distress to all areas of our lives.

The destructiveness of limbic stress can also continue longer because traditional stress-reduction techniques have little or no effect on it. Mentally and physiologically, they frequently address the wrong areas. Further, their calming effects are often too slow to counter the avalanche of negative emotion that limbic stress generates. They simply don't have the power to relieve the inner distress that all too often we choose to perpetuate.

That's right — choose to perpetuate! Have you ever noticed how we tend to stay upset, once a hurt, worry, anger, or fear is triggered? We actually perpetuate the downward spiral by chewing on the hurt over and over again. Granted, this may not be a conscious choice. Nevertheless, it is a function of the mind, rather than the continuation of a specific external event.

The most common example of this process is the way we tend to relive the hurtful event or worry, either by visually picturing the scene and individuals involved, or hearing the dialogue that caused the pain. Each time that memory bubble flashes, all the hurt is felt again. The limbic cycle is retriggered for another debilitating bout of mental short-circuiting.

Naomi is a career professional who recently was teamed in her office with a newcomer named Roseanne. During Roseanne's first few months, Naomi did everything possible to make her feel welcome and supported. Then an event occurred that sent Naomi into a desperate cycle of limbic stress. Roseanne, acting on misinformation and misinterpretation, told Naomi's most respected mentor, Dr. Janes, that Naomi had made slanderous remarks about Dr. Janes.

What Naomi actually said was that other people in the profession had made those remarks. Naomi's intent was to help Roseanne be aware of the undercurrents in the community. Naomi had, in fact, been one of Dr. Janes' strongest supporters.

Roseanne spoke to Dr. Janes to ingratiate herself and gain advancement. That backstabbing by someone to whom Naomi had been so caring and helpful, hurt and angered her. Even more painful was that Dr. Janes initially believed Roseanne and confronted Naomi, calling her, in effect, a traitor. That lack of confidence and accusation, from someone Naomi had admired and supported, exploded in Naomi's limbic brain. She was unable to sleep that night. She kept seeing the incident over and over in her mind. For days she was an emotional wreck. Whenever she wasn't completely busy, she would relive the event, feeling all the hurt and anger again.

Worse still, even after Dr. Janes found out that Roseanne had been misinformed, no apology was made to Naomi. This omission perpetuated the hurt and anger of the limbic stress cycle. Months after the incident, Naomi was still rehashing it in her mind. Not only would she see it, but she would hear the dialogue again. She would also go a step further, thinking of all the things she wished she had said or made more clear. Each time, all the hurts and angers of the situation would resurface. Even the best of days could be tumbled into the darkness of depression by remembering the incident. Naomi's work efficiency plummeted. Her personal life suffered as well. She was irritable and lethargic much of the time.

That is the legacy of limbic stress. It is a mental black hole that consumes us, impairs our abilities, and drains the joy out of life. One of my students, Joyce, described the process as a poison that slowly but inexorably spreads, eventually discoloring every facet of her life. Naomi's case is an example of a limbic short circuit triggered by hurt and anger. With worries and fears, the process is slightly different but basically the same. The mind-numbing anxiety returns with each new "what if?" Each time a different facet of the problem comes to mind without a solution, the feeling of helplessness or uncertainty is restimulated. The result is mental overload. All facets of your work and life are degraded by the anxiety.

Another student, Ann, identified a different element that makes limbic stress so destructive for her. She finds she gravitates to situations that retrigger the cycle. She feels herself almost magnetically drawn to people that push the same buttons and restimulate the same hurt, worry, anger, or fear. Have you ever noticed that pattern in your life?

Can you think of a limbic issue that you would like to stop from repeating. If you could magically banish a particular type of upset from your life, what would it be? Pause a moment and think of a recurring emotional distress you would like to eliminate. Do the Joy Touch a few times if you feel uncomfortable or mentally blocked.

Now take a moment to imagine what your life would be like without domination by that particular hurt, worry, anger, or fear.

- **See yourself smiling and being at ease.**
- **Feel yourself content and inwardly at peace.**
- **Hear yourself thinking good thoughts about yourself.**
- **Know that this is your future, once you learn to break the cycle of limbic stress.**

Shortly you will be shown how to make that future a reality. For now, this simple reflection is just a preparation. It lays a subconscious foundation for learning the techniques to come. Limbic stress can be cleared and you can live the full potential for happiness that is your birthright.

How To Rapidly Clear Emotional Turmoil

To end the broken-record effect of negative emotions, it is first necessary to find the cause of the cycle. Little progress will be made if we try to treat only the symptoms of the pattern. Trying to prevent the downward spiral, or quiet the broken record, won't work if the basic cause of the perpetuation is not addressed.

Assume for a moment that we perpetuate the downward spiral

for a reason. It is said that we never do anything without a reason. Consider the possibility that it is a choice (albeit subconscious) to stay down, as much as a "getting stuck" process.

The reason we perpetuate the hurt, worry, anger, or fear is actually quite simple, but we have to look for it in the right place—or, to be more specific, the right time. The cause actually lies in our past, in our early childhood years. When we were little, we were neither fully capable, nor expected to be, of caring for ourselves (physically or emotionally). As a result, when we really *got hurt* or were *truly frightened*, someone came and comforted us. Someone soothed us to "make it better" or "all right." That *comforting* planted the seeds of the pattern. It was the beginning of our conditioning to look for external sources to ease our discomfort.

In children the limbic system is more easily triggered. Children cry more readily than adults and are more easily frightened. Because of that, and because children are more appealing, they receive frequent comforting during those early years. Further, that comforting is usually very loving. The other person is totally there for them in that instant. The comforting is usually also accompanied by being fed (a key link to why food is so often used compulsively to ease emotional distress). The combination of care, love, and food is powerfully reinforcing. It literally programmed us to look outside ourselves to comfort limbic distress.

As we grow older our limbic system gradually takes a back seat to the cerebral cortex and higher brain functions. The association of limbic stress with the need for external comforting remains, however. It is conditioned into us just as surely as Pavlov's dog was programmed to associate the ringing of a bell with being fed.

Why do we stay down, wallowing in a hurt or worry even though it is unpleasant? We do it because we are crying out subconsciously for someone to come and comfort us. Just like the young child, we will continue and/or increase that cry if comfort is not forthcoming. The inner short circuit continues until someone soothes our raging limbic brain or something (exhaustion, sleep, a new beginning or a positive event) interrupts the cycle.

All too often we expect that someone to be a spouse, relative, or friend. It is much more than a request. Our conditioning makes it a subconscious demand. When for some reason those others can't be there for us (or don't know how to soothe us effectively), our distress deepens. Even if that desired person can be there, all too often they do the wrong thing. They try to solve the problem rather than provide comfort. Solutions don't help when what you want (and need) first is comforting.

Getting that comforting from external sources is a flawed system. You can be disappointed three ways. Strike one is that you can cry out till the cows come home and there might not be anybody there to respond, so you suffer for nothing. Strike two is, even if there is somebody there, they may not care. Equally sad, they may not be paying attention and thus not sense your subconscious signals.

Most tragic of all is strike three. They may be there and may even care, but just *not know* how to comfort. Men are notoriously poor comforters and not because they don't care. Men just tend to have a solve-it reflex that gets in the way of effective comforting. Upon hearing that cry for help, they frequently respond with attempts to solve the problem. One woman told me that her husband frequently stated, "There is no problem that can't be solved in five minutes with duct tape." To which another woman in the audience responded, "Yea, as in across his mouth!" One of the most humorous descriptions of this gender miscommunication was written in *Imazdi*, a *Star Trek, the Next Generation* novel where Wil Riker first meets Deanna Troi.

Deanna is trying to teach Wil the fine points of Betazed philosophy and how to be more sensitive. He has been presented with a hypothetical situation where a female engineer has come to him about a problem she is having with her supervisor. Riker comes up with a solution and is informed by the computer that he has picked an incorrect approach. He is confused and also a little bit angry, asking, "Why did she even come to me with the problem if I wasn't supposed to solve it." Deanna responds with, "She came to you for emotional support, for augmentation of her emotional strength. You could have shared your experience with a similar problem." to which Riker interjected, "and describe how I solved it." Deanna corrected, "No, to describe how you felt, so that she knew she was not alone in her feelings of distress." Exasperated, Riker responds, "Well then, how does the problem get solved?" Deanna answers, "It gets solved in her own right time in whatever manner she chooses (possibly even choosing to just live with it). She is looking for you to support her in whatever she chooses because it is the action she has decided to take." This humorous bit of fiction is all too often played out in many relationships. I have taught for years about gender differences, perceptual types, and sensitivity. I can honestly admit, however, that until I read that passage I didn't truly get it.

If you are a fellow male reader (or a female one) who suffers from an overactive solve-it reflex, absorbing the essence of that scene and approach is a life-changing key for assisting others (male or female) when they are in emotional distress. When you are in emotional distress you don't want solutions. First and foremost, you want understanding and support. Before solutions, you want comforting.

The solve-it reflex is not just a male problem. All people (even women), when they find themselves alone and dealing with an emotional issue, might tend to first think, How can I solve this or make it better? rather than, What can I do that would comfort me in this situation? Because we usually don't take care of that self-comforting, we slip into the old programmed habit pattern of looking for someone else to comfort us. Even if you have a caring, sensitive individual at hand, you can still be thwarted. Strike four can be if the other person is dealing with his or her own distress. He or she may care, but just not be able to be there for you at that time. Life seems almost sadistically comical in how often our significant others have their own crisis at the same time we need their support. Children seem almost psychic at sensing when a parent is the least together. They then pick exactly that moment to be their most challenging.

Why depend on others who may not have the time, the skills or the desire to effectively comfort you? Imagine the change that would occur if you could learn to self-comfort (with something other than food). Think! You could self-create freedom from distress! That is the reward that awaits you when you learn how to trigger your own "Comforting Connection." If you can remember two simple questions, you can self-comfort any worry, hurt, anger, or fear.

The easiest way to begin self-comforting is to simply ask, "What would comfort me in this situation? (What would soothe the hurt or worry I am experiencing?)" In all cases, look for the essence of what will create the comforting effect (not just the external mechanism). For example, having a banana split is the mechanism, not the essence, of the comforting. The real essence is giving yourself a treat. Feeling worthy of something special is the key, not the dessert itself. Focus on the quality or feeling that will make you feel better, not just the object or person that you think is the solution. Avoid falling into the solve-it trap.

Next ask, "How can I give it to myself? (What can I do or focus on that will create the essence of what will soothe me?)" Then see what thought or action comes to mind for you. Finally give yourself the support, nurturing, or activity that you have identified.

This question, realization, and action process is your *comforting connection.* You have succeeded in connecting with your higher brain functions to clear the limbic short circuit! Best of all, the connection can be made easily and rapidly, without the need to rely on others.

There are many therapies and psychological techniques that have the potential to soothe the raging limbic brain. Most, however, take too long and thus allow you to suffer longer than necessary. I have found nothing quicker than these two simple questions: "What would comfort me in this situation?" and "How can I give it to myself?" Answering these questions gets you right to the heart of the matter. It quickly pulls you out of the cyclical pattern of limbic stress and activates the problem solving skills of your higher cortex. Added to the Joy Touch's ability to physiologically elevate your mood, the Comforting Connection gives you a powerful one-two combination for easing short-term and long-term emotional distress.

Note (1): It is helpful to use methods of "giving it to yourself" that match your personality and perceptual type. For example, if you are a visual person, looking at a picture or scene can be better for you than just words. If you are auditory, however, you may find that inspirational reading or saying aloud positive thoughts are your natural keys. For bodily kinesthetic people, whatever you decide to do, do it with movement. Walk and see the sky or write the positive thought or doodle your symbol of comforting. If you are spontaneous and intuitive, give yourself the freedom to release from the issue rapidly. Find the essence. Give it to yourself quickly and move on (knowing that you can come back to it more in depth whenever you choose). If you are highly feeling sensitive, make sure that your comforting-connection process is also physically comforting. Have a cup of tea. Slip into comfortable shoes or clothes. Sit in a comfortable, rather than rigid, chair (believe it or not, many highly auditory or mental types may actually prefer more rigid furniture and desks, as it helps them focus and feel more disciplined). Music can be a helpful addition, whatever your perceptual type, as long as (a) it is music you like, (b) it matches your need (for example a frenzied piece generally does not help limbic stresses where pressure is an issue), and (c) it is at a comfortable volume for you.

Note (2): In all cases, however, the worst thing you can do is sit immobile and stew. That actually makes it easier to be sucked down into a limbic short circuit. Anything that activates the higher cortex of your brain can help pull you out of the black hole of the limbic system. That is why people often feel better just from taking a walk or talking with someone. Strolling and speaking both utilize higher cortical parts of the brain. If you must sit, try writing (journaling) or visualizing to keep you from slipping into a limbic sulk. Stroking a pet or sitting near a window can also be effective, as is rocking in a rocking chair. The mere physical movement of the hand-assisted Joy Touch helps even before you stimulate the septal area.

Take a moment, before reading further, to practice generating a Comforting Connection. (Remember, do the Joy Touch first, or during if you are feeling uncomfortable, or having difficulty getting clear answers.)

- **Do the Joy Touch to start off soothed and mellow.**
- **Think of a worry, hurt, anger, or fear from which you would like to be more free.**
- **Do the Joy Touch briefly to ease any discomfort that issue stirs up.**
- **Ask, "What would comfort me is this situation?"**
  (Identify the essence of what would soothe your distress.)
- **Next ask, "How could I give that to myself?"**
  (What thought, action, perspective or remembrance could you focus on for self-soothing?)
- **Do the Joy Touch again to seal in your realization.**
  (Reinforce the memory of your Comforting Connection and your ability to learn self-comforting.)
- **Mentally congratulate yourself for your learning and progress.**
  (Feel proud of yourself, give yourself a hug, tell yourself bravo, or just know you have done well!)

Even more important than the individual comforter that you figure out, is the *process* of learning to self-comfort. With each Comforting Connection you realize, you not only benefit by immediate soothing, you also grow in self-esteem and wisdom. You take one step closer to freedom from the pain that can be caused by the limbic brain. Imagine the improved quality of life that will be yours, when you learn to quickly clear any emotional turmoil with the Comforting Connection process.

Each of the following sections will provide examples of how to address the different facets of hurts, worries, angers, and fears, as well as sample Comforting Connections. If you had trouble getting the precise Comforting Connection you wanted in the above exercise, feel free to skip ahead to the appropriate section. If you feel totally clear on the Comforting Connection process, you can skip ahead to later chapters that interest you; but first read at least the sections in this chapter on secret pain (pp. 57-59) and depression (pp. 82-96). You can return at your leisure (or need) to the individual sections about the various types of worries, hurt, angers, and fears.

Keys for Self-Healing Inner Hurt and Secret Pain

Hurts are the most debilitating of the limbic stresses. Not only do they impair our performance and interactions, they also drain the joy out of life. Nothing goes well or feels good when we are hurting inside. Physiologically we know that sadness actually causes listlessness and fatigue. Presumably this goes back to early evolution where the lack of energy would keep cavemen closer to a safe place when they were grieving and vulnerable.

Fortunately, hurts are the limbic stress most easily cleared with the Comforting Connection approach. The drained feeling created by hurts can be directly countered by adding the energy of taking action. The mere mental activity of finding a comforter provides an energy boost. The ah-ha! is uplifting. Also, compared to the vague nature of worries and fears or the explosiveness of angers, hurts are more tangible and simpler to soothe. The actions you can take tend to be more immediately applicable.

The first step is to identify the nature of the hurt. While each situation is unique, most hurts usually fall into at least one of the following categories: rejections, betrayals, or loss/loneliness.

Dealing with Rejection

Rejection hurts because we feel unwanted and/or not valued. Feeling wanted and accepted is the essence that will clear the limbic stress of rejection. If you ask, "What would comfort me in this situation?", the answer usually is "to feel valued and wanted." Ultimately the solution is to value yourself. Any technique that stimulates or surrounds you with a feeling of self-value will soothe the hurt and break the limbic short-circuit. Focusing on not rejecting yourself is the key.

It is often hard, however, to be totally self-accepting when you are hurting. A bridge to self-acceptance is always helpful. That intermediate step can facilitate the Comforting Connection process. One of my instructors, Joyce McNelly from Williams, Arizona, has a novel approach. Whenever she feels rejected, she soothes the hurt by going to a place of total acceptance—she visits with her young grandchildren. She always sees total acceptance in their eyes. Those visits dissipate the pain and get her started on a positive new beginning. Enjoying the affection of a pet can also provide a similar soothing.

This is an example of breaking the cycle by replacing rejection in one area of your life with the acceptance you feel in another. Joyce could also clear the ache by simply remembering the love her grandchildren radiate toward her; actually visiting them is not necessary. (Frankly, I think Joyce just plain enjoys hugging and playing with them too much not to go.) When a visit is not possible, however, remembering this variation provides an alternative. It is a way of self-triggering the realization that she *is* of value.

Take a moment and think of someone who has valued you.

- **Remember the smile and positive eye contact they gave you.**
- **Feel the hug or sign of cherishing they shared with you.**
- **Hear the complimentary words they spoke or wrote.**
- **Know that you were and are important to them.**

Because she was highly verbal, Naomi (described earlier as an example of how we perpetuate the cycle) found that her Comforting Connection was positive affirmations. Whenever she felt hurt by Dr. Janes' rejection, she repeated positive affirmations such as, "I do have something valuable to contribute to this office." Then she would remember the projects she had completed and the many people she had helped. These mental affirmations would override the limbic rehearing of the situation's painful dialogue.

For many people, a symbol of valuing themselves is an effective limbic-cycle-breaker. Giving themselves a flower, treating themselves to a movie or a hot-fudge sundae, or just giving themselves the gift of time (relaxation, a hot bath or a massage) can ease the feeling of rejection and break the limbic cycle. The key, however, is to focus on valuing yourself, not merely using the symbol as the soother. Excessive purchases or too many hot-fudge sundaes can definitely have negative side effects. Realizing that you are of value and deserve the treat is the essence of self-comforting for this type of hurt.

Let's practice clearing a recent rejection.

- **Do the Joy Touch first to feel calm and more objective.**
- **Bring to mind a recent situation where you felt rejected or not fully valued.**
- **Do the Joy Touch to ease any discomfort that memory brings.**
- **Ask yourself, "What is the essence of what would make me feel better?"**
- **Think of a way you can give that feeling to yourself).**
  (Try to pick something that can be done or said rapidly.)
  (But at least pick something that provides a feeling of relief just from thinking about it.)

- **See, feel, know, and understand that you are a valuable, one-of-a-kind Soul.**
  (Resolve not to reject yourself.)
- **Finish with a Joy Touch and give yourself a Bravo!**

If you have trouble getting an answer, remember to use the Joy Touch. Triggering the septum pellucidum helps you to pull out of the hurt feeling, so you can connect with insights and creative solutions from your higher mind.

Practice identifying comforting connections in your daily life as you progress through the book. Mere reading only gives you knowledge. Actual practice and experience gives you mastery—the wisdom to achieve greater command of your life. This week if a rejection impairs your performance, try a self-comforting technique and see how quickly you bounce back to greater happiness.

The Pain of Betrayal

Betrayal is in many ways similar to rejection. It is a rejection of our importance. We hurt because we feel the betrayer does not value our feelings or interests. The pain goes deeper, though, because aside from the implied rejection, there is the hurt of the betrayal itself. Betrayal also stimulates additional feelings of helplessness and injustice. These two negative emotions create their own unique limbic short circuits. Here is an example of how to clear them. (See also anger at unfairness, pp. 65-66 and fear of being helpless, pp. 79-81.)

In the early years of my national organization I had an opportunity to process the pain of a major betrayal. Working through the intense hurt of that particular situation was the catalyst for my discovering the Comforting Connection approach. The pain and dysfunction I experienced were so intense, I had to find a clearing method for my very survival.

I felt that an instructor, whom I'll refer to as Monica, betrayed the trust and responsibilities I had given her as a major national representative of my organization. Without consulting me, she modified and deleted parts of our training that I felt were essential. Worse, when I confronted Monica, she rebelled and didn't fully acknowledge my concerns. She saw no reason why she couldn't keep her high-level position, despite this conflict.

If this situation had occurred with a new instructor it would not have been a problem. I would have suspended his or her certification on the spot. Because Monica and I had worked together for years, the situation was more complicated. I felt a deep friendship for Monica and was saddened by what seemed to be less-than-ethical behavior. I felt the trust and opportunities I had given her had been betrayed. I took the betrayal so much to heart that I literally developed cardiovascular irregularities as a result.

Fortunately, the doctor said the problem was not life-threatening. He felt it was a symptom of an abnormally high level of stress. What he didn't know was how this major limbic stress, created by my feeling of betrayal, was adding to my already intense life pressures. On a humorous note, the assisting nurse kindly mentioned that I might consider buying and listening to some stress-reduction tapes (she didn't know that I taught stress-reduction methods nationally). I felt thoroughly chastised to practice what I preach, but nothing was working. Even my earlier stress-reduction breakthroughs (the Soul-Shift and Breath-Control Relaxation) could not reduce the increasing number of abnormal beats I was experiencing. I was also losing the joy I usually felt in my work. Everything seemed a hassle and I dragged through the days. I was depressed and functioning at half my normal speed.

Because of the limbic factor, I knew I had to look deeper for relief. I realized I wasn't facing the pain of the issue. Stuffing my feelings was causing the heart problem, because I was not only stressed but broken-hearted. I felt caught in a hopeless, helpless situation. Monica's refusal to acknowledge her inappropriate behavior made my only choice removing her high-level opportunities. My own feelings of loyalty to an old friend made that option particularly distasteful. I was sure that pushing the issue would lead to her complete resignation. The apparent no-win situation (a professional divorce that I didn't want or the continuation of practices that I couldn't tolerate) made me feel not only betrayed, but helpless.

The feeling of helplessness is commonly associated with betrayal. It is also the key to finding the first Comforting Connection. When I asked, "What would comfort me in this situation?" I instantly knew the solution. *Not feeling helpless* was the answer. Looking for ways that you are or can be in control always breaks the cycle of feeling helpless. There is always something you can do. You can *always* be in control of your state of mind.

I realized that I could not control Monica's behavior, but I could be in command of my own feelings and actions. I couldn't live with compromising our training; I had to be true to my beliefs. Ultimately, I did have to suspend Monica. Rather than mourn her not utilizing the specific procedures I had taught her, I resolved to put my energies into better training (particularly in communication and teamwork skills) for all my instructors. Next, I dealt with my feelings of not being personally valued by Monica. I remembered to respect and value myself for the high standards I believe in. The heart irregularities ceased shortly thereafter. Both my work and life became a joy again. I accomplished more in the weeks that followed than I had in months, but I actually felt less stressed.

Another element of betrayal is the feeling of injustice. We tend to beat ourselves with hurt and anger because of the unfairness of the situation. For this, a good Comforting Connection is realizing that you are also *being unfair to yourself*. The hurt felt by Naomi (described earlier) was compounded by her feeling that Roseanne had betrayed the friendship Naomi had shown her. Naomi perpetuated the cycle by saying, "How could I have been so stupid as to trust Roseanne?" When she realized the unfairness of that statement (to herself) her hurt started to ease. Acknowledging and appreciating herself for the kindnesses she had shown Roseanne helped get Naomi out of the limbic cycle. It made it possible for her to act positively, rather than stay stuck in negative regret.

If you have had a recent or significant betrayal, let's practice how to counter it. Overcome the negativity of the hurts by filling them with positive signs of support for yourself.

- **Do the Joy Touch before and after answering each of the following questions.**
- **Remember that you are not helpless. What actions can you take?**
- **What signs of support can you give yourself?**
- **What can you appreciate about yourself from the situation?**
- **How can you avoid the additional betrayal of being unfair to yourself?**
- **Do the Joy Touch one last time to reempower yourself.**

The pain of betrayal is often magnified by the could-haves and should-haves that rattle around in our mind. It doesn't matter how much you blame the "betrayer"; if you cared for him/her, it is easy to slip into feeling that there must have been something you could or should have done to prevent the problem. It is imperative to remember where the primary responsibility for the betrayal lies. Even if you think of something you *could* have done, the betrayer is still primarily responsible for creating the situation.

This is particularly true for sexual betrayals. Don't make the other person's problem into a weapon that you use against your own self-esteem. Don't let that infidelity, immaturity or fear of commitment reduce your self-esteem. Don't let those instabilities be the basis for your self-worth. That's like giving a thief the key to your house and then being surprised when you are robbed. In sexual betrayals, it is crucial to use the Comforting Connections described in the previous section on rejection. Don't reject yourself by believing that you are somehow not good enough. Look for Comforting Connections that emphasize your value. That is the best way to dissolve the pain of sexual betrayal hurts.

When you do identify could-haves/should-haves, use them constructively. Rather than beating up on yourself, use the "could have" to learn what you will do differently the next time. Instead of wallowing in limbic regret, see and feel yourself carrying out an improved response in the future. It is said that there are four stages of competence: 1. unconscious incompetence (messing up and not even realizing it or knowing why); 2. conscious incompetence (dissatisfied, but at least aware of what needs improving); 3. conscious competence (thoughtfully acting out the better way); 4. and finally, unconscious competence (automatically knowing what to do and acting accordingly). The "What will I do differently next time?" form of mental rehearsal will make the could-have a more automatic behavior when a similar situation arises. It can be the key for moving you from conscious incompetence to conscious competence. Also don't forget to realize that at least identifying what you want to improve is the first step out of unconscious incompetence. You are making progress. Reflecting on what you want to do differently next time continues the learning process.

Take a moment and think of something you could have done differently in the last week.

- **Do the Joy Touch so you view that event dispassionately.**
- **Visualize what you would change and see yourself doing it that way.**
- **Feel yourself being more effective the next time.**
- **Hear in your mind what you will say differently or how you will listen better.**
- **Know that you will be more prepared the next time a similar situation arises.**
- **Congratulate yourself and end with a Joy Touch to reinforce your learning.**

The Emptiness of Loss and Loneliness

In many ways loss and loneliness are the most difficult hurts to deal with. These particular limbic cycles create a feeling of emptiness that can be overwhelming. It can overcome even the best efforts to clear the pain. The secret is to fill the emptiness.

The answer to "what will comfort me in this situation?" is always "anything that successfully fills the void." That is the first step. Clear the immediate feeling of emptiness. Then look for more permanent solutions. As mentioned earlier, however, look for fillers other than food. Here are some examples.

Diane had one of the worst losses to deal with—the death of her only child, Angela, at age ten. For years she ached inside and couldn't sleep normally. She desperately missed her daughter's smiling face and the joy of being with her. She mourned the loss of her daily interactions with Angela. She regretted even more not being able to watch Angela grow to womanhood. She had wanted to guide and nurture her daughter through the perils of adolescence. She felt that opportunity had been lost to her forever. The loss affected every facet of Diane's life. She withdrew from her husband and friends. Her performance at work was so erratic that she was almost fired. Everything seemed to get worse with each passing day.

Diane found the key for turning her life around at one of my workshops. I shared how to be with any Soul, even when they had passed away. One way is through memory. No one can ever take your memories away. I am a total believer in the old maxim that it is better to have loved and lost, than to never have loved at all. When you have the memory of love, you have precious experiences that can always be relived. I call this cherishing rather than missing the loved one.

Further, reliving is more than mere memory. Science tells us that every ray of light ever emitted is still shining somewhere. The same is true for every word, feeling, or interaction. The energies of every event are still radiating somewhere in space and time. To access any event, all you have to know is that the Soul can travel faster than the speed of light. While this can't be measured technologically at the present time, here is a way to prove it to yourself subjectively.

Think back to a time you viewed a star-filled night sky. Have you ever experienced the feeling of being out there, one with the stars? How long did that take? Let's say it takes one second. Also assume you were blending with the area of Orion's Belt, the three stars in a line in the constellation Orion that we know are roughly 10,000 light years away (most of what you see in the night sky is even more distant). In that instant your Soul traveled 315,360,000,000 times faster than the speed of light. In that one second your consciousness traveled 10,000 light years (thus your speed was 10,000 times 365 days in a year, times 24 hours in a day, times 60 minutes in an hour, times 60 seconds in a minute times faster than the speed of light).

With that type of potential there is no place or time the Soul can't reach. All you have to do is be willing to try. That is what Diane did. Instead of regretting Angela's absence, she cherished her memory. When she missed Angela, Diane would bring to mind a joyous memory of their time together. Once Diane learned the Soul-shift technique for tapping higher dimensions of consciousness (see Chapter 3 pp. 115-120), she felt she could make the experience more than just a memory. She found herself surrounded by the bubble of that joyous past event, and relived it.

Whether you believe it is mere memory or Soul travel, the bottom line is, it works. It also works with people you miss who are still living. I proved that to myself during my years as a naval officer. When my ship was at sea for weeks at a time, I missed my new bride intensely. My feelings were so strong that my wife would often receive them full force and get migraines. This gave a new (but painful) meaning to the expression "reach out and touch someone." When I shifted to cherishing her memory rather than missing her, the migraine connection stopped. I also benefited by basking in the warm feelings I had for her, rather than wallowing in my loneliness.

With the cherishing technique, Diane was able to turn her times of regret into joy and get on with her life. She also took my recommendation that she enroll in the Big Sisters program. There she found the fulfillment of working with girls who desperately needed a friend and mentor during their teen years. This filled her emptiness at being unable to guide Angela into womanhood. Once again Diane's life had meaning. At her next job review she was actually commended for her increased efficiency and positive attitude.

Cherishing will always work as long as you have completed your appropriate period of mourning. Without completing the grief process, comforting may only promote denial. While the length of mourning varies from person to person, it is essential for everyone. When you feel it is time for your grief to end, self-comforting can help you get on with life. Cherishing a loved one's memory provides both comfort and positive progress. Rather than dwell on your loss, you are valuing your life and the experiences you have had.

This is equally true for losses other than a death. One of my students, Anna, was abandoned by her father when her parents were divorced. She missed him and grieved for years. When she decided to end her mourning, Anna found that she could fill the emptiness by focusing on her love for him. Anna cherished the beauty of her love. She also cherished herself for the love she felt for her own children. Focusing on those loves comforted Anna. It filled the void left by the lack of her father's love.

The same techniques can be applied to any relationship that has ended. Cherishing the love you gave and felt—which lasts forever—can help with everything from losing track of an old friend to the loss felt in divorce. Don't miss life's joy one minute more. Choose to cherish rather than miss.

Try this Soul cherishing for a moment before reading on.

- **Remember or picture an old friend or loved one.**
- **Bring to mind a particularly happy or playful time you had with that person.**
- **Notice how that thought brings a smile to your face.**
- **Feel the warm glow that fills your heart.**
- **Do the Joy Touch, and seal in that positive remembrance.**

Nothing is ever lost when you can recapture those feelings in an instant. You own those moments forever. Moreover, between here and eternity there is no Soul we won't cross paths with many times. As a result, rather than say good-bye, I prefer "until next time."

Loneliness is similar to loss. It is focusing on what we lack rather than what we have. You can comfort the limbic stress of feeling alone by getting out in nature and cherishing the beauty of the sun, the plants, and the birds. Being near water and listening to its sounds helps many people feel one with a greater whole. The same effect can be achieved by enjoying the majesty of the sky. If you hold strong religious beliefs, you can fill the emptiness by remembering that God and your Guardian Angels are always with you. Take those moments to improve your communication with them. And, don't forget to use the Joy Touch regularly.

What helps you not feel alone? Bring it to mind for a moment before you read further. Resolve to give yourself a renewal of that feeling either by reflection now, or through some specific action later.

Loss of Job or Opportunity

Equally significant is the limbic stress created by loss of job or loss of opportunity issues. The feelings of perceived failure that accompany this type of loss can be just as demoralizing as the loss of a loved one. Often a cycle of hurt and dysfunction is repeated for days, weeks, or even months after the actual end of employment. The effect is worse if the job was a major portion of your life and identity.

One of my students, Karen, lost a job in which she had invested years of her life. Her termination was particularly distressing because long work hours had gradually caused her to drop other activities and interests. She had also put friends and relationships on hold while she had devoted herself to her career. In her words, "I found myself unemployed, unmarried, without friends, and without a purpose." Karen's whole world came apart. She had invested her entire worth in the job. With it gone, she lost not only her security, but her self-esteem and direction. The more she brooded, the more depressed and helpless she felt.

Karen climbed out of her limbic black hole by using a twofold Comforting Connection. First, she got away for a while. In her case she went skiing to recapture the sense of capability and freedom she needed. The same effect can be achieved by going for a drive or taking a picnic lunch to a park near by. The key is getting away from the locations that you associate with the loss. Find a new space so you can look at life with a clearer perspective.

Second, use the loss as an opportunity for creating a new beginning. In Karen's case she used her termination as the motivation to return to school and get her master's degree in a new field. She is now successfully traveling the country as a respected instructor, helping others to get their advanced credentials in physical therapy. New beginnings can also be as simple as rearranging your living room furniture or home-office area.

Most job-loss situations trigger feelings of rejection along with the hurt of the loss. As a result, the Comforting Connections already mentioned for dealing with rejection can be helpful. They begin to clear the limbic short circuits caused by both firings and layoffs. Don't reject yourself. Seize the opportunity to make a change for the better in your life. Sometimes that means starting a new career. Sometimes it means rededicating yourself to your chosen field of endeavor.

The same is true if the loss of job is not a termination, but the loss of a promotion. Frank was an executive vice president of a major corporation. He was crushed when someone from outside the company was picked to succeed the retiring president of the firm. Rather than let the limbic stress of his disappointment poison his life, however, he chose to increase his efforts to learn everything required for the president's job. Frank took a day off and went to one one of his favorite spots overlooking the ocean. He resolved to continue believing in himself and not get discouraged. He also fully supported and assisted the new arrival. As a result, when the new president left the company three years later, he gave Frank the glowing recommendation that led to his ultimately being made president by the board of directors.

The key in all of these situations is seeing the loss as a detour, not a dead end. Whether the loss is as simple as your project being turned down or as devastating as a plant closing, *doing something* is your first Comforting Connection. Keeping active and *feeling* purposeful will ease the sense of helplessness caused by loss.

Find a new avenue for your project or resolve to temporarily file it (rather than forget it). In cases as severe as a company dissolving or a plant closing, use the extra time you now have to do things that weren't possible before. In addition to looking for work or a place to move, cherish and spend more time with your loved ones. You can also donate an afternoon or two to the public-service activities for which you never had time (Big Brothers/Sisters, Red Cross, hospital or hospice volunteer, etc.). Let the fulfillment of giving to others help you maintain your sense of value, as well as your perspective.

In each of the above examples *taking action* is the key. *Do something* rather than sit and mope. Inertia is, in essence, an emptiness of activity. Even if it is only mental, activity starts to fill the void. That is the secret of the Comforting Connection approach. It forces you to initiate action of some kind.

Try the steps below if you have had a recent loss-of opportunity or job (or want to get a new perspective on one from your past):

- **Do the Joy Touch to start off clearer and at ease.**

- **How can you see the loss as a learning?**
  (What can you do differently next time? How can you sense ahead better, or how can you refine the project?)

- **In what ways has the loss made you stronger?**
  (What new qualities have arisen in you? Or have friends and loved ones become closer?)

- **What new beginnings can you create from this detour?**
  (Identify what new training, keys for refining, or new awareness [of what is truly important to you] you can implement.)

- **What can you do that will help you feel purposeful?**
  (What actions can you take? What preparations can you make for your next phase?)

- **In what ways can you congratulate yourself?**
  (Say "bravo" for your effort, perseverence, and determination, or your creativity [with new beginnings], etc.)

- **Joy Touch and reinforce your positive new perspective.**

The library is full of psychology books that list solutions to the hurts of rejection, betrayal and loss. While each has merit, they require you to remember numerous specifics to deal with life. Once you learn the Comforting Connection process, you can be your own resource library. When you know how to ask and answer the simple questions, "What will comfort me in this situation, and how can I give it to myself?" you can find your own unique solutions for clearing *any* limbic dysfunction.

With one simple process you gain greater command of your professional and personal life. You have a defense against the debilitation of limbic stress. Further, you also learn a method for dealing with still deeper emotional issues.

The Shadow of Secret Pain

Sometimes even your normally effective comforting connection is insufficient to clear a hurt fully. You will feel relief, but still have a gnawing sadness or pain that remains. This indicates that the current hurt is just the surface issue. It reflects a deeper secret pain.

Everyone hides at least some secret pain. The pain is secret because we hide it not only from others but—more importantly—from ourselves. We hide it not because we are dishonest or are in denial. We hide it because we don't yet know how to heal it. It would be unhealthy to let these deeply embedded daggers continue to cut away, so we lock them up. They stay buried in our subconscious where they can't as obviously hurt us. The problem is that even when walled off, secret pain can eat away like acid at our happiness. The skills in this section can help you uncover your buried hurts and heal them.

Sometimes secret pains are merely recent hurts that have been suppressed. More often it involves issues from our childhood. Those wounded inner-child issues remain buried, if you do not yet have methods for adequately dealing with them. Now, with the Comforting Connection, you have the skills to heal them.

The same approaches that work in rejection or loss situations can be applied to deeper abandonment issues. The methods that comfort current abuse (whether physical, mental, verbal, or sexual) will work for inner-child hurts caused by abuse. The key is to apply the comforter to the original issue. Using the Joy Touch liberally during the clearing process is also essential.

One of my students, Sylvia, used this approach to clear a long-standing hurt caused by not feeling respected and valued by her father. Although she was never physically or sexually abused, Sylvia was mentally battered. Her dad would berate her for not being logical enough and being "too emotional." As a result she grew up feeling inadequate and valueless. Those feelings affected every facet of her adult life. She drifted from job to job and relationship to relationship, looking for something to give her value. Even when she achieved success, the least little criticism or rejection would send her into limbic dysfunction.

As part of her solution, Sylvia used a variation of Joyce's visit to the grandchildren. Whenever a rejection stimulated the memory of being unappreciated by her father, she would actively cherish herself as a young girl. Her trigger was a picture from her childhood. The photograph captured her at an age when she was particularly aglow with the joy of life. One look at the picture and she realized what a beautiful and vibrant Soul she was and still is. That mental medication and the assistance of a caring psychotherapist helped Sylvia to heal the childhood wounds of her father's disapproval.

In therapy she eventually explored and cleared the issues from her past that were holding her back. Between sessions when a rejection stimulated the secret pain, Sylvia had a way of dealing with it. Her Comforting Connection would break the hold of the past hurt on her present happiness and performance. She also automatically did the Joy Touch every time she looked at the picture. This doubled her relief.

Lets practice how to clear a secret pain and feel good about it.

- **Do the Joy Touch to start off feeling good about yourself.**

- **Pick a worry, hurt, anger, or fear that you think is deeper.** (One that has its roots in childhood.)

- **Identify what event or circumstance created the pain.**

- **Do the Joy Touch to reward your honesty and desire to learn.**

- **Think of a comforter that would have helped back then.** (Would being told you are not alone, being valued, feeling protected, or feeling listened to, etc. have helped?)

- **Decide how you can now soothe that injured earlier you.** (Would saying to yourself what you wish you had heard back then, or giving yourself the hugs you never got help?) (Know your full worth, see yourself as beautiful, growing, and not alone, etc.)

- **Do the Joy Touch to reinforce your insight and new wisdom.**

- **Congratulate yourself for lightening your emotional baggage (even if just a little).**

- **Do the Joy Touch one last time in celebration of your increased freedom.** (Feel lighter. Feel clearer of secret pain. Feel free to be happier.)

Your Comforting Connections can reduce the hurt of any secret pain, especially when combined with activating the septum pellucidum area. For many people the Joy Touch and the Comforting

Connection concept gives them the tools for being their own therapists. For some, having a trained facilitator to work with is essential. You know yourself best. Never hesitate to seek the skill of a professional therapist if you are stuck or need that help to fully uncover inner-child issues.

Whatever option you choose, however, utilize your Comforting Connections and the Joy Touch between sessions. Disconnect the disruption of the limbic cycle until the appropriate time for addressing the core issues. With these two techniques you can break the negative cycle of limbic stress and file the incident until later in the day. Then the issues can be examined at leisure rather than under the pressures of your job or busy family situations.

Either on your own or with professional facilitation, it is important to uncover and clear secret pain. Left buried, it vastly increases your vulnerability to limbic stress. Emotional scar tissue will cause you to overreact to daily hurts. You will stay locked in their limbic short circuits longer. Resolve to use your mental resources to handle more than immediate problems. Clear all the issues that can diminish your abilities and rob you of happiness.

Secret pain often has ties to another limbic stress—anger. Let's explore that area next.

Defusing Your Inner Explosives

Anger is the limbic stress that literally explodes within us. Unless that time bomb is defused before it reaches a critical level, a self-perpetuating chain reaction occurs. The anger can literally take on a life of its own. Like a fire storm that consumes everything around it, anger can turn all facets of your life to ashes. The brightest of days can be fouled and clouded by its smoke.

The first step in defusing the limbic stress of anger is to *diffuse* it. You must dilute the influence of your limbic rage reflexes. Anything that lessens or distracts your focus from angry feelings, prevents them from reaching that critical mass.

In the past, psychology's main advice was the platitude, "Try to take time out and calm down." While this does work, it is frequently not possible to disengage from a circumstance that is angering you, or to calm down quickly enough to keep from restimulating the irritation and exploding. Further, many people feel lost when told to calm down. They don't know what specifically to do to relax and can't keep angry thoughts from popping back to mind.

Now you have something specific you can do that works in seconds. You can use the Joy Touch to immediately start calming yourself physiologically and mentally. The mere action of rubbing your forehead can help you remember to use the technique and start cooling down faster.

The Joy Touch diffuses the anger in two ways. First, the mere focus of doing something helps to pull you up to higher cortical functioning. Second, even if your anger still simmers, the stimulation of the brain's mood-elevation mechanisms reduces the dominance of the rage reflexes. At a minimum, this turns off the heat by distracting your attention and disrupting the fight-or-flight hormone production. At maximum, the mood-elevation boost may also produce soothing endorphins and enkephalins that, chemically speaking, can douse the flames of anger.

Anything that distracts you positively also can be an effective diffuser. Listening to upbeat or soothing music can drown out the inner dialogue of your anger. Getting outside or looking out a window can increase your visual input and pull your attention away from the scene of your upset (just make sure what you view is soothing not irritating). Taking a walk or engaging in other vigorous physical activity distracts you by requiring you to focus on muscular coordination. Physical exercise also physiologically counters anger by burning up adrenalin and returning the body to a lower arousal state once the exercise is finished. For extreme rage, this physical "letting off steam" may be crucial to reducing the anger to a level where other approaches can be considered. The key is activity that is safe for you and not harmful to others (such as running, aerobis, swimming, or punching a bag—not people).

Another way of diffusing anger is to find healthy methods for letting off steam verbally. It is equally important to vent the mental explosion that accompanies anger. Without effectively letting off steam mentally, anger's repetitive cycle of hostile thoughts are like powder kegs waiting to be reignited.

The Joy Touch is also an important first step for defusing anger with appropriate verbal venting. The technique restores the calmness required for regaining a realistic appraisal of the situation. It can help your thoughts progress from, "You always . . . " to "I'm angry because in this situation you did . . . " That clarity and realism also helps you identify what will best clear your anger. See Chapter 1 pages 23-24, for a reminder of how to use it as a first step in dealing with anger.

The second step is to vent verbally either by writing (journaling) or by speaking up. Actually, this venting process is started the minute you identify the anger. Thoughts, when slowed down, usually become word-based understandings. The verbal venting is continued as you find appropriate ways to let your feelings out (rather than keeping them bottled up). Stuffing your feelings doesn't work, because they always come out later, usually in a more caustic form. Holding feelings in can be physically as well as emotionally damaging. That buried acid can lead to everything from ulcers and bitterness to cancer and the inability to love. Accurately expressing your feelings (not just attacking someone) is vital for clearing any limbic stress. It is imperative for effectively defusing anger.

While it always *feels* better to let off steam and verbally vent, it doesn't truly help unless it is done correctly. Experimental tests show that mere outbursts of anger just pump up the rage centers' arousal level, causing people to become even angrier. Specifically stating what you feel angry about, however, does make a difference. It not only lets off steam, but also engages your analytical mind, thus reducing the limbic brain dominance that anger can create.

As much as possible, vent in a way that doesn't hurt you or your loved ones. The intent of venting is to release the internal pressure, not displace the anger onto someone else. The key is being clear about your specific feelings, rather than just blaming. "I feel angry because I was counting on you to be here at the time we agreed!" is better than "You're always late!" "I feel angry because I made a mistake" is preferable to "I always mess up."

Remember also, that asking, "What will comfort me in this situation?" does not mean, "What will end my anger by solving the situation?" The desired comforting effect is created by soothing the pressure you feel. Adding the extra burden of having to solve the situation usually just adds fuel to the fire. For example, if the anger is caused by feeling helpless or powerless, the inability to see an immediate solution can be like throwing gasoline on your existing flames of frustration. When you are caught up in limbic rage, you are disconnected from your problem-solving higher mental functions. Vent and diffuse the anger first, then look for solutions.

Once you have diffused your anger, one of the first solutions is simply getting your feelings heard.

Anger at Not Feeling Heard

Specific verbal venting is a key skill because many angers are triggered by feeling someone is not listening to you. In those situations getting your feelings out and heard is the easiest and most effective way to start venting the pressure and self-comforting your anger. In fact, much of the latest research on anger and emotional intelligence supports this concept. Scientists say that one of the keys to having a high EQ is verbalizing your feelings. Saying "I *feel* angry" is smarter and healthier than exploding into hostile actions. Stating how you feel and why you are angry not only activates the prefrontal cortex (a key area for integrating your emotions and your conscious mind), it also allows you to let off steam. In this circumstance a large part of your Comforting Connection is merely feeling heard.

This doesn't mean you have to speak directly with the person at whom you are angry. In fact, it is usually better not to at this point. Your first explosive outbursts may push the other person into reactive or defensive anger. Also, always do the Joy Touch first to defuse some of the intensity of your anger. Then vent on your own or to a trusted friend or co-worker.

If you don't have someone who can lend an ear, talk out loud to yourself. Speaking helps to pull you out of the limbic short circuit. If you brood, you stay stuck in the loop of limbic rage. The simple physical act of controlling the vocal cords connects you with your cerebral cortex. Writing your feelings down can achieve the same effect. It forces you to access and use higher brain centers. Both methods (talking or writing) also accomplish that initial venting.

Once you have successfully vented, you can start with the final specific steps of your Comforting Connection process. Remember to use the Joy Touch liberally as you identify what it is that you want to be heard about, and then the best time, place, and approach for completing that communication.

Let's clear something you haven't felt heard about.

- **Identify a situation in which you were angry about not feeling heard or when someone wasn't listening to you.**
- **Do the Joy Touch to relax and be objective.**
- **State out loud or write how you feel and why you are angry.**
- **Do the Joy Touch to stay in control and acknowledge your right to be upset.**
- **State out loud or write what you want to be heard about.**
- **Think about the best time, best place and the best approach for being heard.**
  (Prepare a written note, or humorous card, saying, "I need to talk with you about something upsetting me," etc.)
- **Do the Joy Touch to stay calm so you can share without attacking or overreacting.**
- **Congratuale yourself for processing your anger in a way that is healthy and mature.**

One of the benefits of talking out loud is that you *do* get heard—

by yourself, at the very least. Hearing yourself can often help end your anger. First, you hear what you are actually angry about. Verbalizing forces you to outline the issues rather than just be mad. Hearing yourself can also help you recognize the occasional ridiculousness of your anger.

Long before I knew the Joy Touch, I had just such an experience in New York on the publicity tour for my first book, *You Are Psychic!* I had been signing books in the city and was taking the train to Long Island to spend an evening with family. Because I was pulling a luggage carrier, I needed a particular seat. At the ends of each car there are two seats that face three seats. If I could get one of those end seats I could put my luggage carrier in the empty space. It would also make it easier to get off the train.

It wasn't going to be easy, as the platform was full of people waiting for the same train. I decided to use the psychic techniques in my book to sense where the doors I needed would stop. Tapping my intuition, I visualized where to stand, and sure enough, I was right in front of an end entrance as the train pulled to a halt. I stepped on the train and found that I had picked the *one car* that had a bathroom where those seats usually were! Dragging the luggage carrier (only inches narrower than the aisle), I headed for the other end and the three-and-two seats there. To my horror, people began pouring in the other door. I was trapped in the middle.

Now I was in real trouble, because I had to change trains at an intermediate stop. It had been hard enough to maneuver the luggage carrier down the empty aisle. Now there were elbows, legs and feet blocking my path all the way to the door. I might not be able to negotiate this gauntlet during the train's short stop at the intermediate station. Sitting down, I resolved to be positive and rise to the challenge. If I used my best assertive voice I could "excuse me," "pardon me," "coming through" my way to the doors in time.

You know what? I made it! I dragged that damn luggage carrier through the sea of elbows and feet and stepped off the train just as the doors closed behind me. I was exhilarated. I did it! I raised my arms in victory and said, "Yes!" But as I stared at the deserted platform in front of me, I realized that I had succeeded in *getting off at the wrong stop*. Not only that, but the next train wasn't due for over an hour. I went ballistic.

Had I known the Joy Touch at the time I probably could have calmed down quickly. But I didn't and I was furious. I was fed up with the hassles of all big cities and New York in particular. It's a bit embarrassing, but I vented by aiming a series of choice karate kicks at the lampposts and billboards on the station platform, all the while expressing my feelings about being stuck in the middle of Queens. The release and calm I felt from the catharsis of the intense exercise did help to ease some of my rage.

One positive result of the situation was that for ten or fifteen minutes that was the safest train station in New York City. Any muggers or drug pushers in the area probably stayed away saying, "Don't go up there, there's a crazy man on that platform!" The taxi drivers near me actually got in their cabs and backed to the far end of the station.

As I started to cool down, I verbally let go at myself. I was due to be interviewed about my book the next night on Larry King's coast-to-coast radio show. I found myself saying, "Yeah, right! 'You are psychic'!—you can't even get off at the right train stop!" Then I started to laugh. I heard not only the humor in the situation, but I realized how unfair I was being to myself. Just because I had made discoveries in psychic sensitivity, it didn't mean that I had to be perfect. I was still allowed to be learning too. During the interview the next night I remembered that principle. Instead of presenting myself as the infallible expert, I spoke from the point of view of an explorer. I stated on the air, "I don't know everything about ESP, but I have found secrets from brain science that allow you to tap the four psychic senses at will." The show was so well received that I was invited to appear on Larry King's national television show on CNN.

It's a funny story, but it also illustrates two points. First, that venting helped me to cool down quickly. When I arrived at my relatives' house, I was calm and brought humor rather than anger into their home. We all shared a laugh as opposed to my being grumpy and still upset. While this was an extreme example of venting, my method of release really didn't hurt anyone. Vibrating a few lampposts is far better than exploding in displaced anger at a friend or family member. Always look for ways to release your anger without harming your loved ones or co-workers, but *get it out*. Otherwise you become a walking volcano ready to erupt on the next poor soul you encounter. You now also have the benefit of knowing the Joy Touch. The quicker you use it when you start to get angry, the less likely you will be to go overboard physically or verbally. Continuing the Joy Touch as you cool down also helps you get completely calm sooner.

The story also illustrates the importance of verbalizing. Hearing how unfair I was being to myself was the key for breaking the cycle. It had the added benefit of triggering an insight that helped me give one of my best radio interviews.

I chose this story because it also points out a deeper application of the Comforting Connection process. Many of our angers involve anger at ourselves. If you don't deal with that anger, the rage keeps simmering (even after you deal with the other people that angered you). In fact, any time you can't clear an anger (even after verbalizing and venting), it's a sure sign that there is a deeper anger (at self or from childhood) still remaining. In my case I had to clear my self-criticism before I could return to feeling good about life and New York City.

Always add these steps to your Comforting Connection process if anger at yourself is part of the issue.

- **State out loud what has made you angry at yourself.**
  (Remember to be specific with your feelings rather than just attacking yourself.)
- **Do the Joy Touch and remember you are only human.**
  (You are allowed to make mistakes and be learning.)
- **Channel your anger into a disciplined desire to improve or change.**
  (What can you do differently next time; how are you going to work harder?)

Anger at Feeling Helpless and/or Unfairly Controlled

Feeling controlled or unfairly treated is another common cause of anger. In those cases when you ask, "What will comfort me in this situation?" the answer frequently is "not feeling controlled." Most often speaking to the individual involved (after you have verbalized to yourself and vented the initial rage) usually clears the remaining limbic short circuit. It gives the other person the chance to apologize or explain the actions that may have been misunderstood, both of which can help defuse the explosive chain reaction within you.

When there is no apology or clarification, use the comforting concept to regain your inner control. Martha, who lives in San Francisco, felt unfairly controlled by her supervisor, Thelma. Nothing Martha did was going to change the unfair rigidity Thelma maintained over Martha's work schedule. That made Martha furious and destroyed her enjoyment of work. Martha knew what would comfort her: feeling in control. She remembered something I had often taught—that we can't always be in control of everything (as Donald Trump and Leona Helmsley found out), but we *can* always be in command of our state of mind.

Martha decided to apply that concept as her Comforting Connection. She chose to feel free inside despite her external circumstances.

She was free to choose to be happy rather than upset. The change in her quality of life was instantaneous. Rather than being angry and unhappy at work, she was more productive and proud of her inner mastery. She also took pleasure in the fact that the domineering supervisor couldn't get to her.

Try this self-empowering process for yourself.

- **Think of a situation where you felt helpless or controlled.**
- **Do the Joy Touch to stay calm and not overreactive.**
- **State your feelings and think of a healthy way to vent your frustration.**
- **Do the Joy Touch and remember that you are not helpless.**
- **Decide what action you can take that eases your frustration and be productive.**
- **Review the choices you *can* make to be happier.**
  (As a minimum, choosing not to let them get to you is an empowering action)
- **Do the Joy Touch and reinforce your power to choose to be happy.**
- **End by acknowledging the control you do have in your life.**
  (Be proud of yourself and feel your inner power for acknowledging your feelings, seeing the good things in your life, and choosing to control your state of mind.

Anger at Not Being Valued

Sometimes anger is caused by not feeling valued. In these cases valuing *yourself* is the best comforting connection. Phoenix instructor, Katie Bechtel, found a creative method to release anger and appreciate herself. She felt that her computer work in a legal office wasn't being valued. She decided to use a picture she painted as her "self-valuing Comforting Connection" and hung it in a place of honor above her terminal. You see, Katie's father had refused to support her childhood goal to be an artist. To her, the painting symbolized the respect she had for her artistic ability. Anytime she felt that she or her computer work weren't being valued, she looked up at the painting. She used it as a trigger for cherishing her creativity. Seeing the painting helped Katie to instantly value herself.

Try this process for clearing an anger about not feeling valued.

- **Think of a time when you felt angry about not being valued.**
- **Do the Joy Touch to stay calm and mentally clear.**

- State your feelings out loud and specifically identify what you feel is not being valued.
- Do the Joy Touch and remember that you are a unique and valuable individual.
- Think of a symbol of your value you can give to yourself. (Place a note on mirror. Give yourself a flower, or a self-hug. Review your accomplishments, etc.)
- Do the Joy Touch and seal in the knowledge that you are a one-of-a-kind special Soul.

Katie's example also illustrates how an anger can have deeper roots in your past. If you feel the anger ties back to a childhood situation, use the deeper Comforting Connection process described in the Secret Pain section (pp. 57-59) to help you fully clear your distress.

Irritation Anger

Often anger is nonspecific. The many complexities of modern living can create a mood of general agitation. Nonspecific irritability can then lead to angry outbursts over basically trivial hassles. This chain of events is physiologically based and can be best dealt with using the Joy Touch. Irritations gradually build up the level of rage hormones (particularly catecholamines). This slowly escalates the body's level of arousal and thus your susceptibility to explosions of anger.

Using the Joy Touch can interrupt the pattern, preventing your pot from boiling over. Use the technique to soothe your irritation. Doing the Joy Touch often and immediately can prevent your agitation level from heating up to that flashpoint.

If you do lose it, try to identify whether your anger was specific (triggered by a real event that you are justified in being upset about) or just general irritation overload. If the anger is specific, do the Joy Touch and pursue the specific Comforting Connection that applies. If the upset is just general irritation, focus primarily on using the Joy Touch repeatedly to calm down and soothe your level of agitation. In either case don't succumb to the trap of getting angry at yourself for being angry.

Anger at Getting Angry

It is unfair to yourself to think you will never get angry. All emotions generated by the limbic system can (at least momentarily) dominate the conscious mind and our immediate reactions. That is natural because the limbic brain evolved before the higher cortex. The limbic system is designed to command attention and generate an immediate response. It treats every situation as a life-threatening crisis. You wouldn't get angry at your eyes for their blink reflex. It is equally unfair to be unduly upset with yourself for getting angry.

We can't control what gets us angry. We can control how we react to the triggering of the emotion. That ability is a key indicator of EQ and emotional intelligence. That control is difficult enough without adding the fuel to the fire of anger at yourself for getting angry. Realize that it is normal and healthy to get angry. The key is to control the length of the anger.

This is a perfect time to address the issue of the normal, healthy duration of even negative emotions. Once the limbic brain is triggered you are going to experience physiologically a certain minimum of emotional turmoil. This is particularly true of anger. It is virtually impossible to calm the anger reaction immediately. When the rage centers are stimulated, it is the brain's equivalent of turning on an oven. Even if you quickly control your temper, your physiological broiler has been lit long enough to heat up the oven. Turning off the flame will not instantly bring it back to room temperature. The oven will have a specific, natural cool down time. That is the way both physics and your brain's biochemistry work. It is unreasonable to expect your control and return to calmness to be immediate. So, it is totally unfair to yourself to be angry about getting upset. If you must be angry at yourself, let it be for continuing the upset too long, or inappropriately dealing with your emotions, not the fact that you got angry in the first place.

The key is to identify what is the normal healthy duration of an anger once it is triggered. Even if you catch yourself right away, what is the reasonable amount of time it should take for your body chemistry to fully calm down (assuming also that nothing restimulates your rage). In my experience that period is (at a minimum) 5 to 15 minutes, depending on the personality type and gender (men tend to light the flame more explosively) of the individual.

Using the Joy Touch can help. It is the physiological equivalent of opening the door of the oven and cooling it faster. Even then, it will still take time for the oven walls to return to normal temperature. The same is true of your brain. Don't fall into the trap of thinking that just because you know the Joy Touch you are no longer supposed to get mad (or sad, or anxious). You are allowed those emotions; they are normal parts of life. Rather than deny them, strive instead to prevent their out-of-control negative sides from dragging on and dominating your life. Identifying and working within your healthy time limits for them is the answer.

Take a moment and identify what you feel are reasonable time limits for calming your anger.

- Do the Joy Touch to start off calm and objective.
- Identify how long your normal and reasonable time limit should be for being angry.
  (This is without using the Joy Touch. How long are you allowed to take to cool down?)
- Now identify how long you are allowed to stay upset even with using the Joy Touch.
  (Using the Joy Touch alone does not undo the fact that your mental oven got heated up.)
- What Comforting Connection will ease your anger at yourself for getting angry?
  (Saying, "I'm human, I'm allowed to have reactions, I'm allowed to be learning," etc.)
- If desired, do the same identification for hurts, worries, and fears.

You can use these estimates as guidelines for appropriately processing your anger. Shoot for clearing the upset within these lengths of time. As a minimum, try to allow yourself that period of time without reagitation. Also, remember to give yourself a Comforting Connection that reaffirms your right to those emotions. That and the Joy Touch provide a method for truly boosting your EQ and rising above our animal past.

These are just a few examples of how to process angers. Life gives us plenty of opportunities for research. One of the benefits of knowing the Joy Touch and Comforting Connection techniques is that I no longer think of my problems and upsets negatively. I consider them research material for advanced variations and applications of the techniques.

Nowhere in life do we need research more than in the area of preventing worries from eroding our happiness. Let's look at that area next.

How to Silence Your "Worry Machine"

Although not as painful or damaging as hurts and angers, worry is easily the most disruptive of the limbic stresses. Hurts can lead to new growth. Angers can at least serve as motivators. But most of the time worry does nothing positive. It slowly drains you, sapping both your energy and your alertness. When you are caught in the mental wheel-spinning of worry, you literally operate at half speed. Mental capacities you could be using for work and/or enjoying life are tied up in the cyclical inner dialogue of your "worry machine."

Worry is the stress that most embodies the broken-record characteristic of limbic dysfunction. Once a worry gets started, we repeat it over and over in our minds. That mental static causes impaired concentration, irritability, and degraded performance. Worry usurps mental energy needed to operate at our best.

The first step in quieting your worry machine is to stop the endless cycling. Prevent the mental distraction from becoming repetitive, and you are halfway to clearing this limbic dysfunction. First, do the Joy Touch to relieve your feeling of anxiety. Then write the worry down as a way to help break the cycle. Worries are repetitive for a reason; they represent a problem that needs a solution. Subconsciously the repetition is telling us, "Don't forget to deal with this." The broken-record effect is a physiological safeguard for ensuring that we don't forget. When you write your worries down you get them recorded. *That permanence disconnects the "don't forget" mechanism.*

Writing your worries down also helps you identify the exact issues and their scope. Worries always look smaller and fewer once you get them on paper. The mental repetition of worries always makes them seem bigger. The sooner you get them down on paper, the sooner you start to lessen your perceived mental burden. As described earlier with angers, writing pulls you into higher brain functions and out of the limbic short circuit.

If your dysfunction is so severe that even after doing the Joy Touch you have difficulty beginning to write, find another sensory input to override the limbic static. Listening to music, petting an animal, smelling flowers, or soaking in the sunshine can soothe your anxiety and help you begin writing.

Occasionally, however, just writing down the problem will trigger ideas and solutions. If so, all the better. Seize the moment to do the problem-solving or planning that will end the worry. As a minimum, use your list to prevent the mental repetition of the worry. With your list you can file the worry and process it at a more convenient time.

One novel approach is to set aside a designated worry hour. Pick a time after your regular workday or family responsibilities when you can process your worries. That way you can prevent an anxiety from interfering with your day by truthfully saying, "I'll worry about that later." The beauty of this approach is that you are not denying or avoiding the problem. You are simply refusing to let it dominate your day. Write the anxiety down as you become aware of it. Then process it during your designated worry time. With the problem recorded, that can be whenever you choose. Choosing the time also starts to put you back in control.

Feeling in control is a key Comforting Connection for worry. We worry because we feel unsure about a decision or feel powerless to control an outcome we desire. It is an ancient physiological reflex going back to our earliest evolution. Back then high anxiety meant constant vigilance and thus a greater chance for survival. Worry was the biological method of choice for the ultimate control—staying alive.

Nowadays we aren't faced with the same physical survival pressures. We still have a limbic brain, however. Even now the limbic system still focuses on spotting potential threats (real or imagined) and triggering that out-of-control anxiety. How you regain your sense of control depends on the type of worry that is making you anxious. Here are the most common.

Getting It Right

"What is the right decision?" is a universal worry. Anytime you have to decide with only partial information, you are ripe for the stress of "rightness" worry. This form of anxiety is particularly debilitating because of its prolonged duration. Not only is there worry during your decision-making process, the anxiety continues long after in the form of second-guessing yourself. When I refinanced my house I experienced the mind-numbing effect of this type of worry. Until I cleared it, I was unable to function effectively.

I knew absolutely nothing about refinancing and there were so many options to consider. Should I lock in at the current interest rate? Should I let the rate float? Will the rates go up or down? Will the appraisal be high enough to cover the refinancing? Which mortgage broker should I use? Should I go VA or conventional? Which decision is the right one to save my family the most money?

My head felt thick from thinking about the literally hundreds of options. Doing all the research took weeks, and day by day my worry increased and my effectiveness deteriorated. One morning I realized my whole life was paralyzed by the tightness I felt from the worry. My creativity was stifled and I couldn't write coherently. I was grouchy with my family and unhappy most of the time. I knew I had to clear the limbic stress and get on with my life. I did the Joy Touch and then asked, "What would comfort me in this situation?" Immediately I heard, "Knowing that I will make the *right* decision."

In an instant I realized I was overworrying about being right, about making the perfect decision. I was letting a quarter of a percentage point be more important than my peace of mind. Sure, I wanted to get the best deal, but it wasn't that crucial. No matter what I did, I was going to lower my interest rate by at least three percentage points. I was already making the right decision by refinancing. The rest were details that weren't worth ruining my life over. I used the psychic skills I know and the research I had done to make the best decision I could. Then I got back to work.

I felt like a fog had been lifted from my brain. My writing started flowing again. I could once again play joyously with my young children without mentally being somewhere else. My only regret was that I waited so long to ask, "What will comfort me here?"

This story illustrates the Comforting Connection of "putting it in perspective." Often with "getting it right" worries we magnify the importance of details or make our worth dependent on the perfection of a decision. Am I a worthless person because of missing the best deal by an eighth of a percentage point? Of course not!

Even if your job requires critical decision-making, you can only do the best you know how with the data you have. Worry actually degrades your ability to think clearly. Physiologically, we know that worry interferes with working memory (your ability to hold in mind the key data required for completing a task). This can in turn impair your creativity, intuition, and judgment. Make the decision by drawing on the full resources of your higher cortex, not suffering from the mind-numbing static of limbic stress.

Other ways of triggering the put-it-in-perspective Comforting Connection are questions like, "How important will this be a million years from now?" or "If I had only six months to live, how crucial would this be?" When the gloom of an anxiety surrounds you, counting your blessings can literally shed light on your preoccupation with the worry. Realizing that many decisions are not final can also take the pressure off. Think of your plan as a rough draft or an initial direction that can be modified later. Anything that alleviates the rightness worry will lessen the limbic short circuit. In all cases, doing the Joy Touch provides a pocket of inner calm that makes these perspectives and depressurizers easier to see and apply.

Try clearing a worry you have about getting something right.

- **Think of something (past or present) that you worry/worried about getting right.**

- **Do the Joy Touch to start off calm and objective.**

- **Put the worry in perspective. How crucial is it?**
  (Is it life-threatening? Is there only one chance? Does the decision have to be final, etc.?)

- Do the Joy Touch and affirm that you can handle the decision.
- Acknowledge what you have done right thus far.
  (You have spotted the problem and faced it, rather than avoiding the issue, etc.)
- Do the Joy Touch and realize you can self-comfort this worry.
- Decide what actions you are going to take next.
  (More research, consulting others, rough plan, sleep on it, etc.)
- Do the Joy Touch and support yourself for going forward.
  (Realize you are doing the best you know how. Remember your right to be learning).
- Pick the key Comforting Connection you will use if the worry returns.
  (Realize that it isn't that crucial. Realize that you are making progress. See what you have done right thus far. Realize you have a plan for doing the best you can, etc.)

Why do we get so wrapped up in needing to make the right decision? It's because we feel responsible.

The Burden of Responsibility

Responsibility is the yoke we use to chain ourselves to working and living in a stressful environment. When we feel responsible, everything becomes pressured. Worry is the limbic stress that is triggered by uncertainty. Responsibility makes it worse. It opens the door for anxiety about everything that might happen. That burden can make even the most enjoyable work unpleasant. It certainly can pressure your relationships. Compare the difference between being a grandparent and a parent, or the change that occurs from dating to being married.

When you feel responsible, making the right decisions becomes even more crucial. I'm not advocating irresponsibility or not caring. I'm saying, don't use your responsibilities as a pressure. Don't let them make you a victim of the limbic stress of worry. If you have responsibilities, you are going to have worries. It's how you deal with them that makes all the difference. Don't let the responsibility make you feel helpless. Instead of being responsible, be *response able*. You *are* able to respond to any situation. You are not helpless. You can choose how you wish to respond. That conscious choice gives you an instant sense of control. It gives you freedom, rather than the limbic stress of feeling burdened.

When we feel responsible, it is easy to worry about all the what-ifs. The best way to comfort the feeling of being helpless is simply to have a plan. Any plan, complete or not, puts you back in control. Whether providing for retirement or your children's college tuition or wanting to prevent a heart attack or cancer, a plan gives you a method for taking action. It gets you out of worry and into making progress. You are able to respond by making a plan.

Remember also to let your plan evolve. You don't have to have all the solutions at once. A plan merely to start gathering information can clear the limbic short circuit. I constantly juggle numerous projects, instructor relationships, and family commitments. My mind churns out dozens of what-ifs each day. I handle the potential overload with a simple notebook. As I think of problems, I record the worry on the appropriate project's page. Then I take a few moments to list the options available and the deadline for making an initial decision. This clears the nagging worry from my mind and allows me to return unencumbered to my work or family interactions. I accomplish more and have a greater enjoyment of life. I don't let what-ifs paralyze me. I self-comfort by using them to help me plan.

This is what I call worrying constructively. Most worry is destructive. We berate ourselves with all the what-might-happens. That just makes us feel helpless and out of control. In constructive worry you use the what-ifs to generate your plan ahead of time. When your mind says, "What if...?", finish the conversation. Instead of just repeating the worry, identify what you would do if it did happen. Brainstorm on the options available to you. This process puts you in your higher mental functions rather than locked in limbic stress.

Worrying constructively is the key to making worry positive. There was a physiological reason those worry circuits were developed. With constructive worry you can train them to work for you, not against you.

Let's try clearing a worry about feeling responsible.

- **Think of something you worry or worried about because you feel responsible.**
- **Do the Joy Touch to start off calm and clear.**
- **Identify the exact aspects for which you feel responsible.**
- **Do the Joy Touch to realize you have the freedom to be *response able*.**
- **Choose the way you want to initially respond.**
- **Do the Joy Touch and reaffirm that you are in control and can handle this responsibility.**

- **Pick a comforter that you will use when this responsibility worry reoccurs.**
  (Saying, "I am in control, I am response able, I am free, not help-less or shackled," etc.)

and for the second part—dealing with the what-ifs of worry.

- **Make a list of all the what-ifs of your worry.**
- **Do the Joy Touch to stimulate relaxation and creativity.**
- **Now, write next to each what-if, what you could do if it did occur.**
- **Resolve to worry constructively when you feel responsible.**
  (Identify what actions you can take. Develop plans for address-ing your concern, etc.)
- **Do the Joy Touch and reinforce your ability to convert worry into creative solutions.**

Security Issues (Worries about Job, Health, and Money)

Worry about losing your job, health, or money are all basically security issues. Having a plan is again your primary Comforting Connection for these limbic stresses. Writing down your options for job hunting, helping maintain your health, or maximizing your financial security keeps you from feeling helpless. You can clear the anxiety further by taking action on what you have written. Start com-piling a resume, or see what openings are available in your field or other areas of interest. Begin an improved exercise and nutritional regimen. Set aside a little money each week in a savings account. You will always feel more secure when you are actively *doing something*. That momentum gives you a sense of control and adaptability. Iner-tia just leads to vulnerability and greater anxiety.

Sometimes initiating action can be as simple as staying informed. Karen found a unique way to ease her anxiety about being laid off. She worked in a Los Angeles construction firm and had watched it dwindle from 50 employees to 5. Every week she would wonder, "Am I next?" She found she couldn't work effectively with that un-certainty. The anxiety was also making her personal life a mess. Karen resolved to not live and work in that shadow of doubt. Each Monday she checked in with her supervisor and asked, "How is my job security this week?" She received the assurances she needed to work with a clear mind and not let job worry interfere with her per-sonal life. Even if she had received a negative response, the uncer-tainty would be over. She could actively begin looking for new employment.

For health issues, subscribing to a magazine such as *Longevity* or *Prevention* can keep you abreast of all the latest discoveries in health maintenance and nutrition.

Many people worry about investments and losing money. The best Comforting Connections for this limbic stress is a *before* rather than *after* approach. Never invest or gamble more than you can afford to lose. Even if the potential reward is enticing, evaluate if it is worth the risk to your health and quality of life. What good does having extra money do if the worry kills you years before your time?

If a financial loss does occur, remember not to reject yourself for it. Look for Comforting Connections that support your self-esteem. If you earned the money once, you can do it again. Also focus on what you still have (your health, your family, your future, etc.).

Security issues have the double stress of triggering both rightness and responsibility worries. We feel doubly responsible for making the right decision because it frequently affects more than ourselves alone. You may find that no one Comforting Connection is sufficient. That's all right. Find and use the combination of keys that gradually helps you free yourself from the grip of this multiple limbic stress. Recognize also that the stress is multiple because you are feeling responsible for more than one person.

Let's try clearing a worry you have about a security issue.

- **Pick a health, money, or job issue that is worrying you.**

- **Do the Joy Touch to start off calm and thinking clearly.**

- **Identify exactly what you are worried about and list any what-ifs related to it.**

- **Do the Joy Touch and ask, "What exactly would comfort me in this situation?"**

- **Identify the essence of what would soothe your anxiety.**
  (What actions, plans, or preparations can you take? Would seeing the bigger picture help, etc?)

- **Next to any what-ifs, list the specific steps you could take.**

- **Joy Touch and reinforce that you can handle the issue.**

- **Pick the Comforting Connection that best clears the worry.**
  (Having a plan, realizing you are not helpless, putting it in perspective, etc.)

Worry about Family

It is particularly hard to release our feelings of responsibility for our loved ones, especially children. There are so many things we "could" do or "should" know. It is easy to feel responsible for "how the kids turn out." This is where I find the *response able* and *worry constructively* approaches are essential. No matter what the latest mess or stage of development the kids are in, I *am* able to respond. I am doing, and always will do, the best I know how.

I also use the following question to help put things in perspective: Are my kids Souls or lumps of dough? If they are merely lumps of dough, I am totally responsible for how they turn out. If they are Souls, they came into this life with their own individual agendas. I can use my worry to plan how to best guide, nurture, teach, and support them. In the final analysis, however, it is their life. They are responsible for it, not I.

Wray Plunkett, a New Mexico instructor, used this approach when she found herself worrying about her only daughter's future. Even though Chelsea was on her own and in college, Wray still worried. Will she do well enough in her academics? Will Chelsea make the right decisions? Wray comforted her anxieties by shifting to a different perspective. She realized she had done a good job of raising Chelsea and she had to trust her daughter to apply what she had learned. She found herself saying, "Whatever will be, I wish only that Chelsea be guided toward the best interests for her own life's path." Wray then resolved to be *response able* if Chelsea ever did need her advice and support. In this way she could be proud of Chelsea and cheer for her, rather than fret and worry. She could care about Chelsea, rather than worry over her.

We all want to be effective and caring parents. We just have to learn not to let that concern make us slaves. It is not possible to spare our children all of the bumps of life. Those "forging furnaces" are why Souls come to planet Earth. Don't deny your children the wisdom learned from experience. By the way, it is possible to raise children with no problems and no wounded inner-child issues. The result, however, is usually broken parents. The proper balance is somewhere in between.

Practice clearing a family-related worry.

- **Think of a family-related worry.**
- **Do the Joy Touch to start off calm and at ease.**
- **First, congratulate yourself for caring enough to worry.**
- **Next, specifically identify what has you worried.**
- **Do the Joy Touch to ease the anxiety and gain an objective perspective.**
- **What is the essence of what would make you feel better, and how can you give it to yourself?**

- **Identify what you can do to "care" about them rather than just worry.**
  (The action need not be physical. It could be verbal support, or mentally sending love.)
- **Think of ways to be supportive, instead of fussy or critical.**
- **Do the Joy Touch and realize you too are allowed to be learning.**
- **Pick the Comforting Connection that is your key for this worry.**
  (Be response able, list constructive answers to what-ifs, or be caring, not worrying, etc.)

Anxiety about what might happen is where worry starts to transform into fear.

Skills for Dealing with Fears

There is an old story about a youth in deepest, darkest Africa who was separated for several years from his village. When he finally returned home everything he saw lay in ruin. No one was outside working or enjoying life. Everyone was huddled in their huts in fear of the dragon that had taken residence on the hill overlooking the village.

The youth resolved to free his village, but as he looked up the hill he saw an enormous monster. Though he was afraid, he couldn't bear to see his family living in fear. He took his courage in hand and charged up the hill to confront the dragon. Halfway up he slowed down and looked up. Somehow the dragon looked smaller, but it spit fire at him. Terrified, he ran back down the hill. When he looked up again, the monster was even bigger than before. He trembled at the thought of what it might do to him.

Finally, with his spear in hand he threw all caution to the wind and charged all the way up the hill. When he arrived at the top, however, he could not find the monster. He looked and looked but saw nothing. Just then he felt something small biting his foot. He looked down and there was a tiny two-inch dragon attacking him. He picked it up and asked, "What manner of beast are you that appears so huge when it is far away and so small when close at hand?" The dragon responded, "My name is WHAT MIGHT HAPPEN!"

Fear of the UnknownD
Fears are worries that have been blown out of proportion by the limbic brain. One of the most common is the fear of the unknown.

Like the dragon in the story, these what-might-happens always appear more formidable than they really are. Think about it. Haven't the vast majority of futures you dreaded failed to happen, or at least proved less perilous than you had feared?

Deflating that overblown anxiety is the first Comforting Connection for a fear of the unknown. When a fear starts to intrude on my life, I immediately do the Joy Touch; then I remember that two-inch dragon. I resolve not to make a monster out of my fear, but deal with it instead. I look back over my life and realize that most things do work out. I remember that I can rise to any challenge. Then I get back to work and set out to make the future I want a reality.

Let's practice clearing a fear of the unknown.

- **Think of a fear of the unknown that affects you.**
- **Do the Joy Touch to start off calm and unafraid.**
- **Identify exactly what unknown elements are troubling you.**
- **Do the Joy Touch to break free of the fear and think clearly.**
  (Resolve not to make a monster out of the unknown.)
- **Identify what you do know and how you can find out more.**
  (Could you read, speak with others, pray, or meditate, etc?)
- **Review the things you have overcome and/or achieved in your life.**
- **Do the Joy Touch to reinforce your courage and perseverance.**
- **Pick the comforter that best eases that fear of the unknown if it recurs.**
  (Inspirational music, remembering your past successes, feeling your power as an explorer, etc.)

Fear of Feeling Helpless or Being All Alone

Feeling alone and/or helpless always magnifies the limbic stress of fear. Self-comfort these facets of fear with the same solutions discussed earlier for feeling helpless (response able, making a plan, and being in control of your state of mind). Also remember that even in the worst cases you may feel powerless, but you are never alone.

Bob and Sara are close friends of mine who had to face the fear of cancer. Sara was found to have precancerous cervical cells and required a cone biopsy. If the results showed that cancer was present and spreading, she would have to have a hysterectomy. Sara faced the real and obvious fear of life-changing surgery. Waiting the week until the biopsy, and then over the weekend for the results was paralyzing. Sara, an at-home artist, couldn't work effectively. She found herself snapping at her young children. Sara felt helpless to control her future. Bob was also affected. He felt truly powerless for the first time in his life.

Bob had always been able to achieve anything he wanted. Being self-employed, he regularly made things work out through dedication and perseverance. In this situation, however, he felt there was nothing he could do. He could not make the test results come back clear. He felt totally helpless. The limbic stress caused his confidence and motivation to slip, undermining his consulting business (money he would need if Sara required the more extensive surgery).

Bob finally realized he wasn't totally powerless. He could help Sara by being there for her. That night he held her close and instantly they both knew that neither of them was alone. Come what may, they would face it together. They would still have the love of their family and the blessing of the children they already had.

Fortunately, the results were negative and no further surgery was required. The comfort Bob and Sara received by realizing they were not alone made the days of waiting bearable. Religious beliefs can also aid self-comforting through the realization that you are not alone.

Music is another way to trigger the self-comforting realization that you are a part of a greater whole. Whenever I hit times of despair, I find that favorite hymns can lift my spirits. I also particularly like Elvis Presley's rendition of "You'll Never Walk Alone." The music inspires me. To paraphrase the song, when I have to walk through a storm, I hold my head up high and am not afraid of the dark. The realization that I am not alone gets me out of the gloom of the limbic stress. It makes it possible to reach the higher parts of my mind, see the light at the end of the tunnel, and get back to the business of making my goals come true.

Take a moment and identify some of the ways you are not alone. This is not so much to clear a specific fear as to strengthen your sense of not being alone.

- **Do the Joy Touch to start off calm and at peace.**
- **Think of someone or a pet that does care about you.**
- **Identify areas in life where you are part of a larger team.**
- **Verbalize aloud positive aspects of your faith that say you are not alone.**
- **Do the Joy Touch to reinforce your sense of connection and support.**
- **Resolve to be fully there for yourself.**

If this type of fear is particularly difficult for you, you can use the above exercise to help clear your apprehension. The key is to focus only on positive thoughts. If you find negative thoughts creeping in, counter them immediately with positive ones and do the Joy Touch. For additional Comforting Connection ideas see also the section on the hurt of loss and loneliness (pages 51-54). Repetitive and/or paralyzing fears are more serious disorders.

Phobias, Panic Attacks, and Obsessive-Compulsive

This approach is not designed to replace the services of trained professionals, if you have major fears. For these more intense disorders, consistent professional treatment may be essential. The Comforting Connection approach can help, however. Lessening the limbic short circuit will ease both the minor fears we all face, as well as major phobias.

For more intense fears, I recommend a two-step approach. First, expose yourself to small amounts of the fear and overcome it gradually. Then praise and reward yourself for the progress you make each step of the way. A clinic that treats people's fear of snakes has clients handle the animals gradually; starting with briefly touching small snakes, then eventually working up to holding a python. Each step of the way, they are given a congratulatory sticker. You can adopt this approach by doing the Joy Touch before and after each small step you make.

Slowly face a little more of the situation that causes the fear. Each time, reward your victory with a Joy Touch. You can also give yourself a medal for your progress. Buy and wear a pin or piece of jewelry as a symbol of your courage. Honor your bravery in facing that level of the fear.

Fully uncovering the psychological cause of phobias, panic attacks, or obsessive-compulsive behaviors is beyond the scope of this book and the Comforting Connection approach. For that more in-depth analysis, a trained professional should be consulted. Here, however, are a few suggestions for how you can use the Joy Touch to help with these disorders.

For Phobias:

- **Do the Joy Touch several times before entering the activity or environment that makes you nervous.**
- **Do the Joy Touch after each small step you take toward what is making you anxious.**
- **At the end of your efforts do the Joy Touch and praise yourself for your courage and progress.**

For Panic Attacks (add the following steps):

- If you start to panic, close your eyes and do the Joy Touch until you feel calmer.
- Do the Joy Touch once for each panicky thought you have until you calm down.

For Obsessive-Compulsive Behavior:

- **When you feel the compulsion, Joy Touch immediately.**
  (Focus on doing the Joy Touch well, instead of carrying out the compulsive behavior.)
- **Anytime you let the compulsion occur, <u>do not</u> do the Joy Touch.**
  (Specifically think or say, "I am missing the Joy Touch because I did the compulsive behavior.")
- **Give yourself a Joy Touch reward anytime you resist the compulsion.**

Regardless of how great your level of fear is, you can still be proud of yourself. In buying and reading this book you have already won. You are a hero! You have had the courage to face and attack the enemy of limbic stress. What's more, with the skills now at your disposal you can also defeat depression.

Keys for Defeating Mild Depression

There are extensive medical and psychological texts dealing with the physiology and treatment of severe depression. This book is not intended to refute them or to cure severe clinical depression. For those circumstances a trained specialist should always be consulted. The skills described in these next two sections should be used to assist therapy, not replace it. The power of the Joy Touch and the Comforting Connection is that they can prevent the slide into severe depression or lessen its recurrence.

This first section is designed to aid the average individual to counter the short term mild depressions we all experience from time to time. The second section shares keys that have worked for me during times of prolonged depressive feelings.

Depression is the result of limbic-stress burnout. When the hurt is so deep or so long lasting that we can't bear it anymore, we withdraw into depression. It is an involuntary comforting by escaping the brunt of the pain. The same is true of angers, worries and fears. When the intensity or duration of these negative emotions exceeds our coping limits, tuning out becomes the only option. The limbic over-load is so unpleasant that even the blackness of depression is better (in the short term) by comparison.

The problem is that the depression can become self-perpetuating and long-term. Until the issue that triggered the overload is cleared, we can stay stuck in a self-made mental snake pit. Without a resolution, the uncleared hurt, worry, anger, or fear blocks our return to positive activity and traps us in depression.

Depression is the ultimate expression of feeling helpless. It is *giving in to giving up.* You can fight depression, because you are not helpless. What you have learned thus far gives you survival skills and tools for defeating depression. With the Joy Touch and the Comforting Connection process you can defuse negative emotions before you reach overload. The more you clear the limbic stresses in your life, the less often you will succumb to depression. That is the first way to take command and not be helpless. Using the Joy Touch regularly can also help you build the emotional intelligence strengths of optimism and perseverance. The mood-elevation boost you receive from it gives you a ray of hope and enthusiasm to go on.

The specific steps for defeating mild depression are:

- **Joy Touch, Joy Touch, Joy Touch (as often as you can).**
- **Do the Joy Touch one or more times to, at least minimally, lift your mood.**
- **Identify which limbic stress is getting you down.**
  (Anger, worry, hurt, or fear, and then what subcategory of it — rejection, helplessness, etc. If it is more than one, that is all right: just do the steps below for each area one at a time.)
- **Joy Touch to ease your distress and give you clearer insight.**
- **Decide what would best comfort you and how you can give it to yourself.**
- **Do the Joy Touch to feel in control and less helpless.**
- **Check if the limbic stress has a deeper, inner-child issue connected to it.**
- **If so, do the Joy Touch and identify a deeper comforter to soothe those earlier roots.**
- **Finish by doing the Joy Touch several times.**
  (Use it to reinforce your learning and sense of inner command of your happiness. Let it give you one more mood boost and empower you to reengage in life.)
- **Congratulate yourself for not letting depression win.**

This process can help you break free of the grip of mild depression. If you can't remember all the steps or summon the motivation for them, at least do the first, Joy Touch, Joy Touch, Joy Touch. It will give you enough of a boost to get you up and moving. You can then tackle the limbic-stress issues when you feel ready. As a minimum, you will be part way back to the light. Frequently that is the most important step. From there you can cope as you see fit, employing whatever other strategies or therapies that work for you.

Skills for Countering Prolonged Depressiveness

Research for this section was more than just an academic adventure. Because of my family history, it was a personal experience. I know little about my father because he died when I was very young. I do know, however, that at times in his life he suffered from severe depression. In fact, he was hospitalized on several occasions for it. I myself have always been serious and somber by nature. What I tell people is that before learning the Joy Touch, I was serious and moody. Since learning the Joy Touch, I am still serious but more mellow and contented.

That same genetic predisposition to depressiveness that has been a curse in my life, has also been a blessing for writing this part of the book. It not only gave me the personal motivation to discover and develop the Joy Touch technique, it has also provided the circumstances for personally exploring advanced ways to use it to counter prolonged despondency.

During the times in my life that sadness has consumed me, I have been astonished at its debilitating effects. I would find myself completely lost in a hopeless sense of despair, usually triggered by some extreme disappointment, bad news or lack of achievement. I would then castastropize, making all of life feel like a failure. The dark feelings could be so intense that giving up entirely seemed the only option. My commitment to my family and my children was sometimes all that would keep me from letting suicidal thoughts win.

At my lowest, however, even the things I cherished in life started to slip away. I viewed my children, whom I love dearly, as just burdens, obligations and hassles. My emotions for my wife went numb. At one low point I couldn't bring to mind why or when I had ever loved her. Even my love for my work and teaching seemed dead.

Nothing interested me. I couldn't summon enthusiasm for trying again or starting a new endeavor. I had little or no energy for performing even the most mundane tasks. I felt totally despondent. Even though I knew the Joy Touch could help me feel better, I would choose not to do it. The intensity and reality of those experiences were the catalysts for this section's additional list of advanced survival skills.

I am fortunate that even at low points, I am not interested in using alcohol or drugs to escape the pain. I do understand though, how for many, it can become their primary defense against the unbearableness of those negative emotions. With the availability of alcohol and drugs (not to mention the peer pressure and media bombardment), it's little wonder that addictions are so prevalent.

In my case, my addiction seemed to be to staying down. If anything, I would get hooked on the cycle of wallowing in self-pity and despair. I believe that many people who don't drink or use drugs may still get similarly trapped. Feeling lost without avenues of relief is why antidepressant medications can be so enticing. They offer a way out that is considered medicine rather than addiction or a vice. For me, however, I prefer to pursue natural alternatives.

This section is not meant to condemn antidepressants or to say that all depressiveness should be only self-treated. Severe depression should always be taken seriously and professional treatment considered. For some cases and individuals, medication is not only desirable, but potentially life-saving.

In my case those episodes of prolonged despondency actually served as my best research material for this section of the book. I offer the results of those struggles not as a prescription for all people, but rather as a resource that can be freely utilized (even in conjunction with medication and treatment).

Using the Joy Touch in Motion

Because prolonged despondency is far more severe than mild depression, it automatically requires a stronger, more extensive, mind/body approach. The first step is to simply do the Joy Touch more frequently and with a greater number of pulses at each application. Often, that obvious solution never gets a chance to work due to the debilitating effects of deeper depression. Because the desire to "do nothing" is so strong, it's easy to actually do the Joy Touch less. The problem is compounded by the standard way you have been doing the Joy Touch thus far. Or to be more specific, the body position you probably use.

In many ways, sitting is the worst way to attempt using the Joy Touch to relieve prolonged despondency. When you are in the midst of full blown depression, you are pulled out of higher cortex and into the pit of limbic brain dominance. Sitting just helps you to stew in your own juices and sink deeper.

Physiologically we know that sadness tends to sap energy. This reflex may have developed as a safety mechanism in early evolutionary times. The low energy of a loss or sadness would keep you in the cave and less vulnerable than out on the plain where you could be attacked and eaten. Low energy, immobile activities may actually prolong the problem and make it easier for negative emotions to dominate your state of mind.

Anything that shifts your focus up to your higher cortex reverses that pattern and can help. That is basically why talking to someone or writing in a journal provides such relief. Even if you are just sharing or recording the same negative emotions you have been thinking, you feel better. The muscles you use to speak or write are controlled by cerebral cortex areas. Activating those areas pulls your attention out of the limbic blackhole.

Walking accomplishes this effect even better because it activates a greater number of muscle groups and brain areas, thus making it harder to relapse into the suck of limbic distress. The exposure to greater visual stimuli as you walk has an additional externalizing effect that is equally beneficial. You can always walk, even if it is just pacing in a room. You may not always have someone you can talk to. (Using both together provides even greater relief. That is why walking and talking with a friend feels so good.)

The more vigorous the walk or activity, the more you get the additional endorphin pulse that exercise has been shown to provide. This leads to the obvious conclusion that doing the Joy Touch while moving should be better than doing it while remaining sedentary.

This explains why even people who pray or meditate regularly, can still get stuck in depressive cycles. Merely thinking the prayer may not be enough to prevent you from sliding down into the limbic snakepit. Saying your prayers out loud or writing them will be more effective. In the Catholic faith the physical action of mouthing the rosary and fingering the beads can provide a similar result. For meditators, the key is not to let the normal sedentary posture slide you into the limbic trap. Specific visualizations, positive affirmations, or steps that activate higher brain centers are essential or the attempt to meditate can degenerate into internal chanting of negative thoughts. Learning walking-meditation skills is also invaluable.

Once you know how to do the Joy Touch while sitting down it is easy to extend the technique to walking. **Try these simple steps for learning to Joy Touch in Motion.**

- **Start by walking slowly.**
  (You don't have to be outside. Find a area where you have 10 to 20' to walk back and forth.)

- **Focus your vision on something in your environment or that you see out a window.**
  (This pulls your thoughts out of that inner negative dialogue.)
- **As you walk, gently rub your forehead with one hand.**
  (This brings your attention up to the proper level for going in with that mental caress.)
- **Then with one or two fingers, gently press or tap your mid-forehead several times.**
  (As you do, go in with that mental caress you have learned for the Joy Touch.)
- **Try stimulating the Joy Center from above by running your hands thru your hair.**
  (Or try tapping lightly at the center of the top of your head.)
- **Finally, practice doing the Joy Touch mentally as you walk.**
  (Do not use your hands. Mentally caress by going up and in with your thoughts as you walk.)
- **Another option is to pulse the Joy Touch with each inhalation as you walk.**
  (Just as the lungs are bringing you new air, picture the Joy Touch bringing you a new attitude.)

The first key to combating prolonged despondency is to get moving. Do something that gets you out of the chair and active. Gardening, cleaning, building, or just plain exercising can help you to crawl out of your mental morass. Doing the Joy Touch during, or as part of those activities, makes their beneficial effect even stronger. You may even find that doing the Joy Touch as you walk inside (as in the exercise you just finished) gives you the energy, enthusiasm, and motivation to undertake other more physical endeavors.

If you must sit, try a rocking chair or one that swivels. Because movement breaks the cycle of internal focus and withdrawal, rocking chairs have always been great soothers (particularly for worries and despondency caused by worry).

If even rocking seems too much of an effort, you can generate the beginnings of movement by shifting your visual focus. Look from one part of the room to another. Then add the motion of turning your head as you glance around. Next, move your arm and hand to do the full physical (actual forehead touching) version of the Joy Touch. Eventually get on your feet and walk doing the Joy Touch (as described in the exercise).

The secret is to break the rigid pattern of the depression. That effect can also be achieved by varying the direction and location from which you do the Joy Touch.

Joy Touch from Above and Other Alternatives

There is nothing written in stone that says the septum pellucidum area can only be triggered from the front. Going inward from mid-forehead level is just the easiest to describe and teach. Once you know the exact location and what form of activation works best for you, you can mentally caress from any direction.

In fact, some people find that when caressing from the front, coming in from a little to the left of midforehead actually works better. That improved effect may be due to the part of the brain that lies between the left forehead and the septal area. Known as the left prefrontal cortex, this area has been shown to have centers that dampen unpleasant emotions. Stroke victims with damage there (and thus missing that moderating ability) are more prone to catastrophic worrying and phobias.

When negative emotions or prolonged despondency have so debilitated you that your efforts to reach the septal area either fail or don't elicit a strong enough effect, caressing through the left prefrontal cortex may help. Mentally massaging that area as you go inward can ease the despair, making Joy Touch efforts more successful.

Sometimes the main factor is just variety. When you always do something the same way, you can take it for granted. That boredom creates a lack of interest sufficient to prevent you from using the Joy Touch during longer depressions. Any variation that gives you the feeling of something new and different will be effective.

Another such option is to approach the septal area from below and behind. The best way to describe that variation is too picture a hand coming up the spinal column, and then caressing foward from back to front through the center of the head at that septal level (1&1/2 to 2 inches above eye level). Be sure to come up high enough before touching forward so you are above the lower limbic system.

Actually this mental pathway takes you through the cerebellum, an area the Dr. Robert Heath later found to have connections to the septum pellucidum. In many of his later experiments he placed electrodes in the cerebellum because it was safer and easier to access than the septal area. Meditators frequently picture this below and behind approach as a kundalini mediation, with the energy rising through the chakras and then charging the Joy Center. Whatever images or explanations you prefer, variety can be the spice of life. It will make your use of the Joy Touch more regular and effective.

Try these two alternative approach directions for the Joy Touch.

- **First do the Joy Touch physically using your left hand (even if you're right-handed).**

(For many people it is less distracting than reaching across the center line with the right hand.)

- **Instead of the center of your forehead, touch one inch to the left of center.**
- **Now caress the septal area mentally (but coming in to it from slightly left of center).**
  (Follow the normal procedures but focus on caressing more the left side of your head than the right.)
- **Next, mentally Joy Touch from below & behind (be sure to come up high enough).**
  (Don't worry about the exact path, just bring your focus up to the septal level and stroke forward.)
- **Practice any other approach variations you wish.**
  (The key is knowing your end destination, the septal area. Try also just being there and caressing.)

Another approach is to trigger the septal area from above. This variation offers the additional advantage of helping you focus on any beliefs you have in a higher power. In all faiths the divine aspect is generally associated with the space above us. God above, or the Universe above, are common concepts that can be incorporated into the Joy Touch technique. Even science now talks about all things existing in ten dimensions. That extra dimensional and/or spiritual energy (the love of God or the oneness of Spirit, etc.) can be infused into the septal area from above. For many people this makes the Joy Touch more than just a personal triggering of their Joy Center. The technique gains the added symbolism of connecting them with a higher power.

The latter part of Chapter 3, Enhancing the Love in Your Life, has specific techniques for more fully experiencing this Joy Touch approach from above (in the Soul-shifting and Soul-blending sections). Skip ahead to them, if you feel a more urgent need for a spiritually assisted Joy Touch to counter depressiveness.

If you are familiar with the Soul-Shift technique (from the Free Soul Course and/or my other books) it can also be a catalyst for Joy Touching from above. Simply use the technique to shift your focus up to the Soul level and caress down from there. I find that reconnecting with that larger perspective is very helpful if my despondency is caused primarily by physical concerns. You could argue, however, that the relief has brain science roots as well.

Doing the Joy Touch from above is an important option, whether or not you believe in a higher power. Physiologically we know that pulling your focus out of limbic domination is a key for lifting your mood. Connecting with higher cortical areas facilitates that process. Quite possibly, in severe distress, it is necessary to actually focus above the desired area to adequately pull you out of the limbic black-hole. You may be so down that merely focusing at the septal level or stimulating cerebral cortex areas is not enough. Whatever the reason, focusing your attention above the head and caressing down from above is an important option to have at your disposal. Try it a few times before reading on.

Specifically Countering Negative Thoughts

A major obstacle I encountered during times of deep and/or prolonged despondency was the harmful power of my own thoughts. Often the positive effects of the Joy Touch were rapidly undone by my repetitive negativity. In those instances I discovered that a dual approach, based on Dr. David Burns' Cognitive Therapy, was particularly helpful.

As opposed to Reality Therapy that postulates that it is the things in our life that make us depressed, Cognitive Therapy says it is our thoughts that actually cause the depression. In other words, it is not so much the fact that you lost a job or had a relationship breakup, that keeps you feeling down. Rather, it is the way you bombard your mind with distressing reminders of that event, cycle into negative thoughts about yourself because of the event, or even worse, lapse into catastrophizing thoughts (i.e. I'll never be loved, or I'll never be able to get another job, etc.). The key point of the difference is that you frequently can not change the events, but you can always endeavor to change your thoughts.

During my times of increased negative thoughts, the dual approach that worked for me involved the use of tailored affirmations as I did each Joy Touch. The specific affirmation I would use was directly related to the negative thought that was keeping me down. If I was echoing sadness about a rejection or a perceived failure, I would focus on something I *had* accomplished as I did the Joy Touch. If the depressing thought was relationship or family based, I would specifically think of a positive family memory or something I cherished about my loved ones. The key was to shout the thought in my mind as forcefully as I could.

One particularly low point in my life was triggered by recurrent thoughts of failure due to publisher rejections. My despondency was so severe that I felt like giving up entirely on all my work. I had no motivation or enthusiasm for going on, but I then remembered something my father-in-law had once told me.

Al is an engineer and a brilliant inventor. In the 1940's one of his pioneer patents was stolen by the government. Because of wartime security issues he was not able to redress the wrong until documents became unclassified in the 1970's. Even then, the legal case proving that his idea had saved the government millions and granting him compensation, lasted for over ten years. The emotional and financial drain was enormous. During the disappointment of yet another legal continuation, I asked him how he kept going. He responded, "I ask myself if what I am doing is worthwhile. If it is, I don't give up!"

That concept and phrase was my life-saving affirmation that evening as I depressively collapsed into bed for the third night in a row. Each day my insomnia had been getting worse. My slumber consisted more of tossing and turning than rest. The feeling of wanting to crawl away from the whole world grew with my increasing fatigue and sadness. That night I literally fell asleep Joy Touching and chanting in my mind, "What I do is worthwhile. What I do is worthwhile." For the first time in days I slept well. The next morning, although still disappointed about the specific rejections, my motivation not to give up, to get this book out, was restored.

The key is to find a replacement thought that best counters the negativity that is dominating you. Tailor your affirmations to directly rebut the negative thought, or to stop your catastsrophizing (i.e. I am not totally unloved, some people do value me; or I am not a total failure, this area has problems, but others are doing well, etc.).

Sometimes the type of countering thought you require is a reflection of your perceptual type (as described in my book *You Are Psychic!*). If you are a visual person the lack of a clear picture or sense of future direction can be an underlying cause of your prolonged despondency. Counter with thoughts of what you can see thus far, or allow yourself to be browsing for new options (your current direction is to be exploring possibilities).

If you are a feeling person, hostility, negativity in your environment, and/or love issues can be your trip wires for extreme sadness. Counter with memories of being cared about or thoughts of people you love. For high auditory and achievement types, the lack of—or obstacles to—achievement can be the strongest depressors. Counter with memories of what you have achieved and the realization that most accomplishments frequently require continued perserverance. For intuitional people, feeling trapped, limited, or hemmed in can be the most distressing. Counter with thoughts that emphasize freedom and spontaneity.

Equally important can be countering with thoughts that are esteem-builders. Emphasize support for yourself for caring enough about the issues that are disturbing you. Here are a few examples.

Vision, "I value myself for wanting to see a bigger picture and have a plan and/or direction. I know that desire will help me find it." Feeling, "I love myself for the fact that I care about feelings and loving others." Auditory, "I value the builder in me and my desire to achieve. Because of that effort things do get done." Intuition, "I love my creativity and the way I am not rigid."

These last paragraphs should also remind you of the importance of the Comforting Connection for helping to clear the underlying issues that can rekindle a depression and keep you down longer. Don't forget to periodically ask, "What would comfort me in this situation and how can I give it to myself?" The self-supporting answer you get can be the perfect countering thought.

These are just samples. For more information about other facets of Cognitive Therapy, I recommend Dr. Burns', *Ten Days to Self-Esteem Workbook*. As far as using countering thoughts with the Joy Touch, the key is to think them before, during, and after the touch; to say them out loud whenever possible, and to tailor them specifically to your needs and circumstances.

Try doing the Joy Touch as you think of a positive affirmation.

- **First pick a negative thought that can get you down.**
  (Try to use one that frequently echoes in your mind.)
- **Next, identify a positive thought that would be a good counter to that negativity.**
  (Don't get hung up trying to think of the perfect counter thought. If it feels good, go with it.)
- **Say the thought out loud, or at least shout it in your mind.**
  (If you are not at liberty to speak out loud, try mouthing the words silently.)
- **Next, think the positive thought as you do the Joy Touch.**
  (If thinking the thought distracts your mental Joy Touch efforts, use the hand-assisted Joy Touch version.)
- **Try doing the Joy Touch as you say the thought out loud.**
  (Also try doing this as you move or walk.)
- **Last, say, mouth, or mentally shout the thought a final time.**
  (As you do, cherish yourself for that thought.)

Often the biggest obstacle to using the Joy Touch regularly is forgetting to do it. A crucial element of a strategy for making your life better is identifying triggers that remind you to use the technique. Negative thoughts can actually serve you positively. They can be triggers for remembering to Joy Touch. Don't just stand by and let negative thoughts go unanswered. When they happen, counter them and Joy Touch.

As you train yourself to do this automatically, you take a giant step toward revamping the quality of your inner mental environment. It may be possible to go one step further, to improve even the brain's physical environment, its chemical balances.

Recharging Your Brain Chemistry

We are still a long way from fully understanding how biofeedback or even the brain itself works. Exactly what brain areas, or what neural connections, make it possible for someone to mentally lower their blood pressure is still in part a mystery. The same can also be said for how the brain naturally balances and accurately replenishes serotonin, endorphins, and other neurotransmitters that contribute to our feelings of well-being. What we do know is that biofeedback works. Consequently, it's a logical extension that the mind should also be able to help the brain recharge.

The meditator doesn't need to know the specific neural pathway that causes reduced blood pressure, or be able to picture which muscles in the blood vessels need to relax. Using everyday calming thoughts and visualizations is sufficient. In fact, Dr. William Fezler in his book, *Creative Imagery*, points out that nonspecific visualization actually work better than more exact, medically oriented ones. He believes this is because abstract and general images get into the subconscious better. Others believe that visualizations, that will the body to just be as it should, invoke the body's natural healing mechanisms or the effects of a higher power.

Whatever the reason, the result is that you *can* have a positive effect on the body, even if you are not an expert in anatomy or neurophysiology. Just as this has been shown to be true for blood pressure, it should also be applicable to brain chemistry. In my own case I have found that focused thoughts for brain chemistry balancing and recharging have been helpful. They lessened my severe despondency, particularly when used just before falling asleep.

The exact purpose and function of sleep is another area that is still mostly a mystery to science. What we do know is that it is essential. Without sleep, severe mental disorder is inevitable. As a result, it is widely believed that sleep is critical to regeneration and the maintenance of proper brain function. Why not use the power of the mind to support and enhance that restoring renewal?

What I do is mentally picture and feel the brain recharging. I think of it being revitalized and fully rested with all its circuits cleared of static and tension. I don't try to figure out exactly what neurotransmitters need to be recharged or where serotonin should be. I simply hold in mind the thought of the entire brain being replenished. I focus on the feeling of everything being as it should be for maximum well-being.

The key is to think these thoughts in a light, unforced way. It doesn't help you rest and recharge to worry about am I doing it right or "good enough." This is where the Joy Touch helps. By doing the Joy Touch first, I relax that feeling of "have to." It eases the performance pressure and anxiety about getting it right. Doing the Joy Touch, as I hold the renewing thoughts, also reinforces the positive intention with a good feeling. Joy Touching after I finish seals in the desired mood or positive outlook.

If I know that my rest is prone to being fitful because of a specific worry or problem, I add an additional mental technique before starting. I picture taking that worry or trouble and putting it in the chair at the far end of the bedroom. This is not denial. I am such a responsible person, I know I won't forget the worry. This chair technique is effective because it gives me relief during the time I need to sleep. Frequently, I even mentally address what's troubling me and say, "You go over there now. I'll deal with you in the morning when my strength and convictions are renewed. This gives me the ability to focus on what sleep is truly for—rest.

Try this simple process. Give your brain a nudge toward regeneration and renewal.

- **Take whatever is troubling you or occupying your mind and just set it aside.**
  (Picture putting it in a chair, or symbolically taking off that set of work clothes.)
- **Do the Joy Touch to start off relaxed and not over trying.**
  (Be sure not to worry about if your Joy Touch is good enough. Just do it until you feel at ease.)
- **Next, take as long as you want and focus on totally allowing yourself to be resting.**
  (Don't start recharging until you feel that all your "have to's" are released. Just be at rest.)
- **When ready, lightly think of the brain renewing and replenishing itself.**
  (Like a plant naturally soaking up water or absorbing the sun.)
- **Picture or feel all debris and waste products being removed and new energy stored.**
  (At this point use whatever images or feelings most represent recharging and renewal to you.)
- **Let regenerative thoughts caress your mind and total being.**
  (You can add images of spiritual energy renewing your Soul.)

- **Finally, do the Joy Touch to seal in the feeling and effect of the renewing thoughts.**
  (Let this last Joy Touch be like a caress to your whole being, supporting its revitalization.)

This process can be used for any part of the body, but it is particularly valuable for ending the way fatigue always enhances depression. When you are sleep debted or exhausted, none of the exercises are more important than simply getting rest. Rest first. Then decide which approaches will best help restore your well-being.

Finally, don't judge yourself for being down. Guilt just makes depression worse. Take command of your depressions by learning from them. You know the old saying, 169As long as there is so much of it around, you might as well use it for fertilizer." You are not helpless or powerless. You have the skills to create your own happiness.

Preventive Maintenance and Self-Nurturing

Using the Joy Touch regularly is your safeguard against getting sucked into the quicksand of both mild or prolonged depression. It gives you a physiological lifeline to rise above the events, emotions, or chemical imbalances that tend to drag you down. With that first step you can go beyond mental health to mental wealth.

The key is to be nurturing to yourself. Go beyond self-comforting to nurturing the development of a new, stronger you. Turn your problems into growth opportunities. Everyone has peaks and valleys in life. Learn not to let the valleys win. Rename them for what they are—"pre-peaks." Remember, the down times are the forging furnaces where you gather the building material for your next breakthrough (peak). Where do you think the old sayings "it's always darkest before the dawn" and "every cloud has a silver lining" came from? The valleys actually provide the catalyst for new growth. The minute you ask, "How can this situation serve me?" you convert the valley into a pre-peak and begin your self-nurturing growth process.

Sometimes figuring out what will comfort you in a specific situation or facing an inner-child issue is the first step in that growth. In others, using the Joy Touch for the emotional intelligence skills of handling your anger or soothing yourself, is the catalyst for healing and nurturing a new, improved you. In both cases you are regaining command of your life. You are defeating the helpless feeling of depression by taking internal action. The external actions and solutions will follow. Remove the cloud and both your work and life will be brighter.

To understand the full process, think: **mood-elevate, comfort, nurture, grow, and go on.** Trigger the septum pellucidum area and apply your Comforting Connections in the valleys to free yourself from the depressive grip of the limbic stress. Then go beyond comforting to nurturing. Identify not only what comforts you, but also what supports your growth. Remember, you are allowed to be learning. That is your birthright. Nowhere is it written that at a certain age you must be perfect. Be *perfecting*, not perfect. Focus on how the situation can serve to make you wiser and stronger.

Enjoy using the Joy Touch and the Comforting Connection to naturally turn your valleys into pre-peaks. Then pull yourself out of the valleys by pursuing that new learning and increased happiness. Finally, continue your life with a new, invigorated you. Use that energy to replace old patterns of struggle with more time for love— love of others, love of self, and love of life.

In doing the exercises in this chapter you have already faced the darkest of life's issues. You have not merely survived, you have emerged much more emotionally capable than when you began. Life will no doubt still give you future challenges and stresses. It is important before going on, however, to acknowledge the new emotional-intelligence skills that are now permanently yours.

Take a moment to seal in the new wisdoms that you have gained.

- **Joy Touch to start off at peace and appreciating yourself.**
- **Close your eyes and review the new skills you have learned.**
- **Realize you now know a way to mood-elevate in seconds.**
  (No one can ever take that knowledge away from you. It will only get better with time.)
- **Recognize that you know a simple and effective way to clear any limbic stress.**
  (You know the process for getting the Comforting Connection for any distress. You will always remember, "What would comfort me in this situation and how can I give it to myself?")
- **You own these two keys to greater freedom and happiness.**
  (They are yours for life. You now know the gateways out of mental pain and depression)
- **Joy Touch to seal that knowledge into new wisdom.**
- **Cherish and appreciate the new, stronger, wiser you.**

Bravo to you, fellow Inner Technology pioneer, for how much you have learned! Up next is how to use the Joy Touch, the Comforting Connection and other new techniques to have even greater love in your life.

• 3 •
Enhancing the Love in Your Life

Feeling loved is one of the most fundamentally important needs in life. It is crucial to both your total well-being and your health, and not just your mental/emotional health. In a thirty year study at the University of Washington in a division of the Department of Psychology, commonly referred to as the Love Lab, researchers found that women with critical and unloving husbands suffered a higher occurrence of serious illness (cancer, heart disease, etc.)

You may not think of love as being as vital to survival as safety or food and water. Quite possibly, however, your limbic brain does. Think for a moment about the early associations that we have. As an infant, feeling loved was directly related to feeling safe and having your physical needs met. It was frequently linked to the most basic survival need—food. Much of the initial affection you received came as you were being fed. (Is it any wonder that binge eating can be so strongly associated with not feeling loved?) Being held and cuddled also gives the benefit of feeling protected and less vulnerable.

Subconsciously, we may associate not being loved with the dangers of starvation and assault. That connection alone has the power to trigger all of the limbic brain's negative emotions. Not feeling loved can increase your vulnerability to worries, hurts, angers and fears, even without a specific environmental stimulus. Add the obvious anxieties that can accompany such love lost situations as rejection, abandonment, betrayal, breakups, and divorce and your distress can skyrocket. Real worries in these areas have tremendous impact on your feelings of worth, belonging, life direction, and often your financial security.

The overall result is that not feeling loved can trigger a sensation of being at risk that is totally undermining to well-being and happiness. Consequently, enhancing the love in your life is a must for being fully in command of your joy of living. The first step in that command is to take charge of the one love that you can control all the time, that of loving yourself.

There are four main ways you can experience love energy. The three most generally associated with happiness are: feeling loved by others, feeling love for others, and feeling loved by God or the Universe. Each of these requires the fourth—loving yourself, to be fully experienced.

No amount of feeling loved by others is enough to overcome the lack of love from your most significant other—you. When you don't feel good about yourself, you can block out the affection others endeavor to share with you (that self-dislike may even drive people away). When you are not at peace with yourself, it is also harder to feel loving toward someone else or to allow the love of God or the Universe to touch your heart. All three of the major avenues for feeling the beauty of love must cross the intersection of your own heart. If that junction point and your feelings for yourself are clouded or clogged, very little can get through.

This isn't just airy, feel good, philosophical psycho babble. It is the core of health and well-being. If living with a critical spouse can cause distress and health problems, think of the impact of not feeling loved by someone every second of every day. You are with yourself every moment of your life. If your constant companion is hostile and critical, there is no way you can be fully happy. For that reason the first part of this chapter has to address enhancing your self-love. If you identify the limbic traps that erode your self-love, you can learn to effectively counter them. Then, you can live the full joy to which you are entitled.

Neutralizing the Acid of Put-Downs

The first place to start is with that critical inner voice we all have. Mental put-downs are something we all experience. They are those nagging thoughts that echo in our minds far too often, such as "I didn't do that well enough," "I'm too fat," "Why did I say that?" or "What's wrong with me?" I'm sure you are familiar with the process. You probably have your own unique set in addition to the common ones listed above. No matter how seemingly negative they are, it is important to understand that those thoughts are normal. Further, to a certain extent they are inevitable; you should expect them, not judge yourself for having them.

Mental put-downs are a product of the limbic brain. They are the way its ancient survival reflexes endeavor to keep us from the danger of complacency. No matter how enlightened, religious or self-aware you are, you are going to experience mental put-downs from time to time. They are a function of your physiology not your spirituality (or lack of it). Prayer has been around for eons. And yet people who pray still give themselves put-downs. People who practice affirmations and positive thinking still have lapses of negativity. Even the most successful people are not immune. How often have you heard people you respect and admire comment that they have self-doubts and inner criticism? Often the most successful people are the hardest on themselves. Achievement and capability alone do not silence that inner judgement. In fact, they can make it even worse.

The trick is to deal with the put-downs we give ourselves, not love ourselves less for having them. How can you improve your self-love by adding another layer of disappointment and self-criticism? Expect these squirts of mental venom that the limbic brain churns out, but don't let them win. There is a simple and effective way to not only counter their acid, but also to use them to increase your self-esteem. The credit for helping me evolve this powerful approach I must give to my two children.

All siblings can have running conflicts that give their parents fits. In my case I have two very strong and competitive boys. As they each grew more assertive, their interactions started to become a series of put-downs to each other. The oldest wanted to stay on top and hated it when his younger brother did something particularly well (or God forbid, better than he did). The results were particularly poisonous verbal barbs aimed at his brother. The youngest hated being behind and knew exactly what weaknesses his older brother had and how to goad him. Although rarely escalating to physical fights, the verbal results became intolerable.

My wife and I tried everything to curb or change this behavior. We tried time-outs, fines, loss of privileges, etc. Nothing seemed to work. Finally in desperation, we gave up. We told the boys to go to their room and not come out until they had thought of a consequence for themselves when they gave their brother a put-down.

After they got bored with the confinement, they put their minds to work and came up with the solution that we still use in our family. They came out and said, "Mom and Dad, we've decided that when we give each other a put-down, our consequence is that we have to immediately give a *put-up*."

The concept is simple, but tremendously powerful. A put-up demonstrates that the put-down is not the only reality, that there are also positive things associated with you. It can even be tailored to go beyond easing the sting of the criticism to valuing the positive behind what was criticized. For example; Put-Down, "You're such a worrier." Put-Up, "I appreciate that you care enough about me to worry." This could then be followed by a request for a different way of expressing the concern, such as, "Would you be willing to tell me your concerns without assuming that the worst is going to happen?"

The put-up approach is vital in our relationships with others (we will get to that shortly), but it is even more crucial for building your own self-esteem and self-love. The limbic brain is designed to bombard you with a constant barrage of negative jabs. Expect it, but don't let them be the final word. When they occur, counteract their acid by giving yourself an immediate put-up.

The secret to using put-ups most effectively is to learn how to identify ones that are independent of externals (achievements, specific relationships, etc.). For too long our worth has been measured only by outside standards. In fact, most of the put-downs you give yourself are probably based on externals (i.e. "I didn't do that job well enough," or "They don't like me," etc.). If your put-ups are only based on outside achievements or approval, they can't help you when you are between accomplishments or not popular at the moment. When you learn to generate put-ups that are based on your intrinsic qualities, you can always praise yourself.

One of the best descriptions of that intrinsic qualities approach is outlined in *Megaskills* by Dorothy Rich. Ms. Rich focuses on ten skills that she feels are keys to children's success in life. Some of the megaskills are effort, initiative, perseverance, caring, etc. You will notice that these are qualitative rather than quantitative. They emphasize qualities rather than achievements or specific relationships.

This concept of strengthening inner qualities is so powerful to learning that many schools have adopted an expanded form of it called Lifeskills into their curriculum. In Lifeskills the qualities are not limited to ten. Any quality that is internal and intrinsic is usable. Valuing your lifeskills means praising yourself for your intent, not just your results. Even if you are berating yourself for poor performance, you can still praise yourself for your courage in trying, or your honesty in admitting you didn't do it as well as you wanted.

Life is a constant classroom of opportunities for learning about happiness and love. By using put-ups regularly you can reward your progress every step of the way. You can appreciate and love that inner you regardless of how things are going. **Try it for a moment.**

- **Do the Joy Touch to start off at peace and being non-judgmental.**

- **Next, identify two or three common put-downs you tend to give yourself.**

- **Do the Joy Touch again to ease the sting of those criticisms.**

- **Now, think of a lifeskill quality that is a strength for you.**
  (Are you noteworthy for your effort, perseverance, initiative, determination, honesty, caring, or patience, etc.)

- **Then, pick a put-up you can give yourself to counter one of those put-downs.**
  (It can include that lifeskill or another if it is more appropriate.)

- If you like, give yourself additional put-ups to counter the other put-downs you identified.
- Finally, do the Joy Touch to seal in that love and self-respect.

Entire books have been written about the single topic of loving yourself more. This chapter is not designed to replace them or cover all that they contain. This section is included to emphasize the importance of addressing your self-love first. Every time that I have felt unloved or been hurt by the lack of love from another, one element has been the same. In each of those situations I had also forgotten to be loving to myself. I had been so immersed in self-criticism and judgmental put-downs that even mild rejection or hurts wounded me to my core. That lack of self-valuing made me totally dependent on the love of others for my well-being and emotional survival.

That type of dependency is an unfair burden to put on anyone. It also is self-defeating. Clutchy neediness just drives people away. That can result in your feeling even more unloved. Even if the other person isn't put off by that dependent demand for love, you can still lose. You probably aren't fully cherishing the love that they give. When you are empty inside because of a lack of self-love, the love you receive from others never quite fills that bottomless pit. That starvation of inner affection can also cause you to devour love from others without really tasting its sweetness. Worse still, their love is viewed as expected (you are supposed to love me) rather than cherished for the true gift that it is. No one responds well to being taken for granted or used just for emotional survival. Consequently, you can reduce even further the love you receive.

The secret is to have a firm foundation of self-valuing and non-egotistical self-love. Even the Bible says, "Love thy neighbor as thyself." How can you love your neighbor if you despise yourself? When you are secure with your own self-esteem, you can fully cherish the love you receive from others. It also frees you to love them unconditionally in return. That unconditionality is the key to enhancing the love in your life. When we can love without expectations or dependency, we are living the true essence of love. Understanding what may be a root cause behind many lack of love issues is the answer.

Not Feeling Fully Loved

In my world travels I have given thousands of counseling sessions. I have always been amazed at how many people have some area where they don't feel fully loved. At first this didn't make sense to me as I deal primarily with positive, searching individuals. The students I see are, on the whole, loving, caring individuals who seem to be doing all they can to make their relationships and the world a better place. These are the people, who it would seem, most deserve to be fully loved. Why is that not the case? I started looking for a logical answer that could also be a solution to the despair created by not feeling loved.

First of all, let me ask, "do you you believe that Souls evolve?" As a conscious entity, do you believe that you are growing and learning? If you do, then think for a moment; what would come next after a Soul had learned to be loving when he or she is surrounded by love? After you had mastered how to feel good about life and be loving when everyone around you fully loves you, what would come next?

Obviously, it is how to be loving even when you are not surrounded by love. It is easy to be loving when everyone loves you. The real challenge is to be loving when you aren't fully loved. If we are evolving as Souls in our ability to love unconditionally, then it is clear that our journey must pass through valleys of not being fully loved by others.

Look further at this evolving perspective. Would you want Souls that we tend to think of as further along that evolutionary scale (your Spirit Guides, Guardian Angels, or God) to only love you when you remembered to love them? My view is that those higher consciousnesses love us unconditionally all the time.

Why is this perspective so important? Because it can free you from the self-pity and despair that frequently go with feeling unloved. Each person that you feel unloved by literally provides a graduate course for you. They can help you learn how to be loving even when you are not surrounded by love. You can be proud of the Soul courage having them in your life demonstrates. Appreciate yourself for so wanting to learn about loving that you were willing to experience that lack-of-love situation.

It is time to get beyond feeling like a helpless victim when we are not fully loved. No matter how severe, we need to be able to put those issues behind us to fully love ourselves and to love life. The trick is to put it behind you without avoidance or denial. For that, the secret is to embrace it and put it through you. A key to that positive processing can be gleaned from all the work that is being done with abuse and inner child concerns.

Many people are not aware that there are actually two different models of inner child work. In the *victim model* you are considered a survivor of abuse. While it is commendable to get those long suppressed abuses out and exposed, this model is still basically negative. You are considered a victim. Even though you are a survivor, you are still basically damaged goods. The other model is called the *challenge model*. In it, you are not merely a survivor of circumstances. Rather, you are what you are now, not just in spite of what you went through, but quite possibly because of it. You can be proud of yourself for the strengths you have gained in going through those forging furnaces.

By the way, which model do you think is overwhelmingly the most popular? It is the victim model. Why, you ask? It goes back to the pattern described in the beginning of the Limbic Stress chapter for why we tend to stay down. If you are a victim you can be crying out subconsciously for someone to come comfort you. Choose instead to be singing your own praises.

Put the issue behind you by putting it through you (processing it). Cherish the strength and learning it has afforded you. Give yourself the Soul put-up of saying "bravo" for the courage you had to walk through the valley of the shadow of not being fully loved. **Take a moment and try this process.**

- **Do the Joy Touch to start off calm and secure with yourself.**
- **Next, think of a situation where you felt not fully loved.**
- **Do the Joy Touch again to stay objective and not just be dragged into the hurt.**
- **Now, identify how that situation has served to make you stronger.**
  (What learning did you gain or what character strengths can you appreciate yourself for?)
- **Cherish some aspect of how you didn't let that circumstance totally break you.**
  (Or for the fact that you loved, even though it wasn't fully returned.)
- **Do the Joy Touch to feel proud of your willingness to learn about loving.**
- **Give yourself a "bravo" for your courage and perseverance.**
- **Finally, do the Joy Touch again to seal in that challenge model attitude**

Lack of love and not feeling fully loved are difficult challenges. Even so, they can still be opportunities for enhancing the love in your life. You can use them as triggers for remembering to fully love yourself. Don't let love issues stimulate self-pity or you open a pandora's box in the limbic brain. From that feeling of "I don't feel loved" you can slip into the self-criticisms of "I am not lovable" and"What's wrong with me?"

Use the put-up concept to counter that limbic snake pit. Praise yourself for caring, or for your effort at loving. Use the self-praise to heal the wounds to your self-esteem caused by not feeling loved. Let the put-up also reinforce that you have the love of the person closest to you—yourself. Remember also, you don't just have to wait until you criticize yourself or feel unloved to give yourself a put-up.

Seize the Put-Upable Moment

Look for opportunities to give yourself the gift of self-apprecia-tion as things happen in your day. In education there is an expres-sion for teachers that goes, "seize the teachable moment." It means, when you find the student wide-eyed and interested, capture that moment and maximize the learning you can impart. You can adapt that concept and "seize the put-upable moment." Take the oppor-tunity to give yourself that appetizer of appreciation and self-love whenever a window for it arises. Being generous with self-esteem nutrients is essential for creating a life that is a loving banquet. It is also a main course for successful relationships.

The honest support and appreciation that a put-up embodies is equally valuable to enhancing your love of and from others. Put-ups can literally be the keys to saving love relationships. Another inter-esting finding of the University of Washington's so called "Love Lab" involved something akin to put-ups. It was found that whether a couple would stay together or split up could be predicted (with a close to 90% certainty) based on the ratio of positives they gave each other compared to negatives. In other words, if you give your partner more put-downs than put-ups you may be destined for divorce or separation.

Just as you can seize the put-upable moment to value yourself regularly, you can do the same for significant others. Find ways to praise them. Capture the moment to express respect and affection. It can be the foundation for greater love. I have never heard anyone complain about receiving too many compliments from a partner.

When you have a positive thought but the other person is not there, write it down. That scrap of paper can either serve as a reminder to tell him or her later or it can be a simple but meaning-ful love note. With the invention of Post-its, the put-ups that cross your mind can become building blocks for greater romance and love. Don't let those jewels of appreciation be wasted, put them around the house where your loved one is sure to see them.

Remember also that your put-ups can be quality based, not just quantity based. Statements such as "I love you for how hard you are trying." can be just as heartwarming as "I appreciate what you did." Further, you can always give put-ups based on lifeskills. The result; your loved ones can feel appreciated all the time not just when they do something well. It also eliminates the lack of put-ups because you have different standards of what "done well" is. Even if you would have done it differently, you can still deliver the praise for their effort, initiative, or perseverance.

Using put-ups has the additional benefit of enhancing the love that you feel. Each time you generate a put-up, you bathe your own mind with positive thoughts of that person. When you share the put-up, you get the additional benefit of the good feelings that go with giving and pleasing your loved ones. **Try the process briefly.**

- **Do the Joy Touch to start off clear and insightful.**
- **Think of three put-ups you can give a significant other.**
- **Savor the good feeling of having those thoughts.**
- **If you can, (if they are with you currently) tell your significant other those put-ups,**
(If the individual is not present, pick up the phone and call them and share the feelings that way; or write them on post-it notes and place them where they will be sure to find them; or write them down and plan a time to convey the thoughts in person).
- **Value yourself for seeing those qualities in your partner.**
(Feel your love enhancing through that appreciation.)
- **Resolve to give your significant others put-ups more often.**
(Think of a few regular places and times where you could "seize the put-upable moment."
- **Do the Joy Touch to reinforce your appreciation of them and your desire to give put-ups regularly.**

This one skill has the potential to vastly improve any relationship. For too long we have been undertrained in this area. Instead of only random acts of kindness, it is time to make a habit of regular acts of praise rather than criticism. You probably know that, so why don't we live it better? The answer again lies in a facet of the limbic brain.

Easing the Irritation that Undermines Love

Before you feel too guilty about the lack of put-ups and number of put-downs you may give your significant other, realize that the pattern is natural. The bad news is that it is common for people to criticize their partner more than praise them. The good news is that a few put-ups can go a long way toward neutralizing the put-downs. Understanding why you may criticize can also lead to a lessening of the put-downs.

Most criticism in a relationship comes from the fact that you and your partner are two very different people. The old saying that opposites attract is often an unfortunate truism. John Bradshaw has been quoted many times as saying that he could go to a swap meet and within 30 minutes be almost magnetically attracted to a woman who pushes all his buttons. In addition to possible personality differences, most couples automatically face the difficulties of gender differences.

Linguist, Deborah Tannen in her book, *You Just Don't Understand - Women and Men in Conversation* and John Gray in his *Men are From Mars, Women Are From Venus*, have well documented the differences that exist between the genders. Ms. Tannen in particular points out a key problem. Frequently, when we partner up we expect to get a new improved version of a best friend. The difficulty, as John Gray puts it, is that our new best friend literally comes from a different planet. That difference and the frustration or disappointment it causes is what can lead to friction.

This is just the latest way of describing the Eastern concept depicted by the Yin/Yang symbol of opposite polarities interacting throughout all life.

Fig. 17 Yin/Yang Symbol

The genders are opposites but can attract because they fit so well together. In addition to the biology of the sex drive, the bond is made more powerful by the fact that we each have at least some of the others characteristics within us. In the symbol this is illustrated by the spot of the other in each principle. Scientifically we know that each sex has a certain amount of the others hormones. Psychology points out that as conscious beings, each of us has the ability to exhibit the strengths of both the male and female characteristics. In my view you can have the best of both principles because your Soul essence has the power to transcend gender stereotypes. You are a Soul, but you are living through the filter of your gender's body.

While you are more than just those gender characteristics, it would be foolish to discount the power of their filters on your perceptions and values. Even the most spiritual of individuals is affected by the influences of the body's hormones. Women are intimately familiar with the effect of premenstrual hormone changes on their mood. Men, if they're honest, will admit that sexually explicit pictures can shift their focus from the Soul to much lower parts of the anatomy.

These are just some of the more obvious effects. Ms. Tannen's and Mr. Gray's books point out a host of more subtle, but still important others. The bottom line is that for a variety of reasons you are a very different person than your significant other. When the timing of your difference is in synchronicity the result is a positive. Like the Yin/Yang symbol you can complement each other well, adding strength where the other has weakness.

When we are out of synch, our differences are likely to rub each other the wrong way (just as the offset Yin/Yang symbol below clashes). That irritation is what causes us to criticize our partner. The perceived threat to our wants and needs activates the worst of the limbic mechanisms. Feeling subconsciously that our survival (or independence, worth, or stature, etc.) is threatened, causes us to attack. Our significant others are the most likely to be on the receiving end of those barbs, because they are around us at our limbic worst. We let our guard down with them. They see us more often when we aren't fully awake, or are exhausted, sleep-deprived, or stressed-out. This sum total is probably the psychobiological mechanism behind the old saying; "You always hurt the one you love." That hurt is often made worse by the misperception that the partner is being irritating intentionally or just to spite us.

One of the blessings of research on gender differences is that it can lessen that extra fuel for the fire. It gives us the perspective that our significant other's annoying actions are not just done to spite us. They might just be acting in a way that is natural for their needs. This is not just true of gender differences. It applies also to birth order characteristics, family traditions, communication styles, and current environmental pressures.

Villainization of your partner never helps. Using the Joy Touch can be an effective method for cutting off that limbic overreaction. It gives you pause from the subconscious reflex of thinking the worst of the other person. Left unchallenged, our perceptions become our mental reality. With the Joy Touch, you can catch misassumptions before they lead to unnecessary angers or hurts. You can use it to clear enough of your negative feelings to be able to look at other possibilities. That lessening of distress can enhance the amount of love you allow yourself to feel. **Try the process for a moment.**

- **Do the Joy Touch to start off clear and calm.**
- **Think of something upsetting that a significant other does, says, or fails to do.**
- **Do the Joy Touch again to ease your irritation.**
- **See if you can identify a reason they do it; that is for their own needs.**
  (Look for ways that they may be just standing up for their needs, as opposed to being against you.)
- **Feel how that perspective lessens your distress (and makes it easier to love them).**
  (Can it ease your anger or hurt, help you feel less a victim, or stimulate your caring for them, etc.)
- **Do the Joy Touch to reinforce that more tolerant attitude.**

Instead of merely counting to ten when your partner does something that bothers you, use the Joy Touch to help you act not just react. You can enhance the love in your life by preventing your differences from becoming hurtful personal attacks. As a minimum, it can calm things down until you can address them objectively.

This is not to say that we shouldn't endeavor to modify aspects of our behavior that irritate our partners (or to ask them to make compromises on theirs). A large part of civilized behavior is already counter to strict survival biology (serving food to a guest first, waiting in line, etc.). We may be affected by our physiology, but as consciousness we are more than just a bag of cells and chemicals. Choosing to accommodate the desires of loved ones can be a powerful gift of caring and affection. Equally meaningful is complimenting them on their strengths (even though those traits may be annoying to you).

When your differences are not exactly compl *e* menting each other, rather than criticize, compl *i* ment your partner for the strengths he or she has. Use the put-up concept to give a positive rather than perpetuate the unpleasantness. You can even compliment him or her for something you disagree with. Giving a put-up first, before stating your different need, at least lets the other person know that you understand their perspective and do value parts of it. Here are some examples;

"I love the part of you that cares enough about our relationship to want to talk about these issues, but right now I am exhausted and not at my best." or "but right now I have to finish this by a certain deadline." or

"I admire your punctuality and desire to be on time, but right now I need to not feel rushed." or

"I appreciate the financially thrifty part of you that wants to help us save and prepare, but right now I need this expenditure to enhance our living environment." or "I need this trip to restore my/our mental well-being."

The key is honoring the positives in other people's perspective. Giving a put-up to them for those good intentions lets them know that you value them even if you disagree or have different needs or perspectives. Sometimes, widening your view of the other person or the situation is the key to being less reactive and to finding creative solutions to relationship issues.

Self-Solving Relationship Issues Using the Power of the Medicine Wheel

When you have a troubling relationship issue, you can use a variation of the Native American medicine wheel concept to pull through new insight and answers. First, it is necessary to identify what you feel are the key positive characteristics of the masculine and feminine principles. List the core qualities that you associate with the best of the essence of masculine and feminine strengths.

Take a moment and write down (or at least think about) what you feel are the strengths of the two gender principles. Listed below are some of the ones that are common in the workshops that I have given on this topic. (Remember, this is not saying men are this and women are that—both men and women may have all or some of these different masculine and feminine principle strengths.)

Masculine Principle Strengths	Feminine Principle Strengths
Independent	Consensus Builder
Goal Oriented	Supportive of Relationship
Thick Skinned	Sensitive
Analytical	Cares about Feelings
Risk Taking	Protective
Challenging Boundaries	Nurturing of Inner Strengths

Feel free to delete any of these that you don't feel are accurate. Also add any that you feel have been omitted. Remember, however, the purpose is just to get a feel for your view of the strengths of each principle (both of which you have within you).

There are almost as many different medicine wheel traditions as there are Native American tribes. Many, however share several common elements. The first is the concept that a more rounded perspective can lead to creative solutions. Often sacred stones are gathered and placed in a circle with the members of the council or the wise elders sitting around the wheel. Next, the person with the issue either steps into the center and walks within the wheel stating the problem, or voices it from a key starting point in the circle. Then, in turn, each of the individuals sitting around the circle gives his or her view. In this way it is felt that a wiser, more complete perspective is gained. Another frequent element is a cross within the circle representing sacred aspects or the four cardinal directions: North, South, East, and West.

You can use aspects of these elements to set up your own medicine wheel for self-solving a relationship issue. Simply place four chairs in a circle and let each chair represent a specific perspective. The first chair is where you sit and state the problem or issue. The second chair (the first to your right) represents the wisdoms and perspectives of your gender's strengths (If you are a woman it symbolizes the feminine principles strengths. When you sit in it you will speak from the perspective of those wisdoms.) The next chair represents the opposite gender strengths (If you are a woman it symbolizes the masculine principle strengths. When you sit in it you will see and speak from the perspective of those qualities.). Finally, the last chair represents the Soul or Higher Spiritual view. What would be the perspective that would be given by your view of a higher consciousness? This could be from your Guardian Angels, your Spirit Guides, the Universe or God—pick whichever is most comfortable for you.

By traveling around this wheel, sitting and speaking from each chair, you not only get an expanded perspective, you also can identify specific creative solutions for action and/or greater understanding. **Take a moment and try it.**

- **Do the Joy Touch to start off calm and insightful.**

- **Now, sitting in the first chair, think of a relationship issue you have and state it out loud.**
  (What disagreement, area where you feel not understood, not cared for, etc. do you want to process.)

- **Now, move to the chair on your right that represents your gender strengths and speak from it. If you have trouble getting started do the Joy Touch and relax. Then, just talk as you feel a spokesperson for those strengths would.**
  (i.e., If you are a woman, talk from the highest of the feminine principle strengths and wisdoms.)
  (How can nurturing, caring, communication, consensus building, or sensitivity help [you or them]?)

- **Then, move to the chair that represents the opposite gender's strengths and speak from it.**

(i.e., If you are a woman, talk from the highest of the masculine principle strengths and wisdoms.)

(What is the analytical view, what direct action is appropriate, what risks or challenges? Should you take it personally or would being more thick-skinned help?)

- **Next, move to the fourth chair and speak from the higher spiritual perspective.**
  (How would your Guardian Angels, or Spirit Guides handle the issue? What is the universal perspective on this difficulty, etc.?)
- **Finally, return to the first chair and review your insights.**
  (If you feel the need, you can restate you perspective thus far and make another trip around. Make as many trips to each chair as you feel are necessary to resolve the issue in your mind.)
- **Finish by doing the Joy Touch to seal your ability to self-solve like this.**

The insights you get from this process can help you whether or not you decide to talk with the other individual about the issue. If they are communicative and willing to work with you, the information you receive can help you know how to approach them. It can guide you in acknowledging their perspective while still speaking strongly for your needs. If the other person is not willing to address your concern, this technique can help you identify the course of action that will be best for you. You can also identify put-ups you may be able to give them that will lessen their resistance. As a minimum, you will learn insights that allow you to better respect yourself and not take the difficulty personally.

Taking the time to give put-ups and seeing the larger perspective gives you an avenue for respecting your partner a higher percentage of the time. Both give you greater insight and understanding. Most of all though, they improve the environment of your interactions. It makes the time you spend with that significant other more enjoyable. Your physical and verbal exchanges are more positive and your mental associations with them are more loving. Anything you can do to improve your time together and increase your amount of positive interaction will directly enhance the love in your life.

One creative enhancer my wife and I have used over the years is to combine the put-up concept with a special dinner. We each list five things we currently admire about the other. Then, during the dinner, we share one item from our list during each course of the meal. This is a good way to catch up if it has been a while since you have given each other put-ups. It makes for a very romantic and close evening.

Having More Enjoyable Time Together

Enhancing the love in your life is, in essence, surrounding yourself with a higher frequency of loving moments. That process is both an inner and outer endeavor. The amount of inner love you feel can be directly boosted by using the Joy Touch and giving put-ups regularly. These two techniques keep your mental environment bathed in positive thoughts and feelings. Put-ups also help with improving your outer environment. They build a verbal closeness that adds a more loving energy to any setting.

Picture criticism as a foul odor that lingers in the air. You can't see it, but it is most definitely there. The more often the stench is released in the room, the more its odor permeates the fabric of everything causing a permanent negative association. Put-ups are like air freshener. They cleanse the unseen energy of the environment you share with your significant others. They make the space you inhabit more livable and can lead to greater closeness on many levels.

That closeness not only lets greater love and support flow, it can also help to bridge the differences that can be irritating. As with many couples, I have a greater need for watching television to unwind than my wife does. Many years ago, as a result of using Joy Touch-like techniques, I thought of a win-win solution to this difference that was creating friction. I realized that if she stretched out on the couch and put her legs up over my lap, I could rub her feet as I watched. To make a long story short, the amount of TV I get to watch, without complaint, has risen dramatically.

Any creative idea that brings you closer together is a love enhancer. It also doesn't have to be just one way. Often during the couch foot rubs, my wife will give me a hand massage (although this may just be a ploy to keep my hands rejuvenated for an additional stretch of foot rubbing) or a back rub. I carry most of my stress and tension in my shoulders. Even a brief massage there helps to unwind me and make me more loving and harmonious. I also truly enjoy feeling her touch as well. Without being immediately sexual, the physical contact helps to bring us together after long days of balancing our careers and raising two sons.

Whether you progress into the deeper closeness of intercourse or not, mutual back rubs in bed can also be tremendously bonding. Blended with bits of "How was your day?" conversation, they can reunite your energy in a world where the hectic pace of living often pulls couples apart. Head and neck massage can have the same effect.

Scientists tell us that many headaches are caused by tension in the neck muscles. Getting a loving neck massage can keep the pressures of the day from become the tension headache of the evening. When you give a neck rub, one key is too place a hand over the forehead of your partner. This simple step has a dual benefit. First, it supports the head preventing other neck muscles from staying tense to keep the head upright. Even more important, your hand at that position can be sending energy toward your partner's septal area. This helps to trigger the Joy Center mood-elevation effect as the massage releases the physical tightness.

Dr. Robert Heath (the discoverer of the mood-elevation potential of the septal area) also found links from the septum pellucidum area to the cerebellum (the part of the brain just above the top of the neck). When your rub the muscles at the top of the neck at the same time you are touching the forehead, it can help the person being massaged to mentally meet in the middle and trigger the Joy Touch mood-elevation effect. This is another way you can use the Joy Touch concept to increase the closeness, well-being, and love in your life. Aspects of the Joy Touch can even enhance your sexual intimacies.

Joy Touch for Enhanced Sexual Experience

With the marked uplift and inner glow that most people feel from the Joy Touch, it was only a matter of time until someone tried using it during lovemaking. Actually, I started several of our graduates on that exploration without even realizing it. At one training session I jokingly repeated for the group one person's comment, "Oh my God; this is the equivalent of a mental G-spot." Several of the more adventurous participants took the idea from there. They have since told me it was their most enjoyable research project.

One of them, Cara, wrote the following, "The Joy Touch has enhanced my sex life in several ways. At times I am very high-strung. Often when it comes to making love, I need a little help to get me in the mood. Initially, the Joy Touch helps just by relaxing me. When I use it in that prepeak stage, when sexual pleasure is building, I am able to get to climax more easily and with greater enjoyment. Without a doubt I have experienced the strongest and longest orgasms of my life while using the Joy Touch during lovemaking. It is incredible! What an enhancement to an already joyful experience. With it I have also been able to experience more multiple orgasms, each one as strong or stronger than the one before. To all those who feel they need drugs or alcohol to enhance their lovemaking, I can honestly say that the only thing they need is the Joy Touch. I feel liberated—and my partner does not complain either!" Women of all ages (including seniors) have reported results similar to Cara's.

For men, stimulating the septum pellucidum during intimacy seems to enhance their feeling of closeness with their partners. It also makes the intensity of feeling at climax last longer and pulse more through the entire body. For both sexes, the key is being proficient enough at triggering the Joy Touch mood-elevation effect so that you can do it despite being very physically distracted.

At this point, I am always reminded of a comedy routine on the TV show *Saturday Night Live* where their fake news program was poking fun at then President Ford's supposed clumsiness. The reporter said, "The First Lady reports discovering a new contraceptive. She simply gives the President a stick of gum before retiring."

You definitely have to be able to walk and chew gum, so to speak, to be able to do the Joy Touch technique during lovemaking. You have to be familiar enough with how to trigger its mood-elevation effect that you can do it easily with just a quick thought. That may sound artificial, but now-a-days many of the techniques recommended for enhanced sexual response are far more mechanical. At least the Joy Touch has several loving components. As Cara described it can be initially used to release tensions that can prevent or inhibit intimacy. When those tensions and/or irritabilities are cleared, it is easier to feel a desire for closeness with your partner. Finally, one of the main reasons for wanting enhanced sexual experience is to increase the feeling of total union that great sex gives. Being able to fully trigger the septal area at the height of orgasm gives a feeling of oneness that far exceeds the normal climax.

Since this book is not designed to be a sex manual, this section will not have the usual technique or techniques included in it. Feel free, however, to conduct your own research. As a minimum, try using the Joy Touch at times when you know that minor irritations could prevent you from being close. No one should ever feel forced or obligated to participate in sexual intimacies. That is not my meaning. Instead, I am addressing the times when you may be open to, or want intimacy to enhance the relationship or the moment, but know that your current state of mind will prevent it or lessen your enjoyment. In those cases the Joy Touch may prove to be a valuable part of "setting the mood" —yours.

Using the Joy Touch to increase your relaxation and mellowness certainly can't hurt. As a minimum, it can give you enough of a feeling of well-being that you can choose and state what your preferences are (even if they are not for intimacy at that time). When sexual oneness is truly desired, using the Joy Touch before, during, and after, helps the union be even closer with a blendedness approaching a spiritual experience. That concept of increased oneness leads to another avenue for enhancing the love in your life, the area of feeling part of a greater whole.

Tapping the Soul for Greater Oneness

The creative, thinking part of you, the uniqueness that recognizes yourself as an individual, is what I call the Soul. It is that part of you that is your identity. It is also a gateway for experiencing even greater depths of love and oneness.

To me the word "Soul" is not necessarily a religious term. I use it as a label to summarize that complete, conscious, creative you. Whether you are deeply religious, an atheist, or an agnostic, you have a unique consciousness. It is the essence of your humanity. I believe it is the part of you above and beyond the wiring and the physical structure of the brain. For all of our advances in brain science, one thing still remains a mystery. Exactly how the wiring of the brain creates "consciousness" is still unknown.

Consciousness is defined by science as the way you initiate thought and recognize your individual identity. It is, in essence, your Soulness. Just because the exact wiring that creates that unique essence still eludes brain researchers doesn't necessarily mean that science is without possible explanations.

Science and spirituality recently took a giant leap to close the gap between them with the development of a new theory of the universe and subatomic physics. It is called the Superstring Theory, and it promises to end the scientific search for a unified theory that explains mathematically the structure and relationship of all the forces and particles that exist in the cosmos, from the smallest subatomic particles to gravity and nuclear attraction.

What connects Superstring Theory to the exploration of consciousness and the Soul is the fact that its mathematical foundation requires the existence of at least ten dimensions. Physicists are coming to accept that all things -- a chair, a lion, a planet, even you -- exist in ten dimensions (or more) rather than the four we are familiar with. They describe those ten dimensions as the three spatial dimensions (height, breadth and length) a fourth dimension of time, and "six other dimensions that are still beyond our ability to measure with our current technology."

The concept of other dimensions is not new. The term "hyperspace" existed long before George Lucas and *Star Wars*. Astronomers and astrophysicists have long proposed that the material being sucked into black holes may actually be compressed and shot through an extradimensional "back door" to distant portions of the universe -- or even other universes -- where it emerges from white holes. The key point is that Superstring Theory applies extradimensionality to all of us, not just to black holes or to science-fiction stories. Perhaps the unique consciousness that is you, the Soul You, exists in some of those added dimensions.

The Search for the Location of the Soul

Although those other dimensions can't be measured yet, you can explore them because you exist in them. Your Soul and your consciousness actually reside in those deeper dimensions. When you know the general location and pathway for tapping those dimensions you can shift your awareness more deeply into that Soul realm.

During my earlier years I studied and developed methods for enhancing Aura Vision—the ability to see the energy field around someone. I have seen and studied thousands of auras for more than 20 years. As I traveled, I compared how the auras of people doing detailed physical work differed from auras of individuals who were praying, meditating, or feeling closer to their spiritual selves. From that study, I have developed a way to describe, in three-dimensional terms, the location of the Soul and a simple method for tapping it.

It is nearly impossible to fully describe a 10-dimensional energy field in the physical terms of world with which we are familiar. If I had to describe a three-dimensional position for the Soul, however, that location would be an area above and slightly behind the head. If you extend a line from your chin through the top of your head, it will bisect the energy field of your Soul Nature. This is the strongest part of the aura and the easiest to see. That is why most people see their first aura around and above the head area of another individual. They are perceiving the stronger Soul energy field rather than just the body's biomagnetic field. That is also why paintings of saints and major religious figures always portray the halo there. Even if people don't see auras, they sense a consciousness there.

Imagine an upside-down iceberg. It provides a good analogy for the relationship of the Soul's energy to the body. The bulk of an iceberg lies below water; less than a third of it rides above the surface. Turn this image upside down and you have a rough view of the Soul's relationship to the body. Most of the energy that you are, as a Soul, exists outside the body (above the head and slightly behind it), much like the larger normally underwater part of the iceberg. The smaller part of the iceberg (normally above the water) is equivalent to the part of the Soul's energy that extends down into the head area, links up with the brain and physical senses, and coordinates the machinery of the body.

For most of your life you focus your awareness down through the body and out through your physical senses. To tap and experience the deeper dimensions of your Soul, you need to learn to reverse that focus up and out to the more extensive portion of Soul energy above the head. In my national organization, Free Soul, we call this making a Soul-shift. This upward focus shift is what happens when people meditate successfully. You can see it happen when you watch their aura. Around the chest and face the aura dims while above the head it expands, deepens, and moves farther away from the body.

That change can also be measured scientifically. When you shift your focus up to the Soul area, your level of alpha brain-wave activity markedly increases. This is significant because the alpha brain-wave pattern has consistently been linked with higher forms of consciousness such as biofeedback, trance, self-hypnosis, and enhanced creativity. I was able to confirm this connection at a health fair in Glenwood Springs and thoroughly enjoyed myself in the process.

Every year a major television station sponsors health fairs throughout Colorado. At this particular one there was a booth on biofeedback with a toy I had been deprived of during my M.I.T. years. It was a train that you could activate by generating alpha brain waves. I had seen such set-ups before but never was able to try one.

Because I knew how to Soul-shift at will, I could slip in and out of "alpha" quickly. With electrodes taped to my head, I was able to run an electric train in a way I never could as a youngster. By mere thought I could make the train start and run at different speeds. By shifting down from the Soul I could stop it in an instant -- at the water tower, at the station, or, to be perverse, inside the tunnel. The operators of the exhibit were astonished at my ability to quickly generate and easily control alpha brain waves. They thought the alpha state could be reached only by slow and steady meditation. That day their thinking was changed and I was able to verify the clear link between alpha brain-waves and tapping the Soul.

Making the Soul-shift

You now know the location of your Soul energy. Tapping that energy requires learning a pathway for reaching it and a method for attuning your mind to it. The simplest pathway is a mental elevator. As you ride it, gradually shift your focus up through the body and then take a final mental step out into your unlimited Soul energy.

Do not try, force, or overconcentrate while making these shifts of awareness. This applies to all forms of mental and psychic exploration, but particularly to tapping the Soul. These approaches do nothing to speed your journey. They are usually more detrimental than helpful because they increase your level of physical tension; anchor your awareness in its physical orientation; and keep you from the relaxed and open form of consciousness required for extradimensional exploration. In scientific terms, when you try or force, your alpha brain-wave activity drops drastically. Intense concentration pushes you into brain-wave patterns more typical of routine activity than of higher consciousness.

The stereotypes you see in movies or on television, where people squeeze their eyes shut, hold their heads, and strain in concentration to sense psychically or tap higher consciousness are completely inaccurate. This is, in fact, exactly the wrong approach. The correct method is to focus your awareness lightly and guide it gently but firmly.

The key word is focus: to selectively heighten your awareness along the inner direction you are exploring, allowing it to flow along the path of your search. As I pointed out in other sections of this book, the difference between focusing and forcing is similar to the difference between peripheral vision and staring. Staring has an intensity and pressure to it. Seeing something with peripheral vision is more gentle; it requires you to focus your awareness at the sides, heightening your attention there. You are noticing rather than forcing. To experience your Soul learn to focus your awareness gently, like an inner form of peripheral vision.

The process outlined below will guide you in making that upward shift and exploring the fullness of your Soul energy. The effect is like a slingshot, propelling you up and out to your own deeper dimensions. You will feel boundaries dissolve as you step into this more expansive part of your being. You will feel the peace and heightened awareness available to you there. Do not try to analyze what you are sensing during the technique. That will only create tension and cut off or limit your experience. Review your impressions later.

- **Relax, sit or lie comfortably, and close your eyes.**
- **Gradually increase awareness of yourself rather than of your environment. Do not try or concentrate, but gently focus your awareness of what you are feeling from and within yourself.**
- **Next, pay specific attention to your lower legs. Feel your**

feet, your ankles, your calves. Slowly begin to shift your focus up through your legs, hips, waist, chest, shoulders, etc. As you sense each body area and are moving upward, gradually leave behind the parts you have already sensed. Tune them out. Ride this mental elevator upward until you reach the head area.

- As you focus on the head, take time to feel all the thoughts and memories that are You. Briefly let yourself see what comes to mind when you focus on yourself as a person.

- Shift your focus one more level upward to the Soul area. Some people experience this final focus shift as a feeling of stepping out of the top of their heads. Notice how the boundaries seem to disappear and you feel as if you are in an expanding dimension. Feel your awareness of yourself deepen, as if you have stumbled onto a seldom-explored but richer part of yourself. You may even feel you can extend outward limitlessly in any direction. This is the Real You. You have become aware of your Soul Nature.

Note: If you feel any pressure in your forehead or eye area as you make this final focus shift, you are probably trying to turn your eyes backward and force them to look out of the top of your head. They will not go there. Leave them where they belong. Make that final focus shift more as a feeling of letting your mind float, or a heightened awareness of the space above you.

- Explore this deeper part of yourself. See how far you can extend outward. Sense how ageless you feel. Experience the peacefulness that radiates through you as you tap the extra dimensions of your Soul.

- When you are finished, gently shift your focus back down to the head area and note some specific part of your body (nose, mouth, hands, etc.). Slowly move a finger or foot, and when you feel ready, open your eyes. Gently move your body to restore your normal physical orientation.

This technique is only the first step on a long and fascinating journey into the extra dimensions of the Soul. The more you meditate and practice the process, the easier it will be to tune out distractions. The more you experience your Soul, the easier it will be to make that final up-and-out focus shift. Exploring your extra dimensions can also be a natural relaxer. Tapping the Soul, even briefly, relieves the pressure of the physical world. In most instances one's aura will unwind and expand two to six inches by the time the exercise is completed. Once you learn control, the Soul-shift can be used at will throughout your day to enhance your feelings of peace and love.

Being a Soul: Key to Universal Love

I am sure that "soul" is a term with which most of you are comfortable. All major religions include within their framework the concept of the Soul. Whether it is called Soul, Spirit, Atman, or Intelligent Energy, the meaning is still the same. From a scientific point of view, you may think of the Soul as being a unique energy pattern or field that lies beyond the transience of physical matter—outside the limited forms of currently measurable energy. In Superstring Theory terms, it would be those additional six dimensions we all have.

Most people I meet readily admit they believe they have a Soul. This is not enough. To tap your full potential you must go beyond this. You do not <u>have</u> a Soul. You <u>are</u> a Soul. You <u>are</u> a Soul that <u>has</u> a body. This is more than mere linguistics. It is the realization that the Real You, your true self, is that Soul Nature—the conscious, initiating energy beyond the wiring and machinery of the body.

In fact, the belief that you have a Soul is one of the prime causes of people's limitations. If you have a Soul, then you must <u>be</u> something else. That something else you identify with is the physical body. As a result, you impose on yourself all the physical limitations we have been trying to go beyond. Just as the car that you drive is but a tool you use for travel, so your physical body is only an extension of the inner driver that is the Soul. You are the controller, not the controlled machinery. You are the water in the glass, not the glass. You are the electricity that runs the machine, not the motor. You <u>are</u> a Soul. You <u>have</u> a body.

Don't let yourself be trapped into limitations. See yourself as a Soul. Feel yourself as a Soul. Understand and know that your true nature is to be unlimited. Never underestimate how strongly our societal programming has trained us to think of ourselves in a limited way. Even our language leads us away from the concept that we <u>are</u> Souls by causing us to say, "my Soul," when it would be more correct to say, "I Soul."

Now you have a way of breaking the bonds of physical limitations. Being able to make that Soul-shift at will is a major step on the path to experiencing greater oneness. You no longer have to confine yourself to the physical limitations of the body. You now have personal experience with the reality of "something beyond."

Learning to tap your Soul is the gateway to the unlimited potentials that are your birthright. Through it you enter a realm of infinitely flexible energy. Indeed, you <u>are</u> energy. Einstein's $E = mc^2$ equation states that energy equals mass times the speed of light squared. In nonmathematical terms that means all things are energy, only they appear in different forms. The chair is energy. Light is energy. You are energy.

The law of conservation of energy states, "Energy can neither be created nor destroyed, only changed in form." That means that you, as energy, are now, always have been, and always will be. The only question is what you will do with your energy. Will you limit and suppress it? Or will you reach for your unlimitedness?

The first way to prove to yourself the unlimitedness of your Soul energy is to expand your awareness beyond the constrictions of physical boundaries. One of the advantages of realizing that you <u>are</u> a Soul that <u>has</u> a body is that you no longer limit yourself to purely physical capabilities, that you have the ability to blend and be one with all things.

Because we tend to think of ourselves as the distinct physical entity of our bodies, we separate ourselves from other objects, people, and environments. While it is true that these are separate islands of matter, you can still be at one with anything in your environment through your Soul Nature . You can blend into any object and sense it as an extension of yourself. You can gradually become a part of more and more around you.

As with Soul-shifting, the key to success is not trying or forcing. Relax and feel. Gently extend, dropping one artificial boundary after another. Not only does this increase your sense of unlimitedness, but it is a bridge to deeper forms of psychic sensing. **Here is the process for experiencing this Soul skill:**

- **Sit comfortably and close your eyes. Shift your focus up to your Soul energy.**

- **Gently float and enjoy the feeling of You, your Soul Nature. After a short while, allow that awareness to expand so that it gradually includes your whole being. Feel the Real You becoming one with your physical body. Feel your body melt and blend into your awareness of yourself. At this point you may be experiencing for the first time the complete fullness of your total self -- body, mind, and Soul. You should feel like one big ball of awareness, extending beyond the limits of your body but paradoxically penetrating deeper into the fabric of your physical being than you normally experience.**

- **Allow your awareness to expand again so that it gradually** includes all of the chair you are sitting in. Feel your arms melting into the arms of the chair; feel your back gently sinking into the energy of the chair. Feel yourself and the chair becoming one, so that your awareness now includes yourself, your physical being, and the chair.

- Once you feel at one with the chair, explore it. What does it feel like inside? Can you sense all its parts—legs, back, under the seat? Can you feel where the chair touches the floor or the carpet?

- Allow your awareness to expand again. This time blend along the carpet or floor to all corners of the room. Sense the other objects that come in contact with the floor and blend with them. Explore.

- When you have finished exploring, gradually return your awareness to your body. Focus on a specific physical area (nose, mouth, hands, etc.) and when you feel ready, open your eyes. Gently move to restore your normal physical orientation.

Many people experience this blending haphazardly when they are tired, deeply relaxed, or when they meditate. It is, however, a capability that can be learned, controlled, and used in any situation and at any time. The spiritual energy that comprises the Soul is remarkably flexible. Blending with matter is only the first step of what the Soul can do. You can also blend with pure energy and extend your awareness to greater depths. Learning to blend with forms of everyday energy (light, heat, etc.) is a key part of advanced control of the Soul's ability to blend and expand.

Learning to blend and be one with physical objects (your body, the chair, etc.) gives you beginning experience with focused, directional expansion. Energy blending helps you experience expansion in all directions simultaneously. It is the gateway for reaching complete oneness with the universe.

Most of the time your Soul energy is relatively focused. This natural concentration is necessary for you to function through a physical body. The secret to controlling Soul expansion and to experience the Soul's ability to blend without limits is to relax that Soul focus. As you do, you will feel your Soul naturally expanding from boundary to boundary. The more you relax, the further the expansion. You will feel an inner peace and security deeper than any you may have experienced.

"You literally feel one with the All," said William, who when I first met him, had "dropped out" of conventional life soon after getting his degree in business and computer science. The rat race of the corporate world made him tense and unhappy.

At first William searched for contentment by studying world religions. He wanted to feel connected, a part of the universe, at one with his vision of God. William even flirted with various Eastern cults, but chanting on a street corner didn't bring him inner peace. Finally he divorced himself from society. Selling his possessions, he bicycled across the U.S. for a year, searching for a way to feel one with the stars he saw in the clear night skies.

William was near the end of his bike trip when he attended one of my lectures. He was intrigued that someone else with a technical background was searching for unlimitedness as he was. That curiosity kept him coming back until he learned about the Universe Blend Meditation. After that William never had to search or travel again. He had found a way to reach what he called "Home." In a few short minutes, he learned how to expand the boundaries of his Soul energy and journey to oneness with the stars. He came back feeling more at peace than ever before. What amazed him most was that it didn't take an hour of meditation or chanting, and he hadn't needed to find that perfect spot in the mountains.

The key for William had been learning Free Soul's technique of blending with light. He could understand light as energy that was truly unlimited. Riding its beams helped him take the limits off his consciousness for the first time. "I can find light anywhere. I don't have to keep searching for a path to follow to the stars. I can let them come to me wherever I am," he said. William has since returned to society and founded a successful computer software company. He balances the pressures by being able to take a Universe Blend break whenever he chooses.

Blending with the Universe

Beyond the boundaries of matter, blending with light is the next skill to learn. You can see light, you can feel its warmth. Because it is real and familiar to you, light is the easiest form of energy to blend with. Moreover, since light reaches everywhere, you can ride its waves to every corner of the Universe. You can literally be one with all things. This next technique takes the Soul-blending ability you learned earlier and extends it to universal dimensions. **Read the process below and then sit back and enjoy your ride to the stars**.

- **Sit comfortably, and close your eyes. Slip into a relaxed breathing pattern to release tension. Then, shift up and tune into your Soul energy.**

- When you feel in harmony with yourself, begin to sense the light from the room as it falls on you. Feel its warmth and illumination.

- Gradually become one with the light itself. As you feel it passing around you and through you, blend with it. Become a part of its warmth, radiance, expansiveness.

- Being one with the light, travel with it. Extend into every corner of the room and fall upon every object. Go with the light and blend with all the areas it reaches. Feel at one with every part of the room and every object in it.

- Next, sense your awareness extending beyond the room and including the whole building. Sense the different rooms and floors.

- Now rise up and expand even farther. Stretch out to sense the whole neighborhood, and finally the entire city. Feel the various parts of the city as you know it: its center, its limits, the streets, the parks, the highways. Feel as if you have a thousand senses and can extend into all parts of the city at once. Be at one with the city and its people.

- Again feel your awareness expanding. Let your beingness spread until you cover your state or province, your nation, and finally the whole world. Feel yourself becoming one with the entire globe, at peace and in tune with its many lands and oceans. Enjoy this sensation of being at one with our planet. Sense the deeper understanding and kinship you feel for all people on Earth.

- Keep letting the boundaries dissolve. Let your beingness expand even farther, blending with the solar system. Feel the other planets and the sun. Continue expanding past the solar system and to the Milky Way galaxy.

- Completely release your beingness and feel yourself blending with the vastness of the universe, stretching to every portion of the cosmos, being one with every star and galaxy. Let yourself float and enjoy the total peace of this oneness with the universe.

- Feel how that inner peace also gives you a deep sense of love and connection to everything. Feel your love for the entire universe and its love for you.

- After fully experiencing this oneness and love, gradually bring your awareness back to the galaxy, the solar system, the planet, your state, your city, the building, and yourself in your chair.

- Specifically focus on a part of your body (nose, mouth, hands, etc.). Gently move a finger or a foot, and when you are ready, open your eyes. Move easily to restore your normal physical orientation.

Doesn't that feel marvelous? Isn't it exciting to know you can go so far so quickly? Some people spend years meditating before they can reach that same level of macroconsciousness. Now you know how to be in harmony with the universe at any time in only a matter of minutes. The more you practice universe blending, the easier it becomes and the deeper you feel that unconditional love.

Once you are experienced in the skill of Soul expansion, you can quickly touch the peace and love of the infinite whenever you wish. You can take a quantum leap in awareness whenever you need that larger, more "at one" perspective. No longer will you need to feel trapped by the pressures of living. Relief is as close as your next five-minute break. Try it during lunch or a coffee break the next few days and see how refreshed you feel.

This is just a brief introduction to the joyous explorations that are possible through the Soul and beyond. The *Dynamics of Being a Free Soul* Comprehensive Course and Advanced Workshop Tapes have many others. By enhancing your connection with your spiritual dimensions you can boost the level of love you feel in your life. Here are some additional methods.

Other Keys for Spiritually Enhancing the Love in Your Life

Love is not just giving love or being loved by someone else. It is a feeling that fills your very being. Loving life may be even more essential than having someone to love or be loved by. No matter how close your loved ones, they can't always be there for you. As a minimum, their love for you can seem to lessen when they are having a bad day. No matter how much you love them, you can't control that. You can always be in command of your love of life.

Being able to tap the infinite reservoir of love energy that exists in the universe can give you that command.

Blending with the Love Dimension

If, as science tells us, all things exist in at least 10 dimensions, why not think of love as being one of those dimensions that "we don't have the technology to measure yet?" Love is more than just an emotion that you feel. It is an energy that you can sense coming toward you. You can feel it when you are loved. The warmth and caring directed at you is almost palpable. These sensations are recognizable for people of all races, religions, and cultures. For all its universality, however, no love meter or collection device has yet to be developed. Quite possibly, love is another aspect of the Universe that extends beyond the physical dimensions and the wiring of the brain.

With that in mind, consider this option for increasing the amount of time you experience love energy. The same way you can tune your radio to the frequency of a specific station, you can tune your Soul to blend with the dimension (or frequency) of love energy. How do you do that? You simply hold in mind your associations with the feeling of love. Let them draw you to oneness with that radiant, joyous energy. **Here is a step by step process you can enjoy.**

- **Do the Joy Touch to start off at peace and mellow**
- **Gently bring to mind things you associate with love.**
  (Feel love's warmth, see the smile it brings to peoples faces, or hear loving words. Know the sense of acceptance and security it brings, or visualize a color you associate with love.)
- **Feel your whole being becoming one with love energy.**
- **Let that sensation start to attune you with the frequency that is love energy.**
  (Feel yourself blending deeper into it and/or it coming to you.)
- **Bask in oneness with that frequency or dimension.**
  (Be completely attuned with the energy and vibration of love.)
- **Know that you can tap this connection whenever and where ever you want.**
- **Finally, do the Joy Touch to seal in the feeling and your knowledge of how to connect with it at will.**

Love is always all around us. The old song, *Love Is In the Air*, is more than just figuratively accurate. All you need to do is to tune into it more often. The concept of Soul blending with the love dimension gives you a method to increase that frequency. Further, you can combine it with the Soul-shift and Joy Touch techniques to create an even more profound effect.

Doing the Joy Touch from Above

Once you know the feel of blending with love energy and the skill for making the Soul-shift, you can combine them and trigger the septum pellucidum from above. As stated earlier in the Skills for Countering Prolonged Depressiveness section of Chapter 2, there is nothing written in stone that says you must trigger the septal area from the front. That is just the easiest way to teach initially. Once you know the location and feel for triggering the Joy Touch mood-elevation effect, you can approach the area from any direction. Coming down from the top has the benefit of linking you with your deeper energy as a Soul and completing a connection with the Universe.

There are several variations you can try. The first is to just think of that Soul area and focus on triggering the septum pellucidum as you normally would (caressing thought, energy, flow, strumming a harp, etc.) but coming down more from above than from the front. As you become more familiar with the Soul-shift, the second option is to shift your focus to the Soul and specifically direct energy (love energy or any energy) down to your head and flow it through the septal area. You can also do a third variation by starting with the Universe blend technique. Then, as you return from feeling that oneness with the infinite, bring some of it back with you. Extend a finger of its connection back toward you as you return your awareness from Universe to galaxy, to solar system, to Earth, to your body. Fold inward that universal touch and flow its oneness energy through the septum pellucidum area and into every fiber of your being.

These last two techniques lend themselves more to longer deeper meditations. They can be used for deeply recharging your well-being after prolonged periods of stress or before particularly difficult situations you have coming up. They are the spiritual equivalent of taking a full shower as compared to handwashing that the quicker basic Joy Touch gives to your mood. **Take a moment and try at least one of them.**

- **Do the Joy Touch to start off relaxed and in tune.**
- **Briefly Soul-shift or at least focus on your Soul area.**
- **From that above-the-head perspective, caress down thru the septal area.**
  (Picture or feel caressing your Joy Center from above.)
- **Feel the same mellow sensation as with the Joy Touch.**
- **Now let energy flow from the Universe and the Soul to your Joy Center.**
  (Picture, know, feel, or understand that the Soul can be a funnel for Universal Energy.)
- **Feel every fiber of your body being energized.**
  (Let the Universal Energy flow from the septal area to every cell and every atom of your body.)
- **Do the Joy Touch a final time to seal in that total recharging.**

I think of the Joy Touch and the Soul-shift as the two halves of full spiritual freedom. The Joy Touch frees you from being dominated by the animal nature of the limbic brain. It is your key to breaking the survival struggle that the physical wiring of the brain can suck us into. The Soul-shift is your gateway to exploring the dimensions "beyond" in which you exist. Together they give you the ability (the skill, not just the desire) to live what the Bible calls, "Being in the world, but not of it." You have the means for living more as a Soul.

Seeing Souls in Others

There is an old saying from child psychology: "I love you. I don't like what you did." This concept, when added to the perspective of Soul awareness, can be a key for enhancing the love you feel in your life. When you can think of and see others as Souls, it becomes easier to love them all the time. It is easy to love people when all is going well. The trick is to feel loving toward them when they (or you) are irritable.

Many of our negative associations with others are tied to our physical view of them. A look, a behavior, or specific words and body language can trigger feelings that obscure the love we feel over-all. This shouldn't be surprising. The brain is designed to recognize and store distressing visual patterns for our safety and protection. Even worse, old negative memories can be stimulated just by seeing a person's face, even if he or she is not being disagreeable at the moment. You don't have to let that old image negate your ability to love all the time. Seeing and thinking of others as Souls is the way out.

Now that you know the location of that Soul energy bubble, you can direct your attention there. Rather than just see people physically, you can shift your focus to the part of them that is a learning, seeking Soul. All you have to do is look more above their head than directly at their face. When you do this, you will notice that your perspective softens. Even if you don't see an aura or anything other than the space above their head, you will feel less critical, less judgmental.

I find that when I look above the heads of people, it automatically triggers feelings of greater depth to them. I see them more for their full potentials and sense them as the beautiful unique spirits that they are. This helps me to love them even if something in their behavior may be annoying or stimulating one of my biases. When I view teenagers in a mall this way it gives me an immediate perspective shift. Rather than seeing them as irritating, potential juvenile delinquents, I can sense their reaching out for identity. When I do this with people who are bugging me, I can see them as crying out for what they need, rather than being against me. This helps me choose to respond more objectively and lovingly.

When used with loved ones, this technique can help you be less reactive if they snap at you or do something that pushes your buttons. It helps you to sense what may be behind their actions so that you don't take them so personally. Combining this technique with the Joy Touch has been a godsend for helping me do my part to prevent unnecessary arguments in my marriage. This combination also makes it easier to be sure that I am disciplining my children more from my responsibilities as a parent, rather than out of anger or emotional upset.

This skill can also be invaluable for seeing another individual as more than just a sex object. That can be important for both genders when you need to work professionally with someone that you find attractive. It may be even more crucial for men. We don't know all the brain specifics, but it is well documented that men are much more susceptible to sexual arousal from visual stimulation. Neurologically, it may be harder for them to resist looking more at a woman's anatomy than her personality. Consciously choosing to look more at the Soul area than the body can break that cycle. It can help a man to see women more as people than potential sex partners.

Letting your attention be more on that Soul area works because it connects you with the feeling that others are more than just their physical manifestations and personality. Any time you can see a larger perspective of others it automatically helps. Try it for a moment if you have people around you. If you are alone, I recommend taking a brief break to get to where you can view people and do the exercise described below. If neither of these is possible at the moment, read the technique and remember to try it the next time you are in view of your loved ones and/or other people. **Here is the process.**

- **Do the Joy Touch to start off relaxed and open.**
- **Find several subjects and notice your feelings about them.**
  (Identify your perception of them as you look at them.)
- **Next, hold in mind your desire to see others more as Souls than just as bodies.**
- **Now, look more above their heads than at their bodies.**
  (Let your gaze gently fall above them rather than staring at their facial features or clothes.)
- **Feel how your perspective of them softens and mellows.**
  (Notice how you see them in a more tolerant and loving light.)
- **Practice also seeing people who are not physically present.**

(Think of a loved one at home but picture them more as a Soul. Sense them as energy.)

- **Optional: Try viewing yourself in a mirror this way and note the change.**
  (Experience how your sense of who you are expands, compared to just checking your appearance.)
- **Joy Touch one last time to seal in this Soul vision ability.**

Is it the area you are looking at that gives you this more tolerant perspective, or the fact that you are looking with the concept of seeing them as Souls? It's both. There is an energy that exists beyond the mere tissue of the brain. You can even learn to see this aura and its colors. My book, *You Are Psychic!*, contains a whole chapter specifically devoted to seeing and sensing the aura. Even more powerful, however, is the polarizing filter of your intent. When you look to see more, you find it. Being open to seeing others as Souls has the additional benefit of opening your heart. That increased tolerance and love are equally as important to give to yourself.

Remember to see and think of yourself as a Soul, too. Give yourself that same benefit of the doubt. Practicing the Soul-shift technique you learned earlier will increase you feelings of being a Soul. You can learn to tap your Soul in seconds. Then its greater perspective is available to you all the time, not just when you are meditating (i.e. at work, in conversations, and even when you are physically active). My *Dynamics of Being a Free Soul* 10-Lesson Comprehensive Course (available through instructors or self-study in a textbook, or on cassette tape) has specific techniques in each lesson for enhancing your Soul Awareness skills.

The major purpose of this book and Free Soul as an organization, is freedom—freedom for you from dependency. Love is an essential nutrient for the human spirit. True freedom means going beyond dependency on others for love. Anything that boosts the level of love you feel inside is a feast for your well-being as a Soul. There are thousands of books on relationships and romance. This chapter was not designed to replace them. Its purpose is to give you techniques and perspectives beyond their standard approaches. The more you give put-ups and see yourself and others as Souls, the easier it is to be in love with life. Also enhanced is the degree to which you love others and they love you. Love is a choice that is always available to you. Choose to be a seeker of greater love.

The extent to which you love life and yourself is often affected by your self-image and feelings of success. That is another area where a larger perspective is essential. Up next: the secrets for success without the achievement addiction.

— Success —

Without the Achievement Addiction

Almost as important as being loved is feeling successful in life. Take a moment and remember a time when you felt truly successful at something. Reexperience the boost it gave your feeling of well-being. Recall how you felt you were soaring; how it seemed you could do anything. Imagine what it would be like if you could have that feeling more often. Better still, think how your life would be enhanced if you could generate it at will. That is this chapter's focus.

Mastering a greater feeling of success is crucial for creating your own happiness. Without it life can quickly become an unpleasant series of worries and struggles. More often than soaring, the feeling of crashing can become the reality. Let's examine why.

While there are many ways of defining success, achievement and accomplishments are generally accepted as the primary measurement. Overall, that traditional standard has served humanity well. It is probably the motivating force that has lifted us from the cave to the condo. It has driven us to get things done and build a better life. As technology advances, however, aspects of measuring success by achievement may actually work against our well-being.

Addiction is defined as the process of giving oneself up to some strong habit. The habit in question does not necessarily need to be drug related or harmful. In some cases the habit might even be beneficial or at least seem beneficial. It could be said that we are addicted to eating, as few of us are able to deny the compulsion of hunger for very long. We don't think of eating as an addiction, however, because it is essential for survival. Chemical addictions, although biologically driven, are not viewed as necessary to stay alive. They are also thought to have major psychological components in addition to their physiological cravings.

The need for achievement may be an area that crosses the line between physical necessity and psychological dependence. Actually, it has a foot in both realms.

The Biology of the Achievement Addiction

At the dawn of human evolution, achievement *was* essential for survival. The first and most basic achievement was finding food. If not attained, death was the sure result. The longer the period without a success in finding food, the greater the risk of dying. That reality creates a powerful psychological urge to succeed (either at hunting—the aggressive dominating and taking-command type activity, or at gathering—something not too far removed from modern day shopping and/or information gathering). Lack of success would evoke the extreme anxiety associated with the risk of death.

Over the eons, that compulsive urge and its link to anxiety may even have been hard wired into our DNA for the survival of the species. That biological conditioning would result in the need to achieve in order to feel safe and comfortable. Without achievement of some kind, anxiety and discomfort would be triggered.

This may explain why we can so easily catastrophize when faced with the perception of a lack of successful accomplishment. Lack of success with one endeavor or in one relationship can be blown out of proportion to feel like failure in all of life. Those dinosaur parts of the limbic brain are crying out that we are in danger of dying. Why doesn't our rational mind overrule that illogical exaggeration? The answer lies in the psychological addictiveness of achievement.

All our lives we have been rewarded for accomplishments. The benefits have spanned the full spectrum of positive reinforcements, from tangible material comforts (more money, better living conditions, etc.) to the limbic soothers of praise, admiration, increased status and affection.

The result is that we may literally have a biological and psychological need for a specific frequency of perceived success. Without it, the brain may automatically trigger survival reflexes. Lacking regular feelings of accomplishment, our limbic systems can bombard us with worries and anxieties that are out of proportion with actual circumstances. One failure can become, "I may never succeed." One rejection becomes, "I may never be loved."

You can counter that dinosaur reflex. Simply make sure you create that needed feeling frequently enough. This doesn't mean you have to be a workaholic and drive yourself to be achieving constantly. You can use past achievements or milestones along the way in your current endeavors. The key is *feeling* successful. The limbic brain responds to the data it is fed. Its reality is the thoughts you send it.

It is easy to feel successful when your life is filled with tangible achievements. The trick is to maintain your feeling of well-being, even when things aren't going well. This section is designed to help you boost your feelings of success *all the time* without having to work your life away or become an achieve-aholic. It is equally important to feel successful during the lulls between accomplishments. This is especially true when those droughts are longer than usual.

One of the difficulties with our modern environment is that much of our work doesn't generate immediate positive thoughts. Needing to hunt or gather food gives frequent positive feedback and very tangible results. Too often our current-day projects are so long term that the gratification of their completion is weeks or even months away. As a result, even an endeavor that ends in eventual success, can generate weeks of survival anxiety.

Your Periodicity of Perceived Success

The first key to preventing that unnecessary discomfort is to know how often you need to feel successful to feel good about life. This is your personal periodicity of need for perceived success. It can vary through your life depending on your other levels of stress. Time pressures or financial issues can trigger their own survival reflexes. The greater the challenges you face in those areas the more often you will need to feel successful to counter the sense of impending doom they generate. Sleep deprivation makes you even more vulnerable.

Identifying how often you need to feel successful is totally personal. There is no right or wrong answer. If anything, however, it is better to err on the side of too often rather than too little. No harm comes from feeling good a greater percentage of the time. Too infrequently, however, leaves you vulnerable to the time bomb of survival anxiety. You want to know at what point not feeling successful will start to trigger your limbic discomforts. With that knowledge you can counter the survival reflex by self-generating successful feelings before the irrational worry or depression kicks in. Take a moment and try this technique for success related mood-elevation.

- **Identify what you feel is the frequency that you need to feel successful to be secure and happy.**
  (Once/week, once/day, twice/day, once/hour, etc.)
- **Next, specifically think of where you want to remember to feel successful.**
  (At a meal [a type of grace], before the work day, at the end of the day, etc.)
- **Do the Joy Touch to be more relaxed, mellow, and mentally clear.**
- **Now think of something to be proud of yourself for or that you do feel successful about.**
  (It can be something current or even from the past.)

- **Feel the sensation of being capable & pleased with yourself.**
  (Smile and recall another time you were happy with yourself.)
- **Fully cherish yourself for whatever it is and congratulate yourself out loud.**
  (If you are not where you can speak, at least mouth the words or write them down.)
- **Finally, do the Joy Touch again to reinforce and sink in that successful feeling.**

This brief beginning exercise gives you the way to take command of your happiness in relation to success. Feeling successful frequently enough is the key, not the specific achievements. You may not be able to control the timing of completing an accomplishment. You can always generate an accomplishing feeling.

Remember also, what you learned in the last chapter about put-ups that are based on life skills. You can always feel successful for your effort, your perseverance, your courage, or your initiative—not just for your results.

The secret is to remember to reflect positively during your adventures in life, not just at your destinations. Goals, results and accomplishments are important, but they are just one small part of the process. If they become your sole focus for feeling successful, then you can truly become an achievement junkie. That is not success. It is addiction.

True success is being in command of your state of mind, of creating your own happiness. Have goals and achievements in life. Don't let them have you. You can always find something to feel successful about. Just being alive and not giving up can be cause for celebration. Striving for greater learning, joy, and intrinsic self-esteem can give tremendous fulfillment. Merely struggling for results consigns you to all the horrors that go with slavery. Don't shackle your worth and happiness to the pillars of things. Don't imprison your Soul to the treadmill of work. Set it free to explore and enjoy your efforts.

Don't get me wrong. I am now and have always been an achiever. I do have goals. I do appreciate accomplishing. I achieve, yes, but I have tried to make my life a quest rather than a test. I have learned methods for feeling successful that are independent of how the events in my life are going. That freedom can be yours as well.

The first thing to learn is what achievements are truly worth your efforts, what types of success you really value. Chasing after something that is not a true priority for you won't help your feelings of success. Here is a simple exercise to put in perspective what most will create feelings of success for you.

Value Analysis

You have 100 energy points to invest in the value market below. You can distribute the energy points in whatever manner you wish, but you can not exceed an expenditure of 100 points. Also you must allot points in the increments described in the table below (with the points allotted giving the results indicated).

50 = guaranteed all the abundance you would ever want of this quality or achievement

20 = guaranteed a lot of this quality or achievement

10 = chance for obtaining this quality / achievement with ease

05 = chance for obtaining this quality / achievement with effort

00 = no chance for obtaining this quality / achievement

You can add Qualities / Achievements to the list below if, for some reason, something you really want is not shown; but then drop one from the list. The purpose is to have 20 qualities and 100 points to spend. Now, no fair cheating. No spending over 100 points and no spending 1 point on areas - use only 5, 10, 20, or 50 point increments.

Also, no fair saying I don't have to spend points on something because I already have it. For example, if you spend no points on education it means that you would not have the education that you already have. The same for health, family, etc.

Wealth	Spiritual Advancement
Health	Contribution to Humanity
Longevity	Creative Ability
Love	Freedom
Family	Tranquility
Friends	Challenge
Looks / Beauty	Education
Fame	Job Satisfaction
Travel	Professional Prominence
Physical Ability	Positions of Authority

It's an interesting exercise, because it shows what your core values truly are. These are the real areas you should measure your success by. Why pressure yourself and trigger anxiety reflexes about an area that is not really of interest to you? This is where we often fall victim to society's programming and make ourselves miserable unnecessarily.

For example, very few people allot 50 energy points to wealth. Often, however, the vast majority of our feelings of success and worth are related to finances. Even if you allotted 20 energy points to wealth, that is only one-fifth of the total available. Therefore financial issues should only account for one-fifth of your feelings of success. Look at the other areas where you used energy points (such as family, friends, spiritual advancement or creativity, etc.). These are the things you should use to boost your feelings of worth.

Feeling successful is 90% a state of mind. You can use the lifeskills concept from the last chapter and your results from this value analysis to always have something to feel successful about. Cherish your creativity in life. Value your success as a good friend to others. Feel proud of the spiritual progress and learning you have achieved. Remember also to praise yourself for your effort, initiative, courage and perseverance in these areas. Try it for a moment.

- **Do the Joy Touch to clear any anxieties or uncertainties.**
- **Pick an area you gave 10 or more points to that is not traditionally associated with success.**
  (This should be something other than wealth, positions of authority, or professional prominence, etc.)
- **Cherish yourself for your successes in that area.**
  (Acknowledge them out loud, write them down, or at least feel them deeply.)
- **Also, pick a lifeskill that you value about yourself.**
  (Pick a quality such as courage, initiative, determination, teamwork, compassion, learning, perseverance, etc.)
- **Value the inner success you have had in that area though that lifeskill.**
  (Appreciate the ways you have succeeded beyond mere results.)
- **Finally, do the Joy Touch to seal in that sense of value and success.**

The Trap of Desire

We are often faced with a dilemma here in the western world. Our business and personal success standards often stress the need to have it all. Want more, get more, be more are the battle cries. On the other hand religious influences seem frequently to condemn material excesses and wanting them.

In Christianity there are the Bible passages: "The love of money is the root of all evil" and "It is easier for a camel to go through the eye of a needle than for a rich man to enter the kingdom of God." Eastern faiths offer no relief from the conflict either. One of Buddhism's main tenets is that "All suffering is created by desire." Desire is just another way of saying "having wants" (wanting things, wanting to achieve, wanting success, etc.). Both religions echo the thought that striving to achieve only the material has negative consequences.

There is a way out of this dilemma. It is another key for success without the achievement addiction. The secret is to focus on the proper component of your wants. All wants have two components. The first is the "what" of the want, the thing that is actually desired. It is these "whats" that are addictive.

Review for a moment what you know about the addictive pattern. As time goes on, is the same amount of the addictive substance enough? Of course not. More is always needed. This pattern is also true of the addictive part of wants. The "what" always needs more (more money, more clothes, more house, more status, more power) to create the same feeling of success. Sometimes, that "more" means continued performance (the what-have-you-done-lately factor). Sometimes it means bigger achievements. In either case, the result is that you suffer until you get that "more". Lack of continued past performance or lack of achieving the next level up can create a feeling of failure. Either of these perceived lacks of success can then trigger out of control survival anxieties.

The solution is to focus on the why of your wants, the reason behind why you have that want. You may not always be able to get the what, but you can always be making progress on the why. Here are some examples.

When my first book came out, I was very successful at getting media coverage for it. I worked directly with the publisher's publicity department (actually, I had a phone and office in their department) and personally secured over 50 radio, TV, and newspaper interviews. Because I was in their offices daily I happened to see a document that wasn't intended for my eyes. It was from a particular New York TV show that I really wanted to be on. The publisher had approached the show about two books, mine and another they had out at the same time. The show had responded that they could only have one of the two and left it up to the publisher which it would be.

The publisher picked the other book because I had already gotten so much publicity for mine. I was devastated. I had always wanted to be on that show. My disappointment was enormous. I wanted that show with every fiber of my being. I was so discouraged, I felt like giving up on all my publicity efforts. I had to do something to counter those feelings of disappointment. Otherwise, I would sabotage my future efforts to promote the book. I turned to this "why of the want" approach.

The show was the what of my want. I was literally addicted to the feeling of having to have *that* show. When I identified the why of my want I felt relieved and able to go on. My *why* was that I wanted to reach people with the information in the book. I instantly realized that I could always be reaching people (whether or not I appeared on that one particular show). I resolved to focus on the joy of reaching people in all the different ways that were available to me.

I did just that during the evening on the train ride out of New York to my In-laws home on Long Island. I took out a copy of my book and placed it on the seat next to me. As a result, I had several positive conversations with fellow commuters, and actually connected with more media exposure. One of the interested individuals was the producer of a satellite network of radio shows. Realizing I could reach people in almost any circumstance lifted my spirits. My creative approach also led to greater publicity coverage. I was not able to have the specific what of my original want, but I had most decidedly been able to have the fulfillment of its why.

Another common example is wanting more money. The money is the what of the want. When you correctly identify its exact why, you can feel relief even when more funds are not available. Sometimes the why is that you want to be able to do more, to not be limited, or to feel freer. In these cases, be creative. How you can be freer or look for ways to do what you want, but less expensively? Take going on a vacation as an example.

Say you want more money to go to the Bahamas, but the money just isn't going to be there. The what is the Bahamas. Your why is that you want a vacation or possibly warmth, or the ocean. Focus on making progress on these areas. Get yourself some type of vacation time, even if it is just a weekend trip. Get out in the sunlight or to a waterfront stroll (lake if ocean is out of reach). Look for creative ways to give yourself a break and do something special.

The more you are able to identify the whys of your wants, the more you break free from the traps of desires. You then put fewer limits on your happiness. Scott Maley, a Free Soul instructor from Oklahoma, coined a phrase that I think is helpful in remembering to use this approach. He said, "So Pete, I guess you are telling us to go through life with whys (wise) eyes."

In many ways this process is similar to the type of insightful reflection you did in identifying your Comforting Connections in Chapter 2. You are getting to the heart of the matter to more effectively deal with it. With that knowledge you can prevent the erosion of your happiness from limbic survival reflexes that are out of proportion to the exact circumstances. **Take a moment and practice this "why of your want" process.**

- **Do the Joy Touch to start off calm and at ease.**
- **Think of a want you have that you feel is being frustrated or impeded.**
- **Next, separate the what of your want from its why.**
  (Identify the key issue behind your desire.)
- **Then, creatively think of ways you can achieve the intent of your why.**
  (At least make progress toward it.)
- **Feel fulfilled about what you can do.**
  (Also, cherish yourself for your insight.)
- **Finally, do the Joy Touch to seal in the realization and good feeling.**

The whole purpose of these previous sections is to give you skills for feeling good about yourself independent of external accomplishment or things. You may not get the chance to be independently wealthy, but you can learn to be *independently worthy*. Think of the freedom to enjoy life that will be yours when your feelings of success and fulfillment are not shackled to a preconceived set of outcomes. Imagine the increased well-being and contentment that will be yours.

For too long humanity, has suffered more than is necessary. There are enough real challenges in life that demand our full energies. We don't need to elevate minor incompletions to the status of real crises. The limbic brain doesn't know the difference. You do. You can sense an anxiety building and accurately determine if the issue is truly life-threatening or merely a disappointment. Don't let disappointments be the speed bumps in your road to happiness. Use the skills you have learned to be in command of your state of mind.

These approaches will always help you feel better. They will reduce your stress and anxiety; which is often half the battle in handling a crisis. When you are faced with true survival issues, additional concepts may be needed. Lets look at a few of those.

Dealing with Financial Pressure Success Issues

Often there are real financial pressures behind survival anxieties and feelings of lack of success. In these circumstances, just focusing on lifeskills or the why of your wants may not be enough. The tangible financial concerns must be addressed. The key is still, however, to prevent the survival reflex from dominating your every thought. Anything that breaks the cycle of the inner panic can keep you from the debilitation of negative obsessing.

One trick for self-employed individuals is to take the pressure off by doing some math with your savings. Here is an example that occurred to one of my students. Tom is a self-employed piano tuner. When his second child was born he started to worry about being able to earn enough to support his growing family. The anxiety was made worse by a slow-down in the number of tuning jobs he was getting. Tom's distress grew and started to affect his ability to generate new business.

I had experienced a similar feeling shortly after my second child was born. (There must be a gene within men that gets triggered after the second child comes along. It seems to make us feel financially responsible for the whole world.) Because I had had the same experience, I was able to share with Tom what had worked for me.

I had Tom look at his savings and figure the following: How long could he go without any income? Also, how long could he go if he received only half the income he had normally earned each month? Tom saw that, even with no income at all, he could live for three months off his savings. He realized that he had never gone even a month without a new client being referred to him, let alone three months. Tom also saw that at even half of his normal income he could last for six months before things truly became crucial. With that amount of time, he knew he could find new work or put a plan into action for generating revenue. That realization took the pressure off.

Tom had financial challenges he needed to face, but at least he could now do so with a clear mind. His productivity increased and he was able to think of new ways for reaching prospective clients. An additional benefit was that he was able to better cherish the time with his family that the temporary slow down gave him. Rather than being constantly worried, he was able to enjoy playing with the kids and being at home more often.

This same approach can also be used if you are facing the possibility of a layoff or are out of work. If you don't have savings, review your loan options or how long you can go on unemployment.

The key is to at least bring the pressure down a notch, even if you don't use those options. (You may not in fact be laid off or you may not choose to take a loan). Find a way to ease the feeling of total catastrophe. Survival anxiety tends to lead to hasty and unwise decisions. Use your higher mind to keep the limbic animal from taking control of your life. Remember also to fully appreciate what you do have.

Wants versus Needs

Crucial to feeling successful a greater percentage of the time is knowing the difference between wants and needs. Frequently, we mistakenly miss-identify our wants as needs that we equate with survival. This is particularly true when we are living right at or above our means. It can feel like we are barely surviving, when in fact are doing quite well. We have just invested in having many of our wants and as a result don't have a lot of reserves. Take housing for example.

Chances are you are paying more than you really need to for housing. You don't have to have the size or location of housing that you do. There is housing available for less (that would give you greater spending money). Your basic need is for shelter. Everything above that is an investment in satisfying your wants. Instead of bemoaning the cost of a mortgage or high rent, see it as a want you have purchased for yourself. Be happy that you have been able to give yourself that gift.

The same is true for many luxuries enjoyed in America. TVs, cars, telephone, movies, or meals out are not necessary for survival. All of these things are wants satisfied. Don't think of them as needs. If you do, you become increasingly vulnerable to survival anxieties. You can wind up counting your lacks instead of counting your blessings.

Remember, how you feel is directly controlled by the thoughts you have. If you dwell on thoughts of not enough, you will constantly trigger the limbic survival reflexes and all the discomfort they bring. If, instead, you focus on the good things you do have, your attitude and general happiness will be greatly increased. Instead of feeling bad because you can't eat out twice a week, cherish the joy of being able to treat yourself when you can. Instead of feeling lousy because of something you can't have (right now), focus on being appreciative for what you do have.

My world travels as a Naval Officer made me truly grateful for the many blessings we have here in America. I can't walk into a supermarket without feeling incredibly abundant. We are blessed with a selection and accessibility of food that a vast portion of the world can only dream of. Two of my instructors (both engineers) that emigrated from the Soviet Union tell me that during the dead of winter an orange used to cost them a day's pay, a pound of coffee a week's pay. They also had friends who were imprisoned merely for teaching yoga.

Here in America we are also blessed with incredible freedom of information. Walk into any bookstore and be grateful for being able to explore almost any topic that interests you. The glass ceiling that limits opportunity to women is unfair, but it is infinitely better than the shackles that still bind women in many other countries.

I am not saying to not want more. There is nothing wrong with wanting a better life and striving to have it. Just remember with each want, to give equal time to cherishing what you have. Otherwise, life can become the ultimate carrot on a stick and can feel like climbing an endless staircase. Be sure to look down and also see how far you have come. There are always things around us for which we can be grateful. Taking the time to recognize them is a key for increasing your frequency of feeling successful and happy. **Take a moment and do this brief "counting your blessings" technique.**

- **Do the Joy Touch to start off mellow and insightful.**
- **Identify the things for which you are blessed.**
  (What can you feel grateful for?)
- **Cherish the freedom and good fortune of those blessings.**
  (Feel deep within you an appreciation for what you do have.)
- **Do the Joy Touch to seal in that feeling of appreciation and being blessed.**

We are truly blessed in many ways. Next, let's extend that feeling of good fortune to the location where many success issues are triggered, the workplace. On average, at least eight hours a day are spent working. A major factor in feeling successful is making that one-third or more of life more enjoyable. Anything you can do to enhance your work environment will definitely help you be happier.

Creating Happiness While You Work

Regardless of whether you work in an office, for yourself, or at home, take a moment and do this simple exercise. If you were going to have a new boss and could choose the type of boss he or she would be, what characteristics would you want that person to have? Actually write them down. Would you want a boss to be patient? Would you want him/her to be a good listener? What qualities would make someone a "Good Boss" for you? Now, list the traits you wouldn't want a boss to have. What qualities or styles would make that person an unpleasant or "Bad Boss" for you?

Most people come up with two categories of positive qualities: skill traits (organized, efficient, good communicator, etc.) and supportive characteristics (empathetic, patient, good listener, etc.). On the negative side the list tends to include the characteristics that make all of us feel uncomfortable (critical, judgmental, impatient, etc.). Here is a sample list that was compiled at one of my "Master the Business of Life" workshops.

"Good Boss" Qualities

Positive Supportive	Positive Skill-Oriented
Patient	Dynamic
Supportive	Decisive
Empathetic	Efficient
Good Listener	Organized
Mentor to You	Achieves Goals
Nonjudgmental	Good Communicator

"Bad Boss" Qualities
Critical
Impatient
Dictatorial
Closed-Minded
Picks at Your Faults
Attacks/Undermines

No doubt creating your list was relatively easy. Now comes the difficult part. Honestly evaluate what type of boss you are being to yourself. Do you spend the majority of your time treating yourself with qualities from your Bad Boss list or from your Good Boss list? Do you tend to be critical and impatient with yourself? Do you pick at your faults rather than being supportive and a good listener to yourself?

Whether you are a homemaker or career professional, whether you receive a paycheck or are self-employed, you are the boss of your own life and growth. You are the CEO (Chief Evolving Officer) of the business of your life. Every minute of the day, first and foremost, you work for yourself. The type of boss you are, *to you*, directly affects your every waking moment.

The concept of Inner Technology is learning how to mentally enhance your performance and quality of life. The kind of boss you are being to yourself determines the primary conditions you work in every minute. How can you possibly achieve your best if you are met at each turn with an attacking and judgmental inner boss? Even if you are able to perform well in a negative inner environment, why tolerate that form of abuse when you can instantly end it? You can't always be in command of how other people treat you; you can always be in control of how you treat yourself!

Even those of you who are caring and successful managers may find that, with yourself, you draw more often from your Bad Boss list. Frequently, when we fail to exhibit fully our Good Boss skill traits, we attack ourselves with qualities from our Bad Boss list. For example, when you aren't as organized, decisive, and efficient as you would like, do you tend to be self-critical and pick at your weak areas? When you fail to achieve your goals, do you tend to put yourself down rather than be patient and supportive? Do you ever tend to be closed minded or dictatorial with yourself ("I just can't do it" or "It has to be this way or it's no good")?

You can change that pattern. All it takes is the ability to identify what traits you want in a boss and apply them to yourself. When you find yourself being self-critical, choose to shift into your Good-Boss mode. Be supportive and nurturing instead. When you encounter difficulties, remember to be a mentor to yourself. Tap your self-teaching and encouraging traits. Think, "What would help me in this situation?" Then give yourself that support.

Don't put up any longer with a tyrant in your inner office. This simple technique gives you a method for dynamically improving both your performance and quality of life. Everyone works better and feels better when they are supported, encouraged, and nurtured. Why be dependent on others for these crucial life nutrients? Why gamble your life and fulfillment on whether your spouse or an office supervisor is able to provide that support, or is even in the mood to try?

Resolve every day to be a Good Boss to yourself and you will take the first step toward full freedom. You will truly be working for yourself in everything you do. This inner technology key unlocks the gateway to achieving your full potential for success and happiness.

Working Three Jobs, Getting Paid for Only One

It's easy to slip into Bad-Boss traits with ourselves because we are all overworked in today's society. Most of us are holding down at least two jobs—our professional work and the business of our relationships. If you have children, you are actually working three jobs or more.

Not realizing you have these multiple workplaces is a major contributor to feeling overworked. Because interactions with relationships and children take place in the home or in supposedly "off-work" environments, you might not think of them creating job-type pressures. They can, in fact, create stresses that make the professional world look easy by comparison. Take the following example:

Imagine having a job where, every day, you must be working as soon as you wake up, even before your feet hit the ground. The job entails constant responsibility, but has insufficient breaks and no guaranteed vacations. You can count on regular sleep disruptions to deal with emergencies and problems. You are also consistently challenged, questioned, rebelled against and underappreciated. You will be required to be a supervisor, teacher, judge, policeman, medical specialist, therapist, and mentor with changes in roles needed at a moment's notice. Furthermore, once you begin you can't quit for at least 18 years (frequently much longer). And for all this you are paid not one dollar. Even Charles Dickens never imagined such stressful, unfair working conditions. All of you who have children endure these circumstances every day.

I have often wondered if God didn't make sex so enjoyable to trick us into a work situation we would never otherwise volunteer for. Kidding aside, children are work. They do give us great joy. They provide an opportunity like no other for loving and being loved. But they, most definitely, <u>are</u> work.

Stress is frequently defined as being under pressure without the ability to control the circumstances causing the pressure. Many of you tackle a form of stress every morning that rivals the pressures faced by air-traffic controllers or commodities brokers. It's called getting the kids out the door on time.

Relationships are equally challenging. Whether you are single or married, you are faced with wanting to please someone that is infinitely closer to you than any business contact. Rejection or loss in a business setting is discouraging. In a personal relationship, it can be devastating. The first is merely displeasure with your performance. The second is often felt as a rejection of *you*. Which do you think has the greater potential for stress?

Because we don't think of relationships and children as work, we give ourselves all the responsibilities they entail without the breaks, benefits and perks we would demand in a business setting. We also don't apply the stress-reduction techniques and relaxation time we know are essential for fulfillment and maximum performance in the professional arena.

Life's stresses have been made still worse by the blurring of gender roles in the last twenty years. Increasingly, women have entered the workplace and men are contributing more to home maintenance and child care. That sharing of opportunity and responsibility is a positive step, but it has led to a doubling of burdens rather than a division of them. We have added pressures to each gender without really lessening the original core worries.

Even if the husband helps at home, many women still feel responsible for the house and children. A working mother whose children are having problems is viewed, not only by others, but frequently by herself, as failing them. She has added all the stress of the workplace without lessening her burden of responsibility for being the primary nurturer of the family.

Men have a similar dilemma. Even when their wives work, men may still feel financially responsible for the family. If the family doesn't have enough money, the man can feel he is not being a "good provider." He has the same internal financial pressures in addition to new worries about helping with the house and children.

When gender roles were more clearly defined, things were simpler for both sexes. The current system is fairer. The drawback is that life has become much more complex. Old approaches to success and happiness are no longer enough. We need new methods to handle the pressures of our changing times and expectations. A whole new technology with skills for living in the 21st century is required.

This is where the Joy Touch and the skills you learned from the Value Analysis and the Whys of Your Wants comes in. You now have the ability to regularly trigger the brain's natural mood-elevation mechanisms during your workday. You can give yourself an esteem boost when you feel the need for a perceived success to prevent survival anxiety. You can stay in touch with what you truly value even during work pressures.

Take a moment and try putting it all together in this brief exercise.

- **Do the Joy Touch to start off calm and clear.**
- **Think about your work and a particular pressure or concern that troubles you.**
  (Is a project not going well, a relationship strained, or do you feel unrecognized, etc?)
- **Ask, are you being a Bad Boss to yourself about this area?**
  (Are you being critical, pressuring, impatient, etc?)

- **What Good Boss trait would best support you here?**
  (Would being mentoring or more patient help?)
- **Do the Joy Touch and feel/picture yourself acting from that Good Boss trait.**
  (Talk to yourself from that perspective or feel that trait surrounding you.)
- **Review how to combine the Good Boss trait with a key value and/or a why of your wants.**
  (i.e. [trait = mentoring, value = learning, why = to best serve my clients/friends] What can I learn for the next time to be better able to help everyone in the endeavor be more successful?)
- **Do the Joy Touch to seal in and make automatic what you have learned.**

The skills that you have learned thus far in the chapter give you the tools to break free from the achievement addiction. Individually they provide you with a variety of approaches for breaking the old patterns that lead to unnecessary survival struggle. Combined they yield a dynamic approach that gives you the freedom to enjoy your work rather than having it control you.

Play at It, Don't Work at It!

How can you be truly successful if you are unhappy during your work? If work is burdensome then even the greatest of achievements is nothing more than slave labor. Just as important as what is accomplished, is your attitude while you are working. Here is where the Joy Touch is immediately valuable. Triggering the brain's natural mood-elevation mechanism regularly during the work day helps to keep you positive. It prevents the struggle reflexes created by time pressures from taking over your state of mind. You can do even more, however.

There is no reason that work and fun have to be mutually exclusive. Working and enjoyment can go hand-in-hand. The key is creativity and learning. Learn to be creative about the way you do your work. Look at it as an adventure that offers opportunities for something beyond just getting the job done. You know you can do the work. Give yourself the bonus of having some pleasure from it.

There are many ways to spice up even the dullest of tasks other than just doing them in a different way. You can explore learning some new facet of the project. You can picture the people that it will touch and feel good about the benefit they will receive. If you interact with other individuals during the project, you can take the opportunity to learn something new about them or cherish a brief but positive interaction. Truly work for yourself by being in charge of how you accomplish the task, as opposed to being owned by it.

If you are creative and learning, rather than merely working, you will still be just as productive, possibly even more so. You will have the added benefit of completing your work energized and excited rather than drained. Nowhere is there a better example of this than in children. Kids are masters of accomplishing through play. Their games and projects are always fun and innately creative. They also can be tremendous accomplishments. We need to recapture that energy and spirit.

You are a child of the universe. No cosmic law requires you to stop having fun just because you have a job (at an office, in the home, or raising a family). People long to be able to return to childhood times (or get to that second childhood of retirement) because they are starved for more fun in their lives. There is no reason you can't have that greater happiness now. You probably do have greater responsibilities than when you were a kid, but you still have the same right to enjoyment of life. Instead of being burdened by being responsible you can be *response-able*, able to respond in a different way to make your responsibilities more fun. The key is choice.

People tend to distinguish play from work based on the feeling of having a choice. Work you have to do. Play you choose to do. The secret is to choose to play at your work. Choose to have fun at it, rather than to be miserable. Choose to look for creative options as you go through your day, rather than shackle yourself to the grindstone. It does take a bit more thought and energy to be creative, but it is worth it. The mood boost you get from doing something that is enjoyable and exciting is invigorating. Further, the enhanced enthusiasm you feel also leads to greater productivity and insightfulness. The single investment of choosing to play at your work yields a two-fold return.

Also choose to invest in some recreation each day. Give yourself the gift of two forms of regular recreation. First, remember that recreation can also be written as re-creation. Re-create yourself and your interest in your work by following a more playful approach. Rather than say, "What am I going to work on?" say, "What am I going to play at next?" Play at it, don't work at it.

Second, fit some form of pure enjoyment recreation into each day and not just after the workday. Robert Fulgrum in his book, *All I Needed to Know in Life I learned in Kindergarten*, says "Work a little, play a little, and rest a little each day." Listen to music as you work. Take time at lunch to read a chapter of a book or browse the internet. Go someplace different for lunch or meet someone new. Find shorter forms of recreation that can be interspersed throughout your day to refresh your attitude.

The same daily requirement also applies to rest. Long hours are made longer by not taking adequate breaks. The body and the spirit need pauses to regenerate. Re-creation of your motivation is equally important to your well-being. Even if you are behind, no project is going to be made that much later by taking a five-minute stretch break. Moving or walking for a drink of water not only helps the body, but also recharges the mind. Periodically get to a window and expand your view. Long periods with too narrow a focus can make anyone feel imprisoned. Another option to consider is resting by taking a nap.

Science has now shown the value, both mentally and physiologically, of taking brief naps. You work slower when you are drowsy and fatigued. Setting a clock and allowing yourself to doze for fifteen minutes (after lunch if you can't during the day) can be tremendously restoring. You will feel better and probably accomplish twice as much than if you just plodded tiredly on. **Take a moment and try putting all these "play at it" concepts together**.

- **Do the Joy Touch to start off unstressed and open-minded.**

- **Pick some area of your work that is normally a drudge.**

- **Identify creative ways you could liven it up.**
  (Think of a new method of doing it. Sense the people the project will benefit. Learn something new about the project or the people involved in it, etc.)

- **Think of how you could make it more play or recreation.**
  (Make it a challenge, play music, work in a different setting, etc.)

- **Plan something you are going to do just for fun today.**
  (Identify something for both during work and after work.)

- **Feel, see, hear, yourself doing that project more enjoyably.**
  (Picture and sense yourself being happier as you do it.)

Note: For people who are very intuitive, thinking how to be creative ahead of time may feel imprisoning. The key for you is to allow yourself to be spontaneous. Just know that when you get to it you are going to look for a way to do it differently.

- **Cherish yourself for giving yourself the gift of fun while you work.**

- **Do the Joy Touch to seal in and reinforce this more enjoyable way of working.**

The more you play at it rather than work at it, the more you will enjoy life. That is what true success is all about. The skills you have learned in this book give you the ability to enjoy life more because you can *in joy* it as well as *and joy* it. With the Joy Touch you can put joy in by triggering natural mood-elevation whenever you want it. With the "play at it, don't work at it" concept you can do your work and have joy by making it fun.

No one can take those abilities away from you. They are yours for life. Only you can forget to use them or allow the limbic brain to prevent you from living the full happiness you deserve. One of the most common ways we let the limbic brain win is time pressures.

Feeling Behind

Nothing kills enjoyment and the spirit of play more than time pressures. Feeling behind puts you in an immediate survival state of mind. This is probably a throwback to an ancient genetic memory. In prehistoric times, feeling behind was undoubtedly associated with a predator gaining on you or not gathering enough food for the winter. Put simply, *behind* equalled about-to-be-eaten or starve. Those perceptions/associations will trigger every limbic stress anxiety you have. Enjoyment is shoved out of the way in favor of survival.

There is a way out of this emotional highjacking. Simply evaluate if the time pressure you are feeling is truly as big a threat as you are making it. If it is, then definitely let that sense of urgency spur you on. If not, don't let your dinosaur brain ruin your enjoyment of life. Using the terms that John Bradshaw coined, don't let it make you a Human Doing instead of a Human Being.

There is never enough time in life. The TV show Saturday Night Live humorously illustrated this point in one sketch that showed a Time Bank with a drive-up window. People asked for more time on a project, or "Could I have just a few more hours today, please!" To quote *The Circle of Life*, the title song from the movie *The Lion King*, "From the day we arrive on the planet.....There's far too much to take in here..... More to do than can ever be done." Don't let the overwhelming abundance of opportunity sacrifice your feeling of successfulness

If you let it, being just a little behind can make you feel like a constant failure. Each thought of "I'm behind" can trigger a sense of lack of success. The result can be a major esteem drubbing over a very short period of time. Even worse, is not truly being behind, but just feeling that way until the project is completed. That perspective causes you to feel badly the entire time for no real reason. The concept of finding *adequate time* can help you avoid these limbic traps. It also gives you some fulfillment instead of none at all.

I define adequate time as having enough to give you, at least, a sense of progress in the area involved, a feeling that you are making a dent in it. For example if you are behind on your correspondence, you can feel lousy eternally. There's always some letter that needs answering. (I can imagine, with a grin, the possibility of getting kicked out of Heaven for failing to write God a thank you note for being allowed in). By seeing and taking the adequate time approach, you write the letters, or e-mail, etc. that you have time for, at the moment, and take fulfillment in what you did get sent. There is never enough time. The secret is to make *adequate time*.

Do a little each day on every project. Pause for a moment to smell the roses, or to enjoy the view. Once, when my children were preschoolers, my youngest son came up to where I was writing to give me a hug. I was behind on that particular project and also had more to do than I could complete by the end of the week. At first I felt bothered and annoyed by the interruption, and started to tell him I'd hug him and play with him after I finished the chapter. Then I realized, "How much later is it really going to make me to give him a hug and playful tickle right now?" I didn't have enough time to fully rough-house with him, but I did have adequate time to help him feel loved.

We, as adults, are no less worthy of that consideration. Give yourself the gift of pauses, breaks, pacing, and enjoying what you are doing. When you don't allow time for feeling good, you place yourself in a prison of your own making with time as its warden. Use the deadlines and requirements as guides and structure to channel your energy and focus. Don't bar yourself in, however, by blocking out the sky, the people around you, or your view of opportunities ahead.

Start to train yourself out of the old limbic brain deception that being even a bit behind means disaster. Instead of allowing time to shackle you, learn how to find adequate time and feel in command of your own schedule. **Take a moment and practice the process.**

- **Do the Joy Touch to start off calm and unstressed**
- **Think of an area in which you feel behind.**
  (Work project, correspondence, home chores, etc.)
- **Identify what portion or facet you could get done now with the time you have.**
  (Make a start, draw up a plan, do one item on the list, one call, one letter, etc.)

- **Explore ways to find pockets of time for making progress on this area.**
  (Pick a designated hour each day, set a day for focusing mostly on it, delegate, or collaborate, etc.)
- **Feel the fulfillment you will have from getting at least that much done.**
- **Sense yourself taking the pressure off and feeling more successful.**
- **Do the Joy Touch to seal in this more realistic perspective.**
  (Reinforce your sense that you are in command of your time.)

Seeing that you will get the project completed and still have options, takes the pressure off. It engages your higher thinking skills and releases the dominance of the limbic system. It puts you in command of your time, instead of time controlling you.

Another way that we unfairly pressure ourselves is by feeling behind our inner image. In every area of our lives we all have an inner image of how capable or far along we should be. It is important to realize that this inner image is always ahead of you. All too often, because you can see it, you think you are supposed to *be* it. This is not true. Your inner image is where you are headed in your development. As you get there, you will always see farther. When you use that inner image as a negative comparison, you always feel behind and unsuccessful. It can become the ultimate carrot on a stick.

The secret is to realize that your inner image is your view of your future. Instead of using it against yourself critically, let it empower you with a sense of direction. Appreciate yourself for having a vision of what you want to achieve. Then ask, "What step can I take to make that vision a reality?" That identification gives you the ability to create your own success faster. **Try it briefly.**

- **Do the Joy Touch to start off clear seeing and objective.**
- **Pick an area in your life where you have been a little disappointed in yourself.**
  (Relationship, communication skills, some ability or task completion, etc.)
- **Reflect on what you inner image is in this area.**
  (What do you think you should be?)
- **Realize that this is your future potential.**
  (If you could be it right now, you would be.)
- **Cherish the fact that your vision is a direction.**
  (You know what you want and have a guide toward it.)

- **Identify what you can do next to move you toward that vision.**
  (What action can you take that will help make that future a reality.)
- **Do the Joy Touch to seal in your sense of purpose and success.**
  (Acknowledge that you are motivated and making progress rather than being behind.)

This concept and simple technique give you a way to cherish your desire to improve, rather than judge your behind (we'll save that for the next chapter on weight control!). Using your inner image as a positive motivator is a key for being that mentoring Good Boss to yourself, rather than a derogatory self-critic.

Sometimes the put downs we give ourselves are based on specific goals that we have failed to achieve. This is another area where old patterns can limit the frequency of your feelings of success. Often we set goals that are too high or too out of reach. When our goals are too challenging we may not achieve them frequently enough to prevent survival anxieties. Here is a simple solution that allows you to keep your high ideals and desires without sacrificing your feelings of accomplishment.

For each project I undertake I always set two goals, my ideal goal and my minimum goal. My ideal goal represents the high standards I have for myself. It is the peak performance I would like to achieve. I always have it in mind so that I can strive for the best I can be. My minimum goal represents what I want to accomplish as a minimum. If I get at least that done I will feel fulfilled.

Timing, family pressures, circumstances, or just an off day may prevent me from reaching some of my ideal goals, but I almost always achieve my minimum goal. This two goal system is a lifesaver because it gives me a way to feel good about myself a higher percentage of the time. Rather than being miserable because I barely missed an ideal goal, I can see that I was well above my minimum goal. I can focus on the fact that, overall, I was successful. It keeps me from being dependent on perfection for happiness.

The truth is that you are wonderfully successful just for being you. You are always doing the best you know how. You may know of a better way, but if it were fully within your state of consciousness you would be doing it automatically. Remember, you are a work in progress. You are perfecting (even when you are not perfect). At any given moment, you are always the best you there is.

You Are Unique

The bottom line is that success is primarily a state of mind. It is a sense that you are special and can be proud of yourself. Without that inner feeling, even the richest or most powerful among us can feel like a failure. Being fully in command of your success is ninety percent being able to generate that sense of specialness and value.

You don't have to have achievements to generate that esteem. It is a gift that is intrinsically yours to give yourself. You are always special. You are always noteworthy because you are the only one of you there is. You are a one-of-a-kind, unique Soul. No one else is exactly like you, which means you are automatically the best you there is. It is time that we learned to take pride in that uniqueness, rather than abuse and deprive ourselves by only feeling successful based on externals. **Try this brief uniqueness meditation technique. Feel the power of it and reflect on its concepts as you read through it.**

- **Do the Joy Touch to start off open and receptive.**

- **Bring to mind and easily review the various aspects of your life that make you different from other people and unique in the world. Recall aspects of your childhood (how nobody else's was exactly the same). Remember some of your emotions and feelings. Realize how nobody else has quite the same inner experiences you do. Let yourself go, reviewing all the things that make up the you that you are–your hopes and dreams, your accomplishments, the people you have known and the friends you have, the pasts you have lived through, and the exact present you are experiencing. As you do, bask in the growing knowledge that you are as unique in your total being as is your individual fingerprint.**

- **Begin to see yourself as a massive storehouse of experiences, feelings, knowledge, and awarenesses. Begin to realize just how intricate and extensive that storehouse is, and therefore the uniqueness that it has. No matter how extensive anyone else's storehouse may be, none can be exactly like yours with all its special and unique experiences.**

- **Feel yourself as that Soul storehouse. Feel the fullness and beauty of the myriads of experiences you have had. See each experience as a shining crystal with its own color, brightness, and size. See individual experiences sparkling. Gradually move away and see more and more sparkling,** shimmering experience crystals until finally you see your whole self—one huge, billion-sided jewel, sparkling, shining, and reflecting all the experiences and feelings you have had.

- Feel the beauty and complete individuality of this valuable, precious jewel—yourself. Hold the feeling and soak it in. Feel how great it is to be truly one of a kind, that you are the best you there is in the world.

- As you hold these images, focus on the value, appreciation, and respect you feel for that beautiful jewel, that best you there is in the world.

- As you build these sensations, gradually raise one of your hands and feel the energy of that appreciation, acceptance, and value flowing out through it like a beacon of worth and success.

- Now slowly bring that hand to you and give yourself a pat on the shoulder or a touch over the heart (or you can do this with two hands bringing them across and down on your shoulders in a self-hug). As you do, feel all the appreciation, acceptance, and worth penetrating deep within you, filling you with inner satisfaction and contentment.

- Let that feeling engulf and relax you. Let it put you totally at ease, at peace with your own sense of value and success. Absorb that feeling and make it part of your consciousness.

- Do the Joy Touch to seal in your feeling of success for just being you.

This simple technique is designed to help you fully experience and cherish your intrinsic value. You are the one you live with every second of every day. Seeing and feeling the worth and success that resides within you is a precious gift that you deserve regularly. It's free, its always available, and it accurately reflects the value that you have for being a seeker.

Bravo to you for the beautiful unique jewel that you are. I'm proud of you for questing to learn more about being in greater command of your happiness. Before leaving this chapter take one more moment to be proud of yourself. Congratulate yourself for your courage, your effort, and your perseverance in the adventure of life.

Probably more than any other, our next topic, weight control truly requires the attitudes of adventure and self-worth. With those weapons firmly in place in your arsenal, lets head off to victory in "the battle of the bulge."

Weight Control - Five Simple Steps for In-Joying Your Diet

This chapter is not designed to be a new fad diet or the encyclopedia of weight loss. Tons of such books have already been written. Despite that immense poundage of literature, millions of Americans still find the effort to take off weight (and keep it off) a losing struggle. There may be no other area of life that so contributes to feelings of failure, depression and low self-esteem. For many of us, the sad truth is that just as tragic as a mind wasted, is a waist that has to be to minded.

What this chapter offers are five simple steps for dealing with your weight without making life (yours and your loved ones) miserable. It is time to end the pain, struggle, and deprivation. Each of the five steps is designed to change the pattern of struggle that so often accompanies efforts at weight management. Weight control keys should be short and sweet. Their essence should be grounded in common sense and linked to the parts of the brain that automatically make you feel better. Each of these keys is easy to remember and can be used with whatever weight control program you choose. If you practice them regularly you will be able to enjoy what you eat for the rest of your life.

Step 1: Feel Good About What You Eat.

There is an old saying that war is hell. For those of you fighting the battle of the bulge, you literally live that hell too many hours of the day. It is time to stop fighting with your food. Instead, enjoy letting it nourish you as you control your weight, rather than letting your weight control your life.

Struggle automatically sets you up for failure because it triggers the body's survival reflexes. Genetically our bodies haven't caught up with the abundance of food that is available in our modern world. Our metabolisms have evolved to handle scarcity and famine, rather than the problems of too much food. If you worry about food, your subconscious interprets the message as a sign that starvation is threatening. When that mental signal is matched with the reduced calories of dieting, is it any wonder that the body's metabolism slows down? Our physiology is designed to try to prevent, or at least slow down, the perceived starvation threat. For that reason, you should always think in terms of weight control rather than weight loss. Loss is mentally equated with deprivation and denial.

No diet will work in the long run if you are miserable and suffering. Feelings of deprivation in the end will eventually trigger binge eating. Or worse, the emotional distress created by denial will lead to out-of-control anger, depression, or substance abuse. Those side effects might be worth it if in the long run depriving yourself worked. But it doesn't. Studies show that the majority of diets simply lead to regaining the weight lost or adding even more. Your biology is designed that way. The body seems to say, "You never know when there is going to be another famine like that last one, so I better pack on a few extra pounds just to be safe." The result is that you can be miserable for months and still wind up worse off than when you started.

This doesn't mean that all diets are no good. In fact, some of the most successful diets, such as the Scarsdale Medical Diet, mirror this principle of weight loss without extreme deprivation. With Scarsdale the portions are generous and there is a variety of enjoyable menus from which to choose. If you have a regime that is successful for you, don't abandon it. Keep what is working and add these five simple steps. Use them to approach your weight control differently. They will make eating a positive experience, rather than a survival struggle. The first of those keys is to always feel good about what you eat.

Eating and everything associated with it should always be cast in a positive light. Each meal, even if it is a small snack or just a diet shake, should be a celebration of life. The minute you introduce negative feelings into food situations, you trigger all of the body's scarcity reflexes. When that happens, it will be twice as difficult to keep from overeating.

How can you fully enjoy restricted meals? Make the meal an event. Even if all you have is a brief lunch break, find ways to savor your opportunity for replenishing the body. Cherish the joy that you are getting to eat. Food is wonderful, appreciate it.. Relish the food itself, not just the quantity. When you truly cherish each bite, you will need less to help you feel happy about life.

As much as possible, take time to enjoy the handling and preparation of your meal. Wherever you can, enjoy looking at the food and smelling it. Getting additional sniffs of food's aroma has been shown to reduce the amount you need to eat to feel full.

A University of Minnesota study discovered that the brain has a smell counter as part of the body's natural appetite suppression mechanisms. It literally, by smell, counts the number of forkfuls you lift up to your mouth. Tests using artificial smell sticks (where participants took 20-30 sniffs prior to eating) were successful in reducing appetite. There is a common experience with this brain phenomena. The individual cooking the meal is never quite as hungry when she or he sits down to the table as the rest of the family. The prolonged period of smelling the food during preparation dulls the appetite.

The benefits of decreased preparation time with modern appliances may have had negative side effects on our weight. Less time enjoying the aromas may literally equate to extra appetite and poundage.

Another easy first step is to eat in courses. Have a low-fat appetizer (carrot sticks or celery dipped in nonfat salad dressing) that you can munch while you are preparing the main, higher calorie, course. Smelling and slowly savoring a soup dish also can be an appetite suppressant. Here is one place where the speed of the microwave can be useful. Low calorie broth based soups can be heated rapidly and their aromas inhaled steadily as you leisurely consume them as a first or second course.

For hurried meal times, such as sack lunching at work or needing to grab a quick bite out, you can still use some of these principles. Pack carrot sticks as an appetizer. Recent studies have shown that beta carotene's healthful side effects are best when received from natural foods, rather than from supplements. If you must grab something at a fast food place, sit and smell the aromas for a few minutes. Then, have a beverage with your carrot sticks first. You will find you order less when you do go up to the counter for your main lunch item.

This also brings up the point of advanced preparation for successful weight control meals. What you snack on and/or use for appetizers is directly linked to what you have in your refrigerator. The key is to shop for things that will make good weight control meals. Certainly, you have heard this many times before. What you haven't heard is that you can use the Joy Touch to help you with healthy shopping.

The same way you should never go shopping when you are hungry, you shouldn't even step into the market without first doing the Joy Touch several times. One of my students, I'll call Pamela, told me this concept totally changed her shopping and eating habits. She shared, "I know that if it gets in my refrigerator, I'm going to eat it.

I always tell myself when I'm in the market that I'm getting that treat just for the kids or for some possible special occasion. The result, however, is sadly predictable. If it gets in my shopping cart, it's going to wind up in my mouth and then on my hips. I found that using the Joy Touch helped me with this. Before even stepping through the door of the market, I do the Joy Touch three to five times. I also do it once each aisle. The result is that I feel more satisfied as I shop and I don't reach for things on the shelves that I know I don't want in my refrigerator." Try it yourself. At worst, it will make grocery shopping a more mellow experience. At best, it may give you the same benefits it has given Pamela.

Another important reminder is to prepare your healthy, low calorie appetizers as soon as possible after you get home from the market. Cut up the fruits and vegetables (or buy baby carrots or berries that don't need cutting) and place them in easy-to-open containers or baggies. That way you can grab them quickly, when you want something to munch, instead of reaching for a more fattening snack. Preparing the next days appetizers as you cook that night's meal can also give you the appetite suppressant effects of increased aroma exposure. In fact, a major element in appetite suppression is directly linked to the second simple step.

Step 2: Wait Control

Study after study has shown that if you eat faster you will eat more. The key is to slow down all stages of your eating. Take more time with your food preparation. Make meals more lengthy without increasing the quantity of food consumed. And in particular, chew each bite more slowly and longer.

The appetite suppression benefits of chewing longer and more slowly are enormous, particularly considering how easy it is to do. Further, chewing more slowly actually aids step 1, as it allows you to more fully enjoy each mouthful. Another way to slow down your pace of eating is to do the Joy Touch between bites or as a minimum between courses. Using the technique as a focal point for appreciating the meal and your food adds to your feeling of feasting rather than dieting.

This brings up a similar way to lengthen the meal time that adds mental satisfaction to physical satiation. Take the time for a truly heartfelt blessing. We live in an incredibly abundant country in comparison to much of the world. Even a smaller portion of your meal is vastly more satisfying than what many in third world nations have as their only option.

Speaking of that smaller portion, a practical tip is to put only your plate (with the portion you intend to eat) on the table. Keep serving dishes in a separate place, or if possible, even in a separate room). The desired effect is to get up out of your chair to get more. That doesn't mean you can't have seconds. You just have to think about your choice more consciously. It also gives you the opportunity to do the Joy Touch either before getting up or on the way to the serving platter.

Sometimes the step of *wait* control means just pausing long enough so that you are not as susceptible to binge eating. This is another area that the Joy Touch can help. When you feel a craving or know you are experiencing emotionally driven hunger, do the Joy Touch first. Ease the upset first. Then decide if and what you truly want to eat.

Sharon, one of my students who has battled weight issues for years, described how she used the Joy Touch to help her. She says, "I'm one of those people who is always on a diet. Unfortunately, too often I'm on a see-food diet. I see food and I eat it. For years I have been unable to break the cycle of see it, want it, eat it. When I learned the Joy Touch, that changed. I saw the results the day after learning the technique. Driving home from Pete's seminar, I pulled into one of those everything-under-the-sun truck stops for a break. You know, the type of place where every area is designed to lessen the weight of your wallet. Well, the restaurant area was no exception. Pastries and greasy foods beckoned. Before, I had always been unable to resist their siren call. This time, using the Joy Touch, I could. Stimulating the septal area made me feel at peace and satisfied inside. As a result, I had a sensible small snack, rather than bingeing on all the goodies that were dangled in front of my face."

This is just one example of the numerous ways you can use the Joy Touch to help you with both *wait* control and feeling good about your food. The ultimate result is that weight control becomes less miserable. Try this simple exercise that combines key aspects of these first two steps at you next meal.

- **Do something to make the meal special.**
  (Use special plates or napkins. Add a soup course or scented candles.)
- **Think about what you are eating and appreciate it.**
  (Feel good about the joy of eating and something specific you like about that meal.)
- **Fully enjoy the aroma of the food as you get the meal ready.**
  (And, whenever possible, smell the food at least two or three times before eating it.)

- **Take the time before eating for some form of appreciation and blessing.**
  (Feel thankful that we live in a land where food is plentiful and available in such a wide variety.)
- **Do the Joy Touch before each course (at a minimum).**
  (So you eat out of true hunger rather than emotional distress.)
- **Focus on chewing more slowly and fully savoring each bite.**
  (Enjoy noticing the full flavor, spices, and texture of the food)
- **Whether or not you have dessert, do the Joy Touch as a mental final course.**
  (Bask in the feeling of well-being that comes with enjoying your meal.)

This approach makes managing your weight more pleasant. You have enough stress in your life without adding day long anxieties about food. What we need in life is less criticism and worry and more nurturing and support. That leads us to step number three.

Step 3: Care about Your Diet Rather Than Worry about Your Weight.

Weight loss and/or control should first and foremost be about improving your quality of life. Primary to that goal is improving your health. Your physical well-being is far more important than your appearance. Nobody looks good dead.

Why such a strong statement? Because our national obsession with weight loss is becoming an ever increasing health risk. Aside from the problems of anorexia that are well documented, a new danger to dieters is on the rise.

Serious complications and deaths are now being linked to the latest trend in diet pills, nicknamed the phen-fen approach. The drugs phentermine and fenfloramine (sold as ionamin, factin, adipex and pondimin) and most recently dexphenfloramine (sold as redux) are showing an alarming link to primary pulmonary hypertension. Once contracted, this condition is irreversible and can lead to death in as little as three years. It can place even those in their twenties on the waiting list for a heart/lung transplant. This type of risk is just not worth it unless you are so obese that the negative health effects of your weight exceed that of lung failure.

Rather than waste time worrying about weight, invest your energy in providing yourself with a healthy diet that lengthens your life as well as narrows your waist. Instead of spending your hard earned cash on risky pills or fad diet foods, put it where your mouth is. Gift yourself with quality low fat foods that taste good. Let your efforts benefit your body, rather than the weight-loss industry's stockholders. Care about your health, instead of worrying about weight.

First of all, worry just leaves you prone to emotional binge eating. Also, at best it is wasted energy. At worst, it becomes destructive self-criticism that torches your self-esteem. If you are going to burn anything, burn calories or fad diet books. Put your energy into the little bit of extra work that is necessary to eat healthy.

This book is not going to try to define the perfect healthful diet. In fact, obsessing about that could just as easily lead you to overeating out of emotional anxiety. You know what's good for you and what's junk. Use your common sense and have those types of food always close at hand instead of just high-calorie and high-fat options.

Also, drink plenty of fluids. Even with a reduced calorie diet, your body can't metabolize fat as efficiently if you are not drinking enough water. Increasing your fluid consumption can lessen your urges to cheat on your eating plan. Use a low-calorie flavored drink or treat yourself to a cup of special tea as a break in your day.

We need special treats during the day, or life quickly becomes a bread and water prison. That sense of deprivation just kicks the body into survival mode and your mental state into a hunger for overeating. Keep the sense of a special treat, lose the out-of-control overindulgences. Small treats through the day can keep you from gorging at main meals. Medically, it is actually better to eat smaller portions more often than one large meal. **Take a moment and identify the following**:

- **List a variety of low-calorie/low-fat special treats you could give yourself.**
  (Include teas, vegetables, fresh fruits, low-fat yogurts, etc.)
- **Identify what quantity is sufficient for creating the feeling of a special break without overdoing it.**
  (Decide what combinations will work, i.e. tea and fruit, or salsa and baked chips, etc.)
- **Pick the times during your day for your treats.**
  (what time and place that will refresh you yet keep you from overeating at the next meal?)
- **Decide how to use the Joy Touch to enhance the sensation of the treat.**
  (Joy Touch during each bite, before beginning as a blessing, or at the end as an extra dessert.)
- **Remember to end any healthy treat with the Joy Touch.**
  (Reinforce your eating well and taking care of yourself.)

It is possible to lose or maintain weight without being miserable. Simply pick life enhancers that are good for you. Make your treat times celebrations of healthy living rather than eating out of a sense of struggle and survival. When you focus on caring about your health rather than worrying about calories, you get a double benefit. First, you eat a more balanced nutritional diet. Second you will feel better. You can be proud of yourself for choosing wisely.

The self-esteem boost you can receive from that realization is in itself an appetite controller. When you feel good about yourself, you are less likely to eat just to satisfy emotional hunger. This leads us to the next simple step.

Step 4: Value Yourself, Not Your Size.

For too long our society has been fixated on appearance and weight as a measure of worth. Women have been particularly victimized in this regard. In fact, they have been bombarded since childhood with unrealistic standards. It has been well documented that the model held up to young girls for decades (the Barbie doll) is not the normal female weight, figure, or body type.

The psychological misrepresentation is continued into adulthood by the plethora of advertisements that feature models that are not the norm and in some cases are even unhealthy, underweight extremes. Is it any wonder that over five million Americans have eating disorders and that 1,000 women die from them each year? The old saying, "You can never be too thin or too rich!" is the ultimate example of how our society over relates weight and figure with worth. Since the standards being touted are not the norms, the vast majority of women can inaccurately feel less attractive and desirable.

My own wife is a classic example (in several senses of the word). Debbie is very attractive, but she has always bemoaned here pear-shaped figure. One day when she hadn't been exercising as much as usual and was feeling on the heavy side of her monthly weight, she was being particularly disparaging to herself in front of our two pre-teen boys. I didn't want the boys thinking that only the Cindy Crawfords of the world were beautiful, so I made a point to compare their mother's figure with beauty through the ages. There happened to be a coaster on the coffee table with Botticelli's masterpiece, *The Birth of Venus*, (the Venus standing on a giant clam shell). Although my wife has dark rather than blonde hair, the figure is the same (pear-shaped with smaller breasts, rounded hips, and adult [not 12 year old] thighs). I pointed out the similarity to the boys and said, "See, your Mom is what has long been thought of as a classic beauty."

Even though I probably scored some good intentions points with my wife, the bottom line was that she still thought her figure was not good enough. This, despite the fact that she has taught classes to adolescent girls specifically focusing on the unrealistic images of women portrayed in advertising.

It is time to get real and counter this media programming that has been bombarding your limbic brain for years. You are valuable for you, because you are a unique Soul, not because of your waist size. It's bad enough that advertising manipulates our purchasing choices, don't allow it to control your self-esteem. If this is an issue for you, I strongly recommend *Self-Esteem Comes in All Sizes* by Carol Johnson. I haven't read the entire book, but I love the title and know that we share similar views on focusing on health not just weight.

In fact, what you actually weigh can at times be a poor indicator of your progress. Often when you begin a more extensive exercise regime, your weight may actually increase due to adding muscle. How you feel is more important. If you feel good, you will be more active and therefore burn more calories. The heart of the matter is self-esteem that is independent of body issues.

I'm not saying to forget about your appearance, but rather to put it in perspective. Think back to the Value Analysis you completed in the last chapter. How many points did you allot to appearance? Even if it was an important area for you, that value would still be only one-fifth to one-tenth of your priorities. Don't make it 100% of your self-esteem.

The true essence of this step is to value your *self*. Remember what you learned in Chapter 3 about how to give yourself put-ups that are independent of externals. Focus on the megaskills that you can value yourself for regularly. As a minimum, use the put up approach to counter times when you have negative thoughts about your weight. Further, don't just deny your concerns. Use them to *care about* (rather than criticize) your weight. Let your thoughts motivate healthier behavior, rather that malign you. Then, mentally praise yourself for dealing positively with your weight concerns. **Here is the step by step process**.

- **When you have a negative thought about your weight, immediately put it in its proper perspective.**
  (How are you doing overall? Have you made progress? How close are you to the norm?)
- **Next, counter the thought with a put-up that values your *self*.**
  (Emphasize your good qualities, your desire to improve, your worth as a human being, not just as a body.)

- **Then, let your concern guide you to helpful actions.**
  (Try healthy snacks, more exercise, drinking more water, smaller portions, etc.)
- **Finally, praise yourself for your caring and your discipline.**
- **Seal in your independent self-esteem by doing the Joy Touch.**

If weight is an issue for you, you are going to have occasions when you think negatively about it. The key is not to let those thoughts control you. Don't let them dominate either your time or your mood. That approach is the focus of the fifth simple step.

Step 5: You Control Your Weight. Don't Let It Control You.

The primary purpose of weight control is to learn an approach to eating that is sustainable and livable. If you are going to live normally, life must be more than food. This fifth simple step emphasizes that reality. Unless your situation is life threatening, don't let weight issues consume your days and your happiness. Use the techniques you have learned and the control you *do* have to make a peace through strength with your battle of the bulge.

There are many ways to be "in control." The first and probably most important is to control distress eating. The key to success against emotional binge eating is using the Joy Touch effectively and often. Manage your moods and your waistline will follow.

Emotional distress is a powerful overeating trigger. Instinctively you know that the sated feeling of a full stomach can ease the pain of hurts, worries, or angers. With the added temptation provided by sweet, salty and high-fat foods, it is easy to give in and eat until you are stuffed. Use the techniques you have learned for dissipating emotional turmoil before you lift the first forkful.

Do the Joy Touch several times to provide enough of a mood lift that you are willing to look at the core issues and clear them. Then, apply the Comforting Connection approach from Chapter 2 to address the cause of your distress. You can still have the snack if you are legitimately hungry. Instead of bingeing, use your control to have a sensible portion of healthy food and savor it as a reward for your insight and discipline.

You also exercise your control each time you use the Joy Touch in the practical situations described in the earlier steps, such as between bites, to slow down your eating or to enhance and savor each mouthful. You can also use it as an appetite suppressant before you pick your snack. Just make sure you start it soon enough before eating.

One Free Soul Instructor tells me that if she waits until she opens the refrigerator door to do the Joy Touch she is lost. Chances are she will take out more than she should have. The visual stimulus of all the food and the urge to eat is just too powerful. If, however, she starts doing the Joy Touch as she walks down the hall toward the kitchen, her will-power is bolstered by the time she gets her hand on that doorway to delicacies.

Exercising control also means exercising. No single approach to weight management is more important than increasing your metabolic rate. Here too, the Joy Touch can be helpful. The secret to exercising more often is to make it fun rather than merely fatiguing. Sometimes the first obstacle to exercise is mood. When you feel despondent or anxious, the work of exercise can seem unbearable. When you feel better and have more energy, it is easier to motivate yourself to get out for a walk or do some other aerobic activity. Exercise doesn't have to be vigorous to be effective. In fact, merely walking has been shown to have significant weight-loss benefits. Do the Joy Touch to help you feel like getting out for a stroll and then do it as you walk to make your exercise period more enjoyable.

As you perfect your ability to trigger your septal area, you can even do the Joy Touch during more strenuous exercise. You will find it helps you to stay at a particular activity level longer with less perceived effort. This is, in effect, the equivalent of self-inducing the second wind of the so called "runner's high." The sensation is also similar to the way that music can make doing aerobics or step exercises easier. Whether vigorous or gentle, find some regime of exercise that is comfortable for you. That discipline is a key element of controlling your weight.

Most important of all, be in control of your state of mind. Be in command of your *in joy ment* of life. Happiness is primarily a state of mind. Even when you are totally helpless to control the events and circumstances around you, you can always be in command of your own state of mind. You are more than just the animal brain. You have the conscious ability to rise above the wiring and live life as a Soul. Use all the concepts and techniques of the previous chapters to be working for yourself and enhancing the love in your life. Your life was meant to be joyful. Don't fall victim to the misery mechanisms of the limbic brain.

Being fully nourished is more than just staying well fed. It is also providing food for the Soul. Get your daily spiritual nutrients of self-acceptance, love energy, and the connection with a greater whole. That original "Soul food" is vital to your complete well-being. Strive each day to learn a little, love a little, and even cry a little. Accept the full gamut of ups and downs as the stuff of living and enjoy the adventure.

Through it all, resolve to fully and completely cherish yourself as a growing seeking Soul. Give yourself the daily quota you require of appreciation and respect. Here is a simple way to experience the feeling of acknowledging your worth regularly.

- **First, do the Joy Touch to start off open and receptive.**
- **Second, feel, see, know or understand being pleased with yourself.**
  (Feel good just for being you, the unique, one-of-a-kind Soul you are.)
- **Next, place your right arm and hand across your stomach.**
  (This gives you a safe, protected and full feeling.)
- **Then ,place your left hand and arm over your heart.**
  (This gives you the feeling of being valued and cherished.)
- **Finally, just bask in the sensation of being at peace and content with yourself.**
  (Fully feeling your worth, your uniqueness, and your independent value.)
- **After a few moments do the Joy Touch to seal in this realization and feeling.**

You deserve this period of inner peace and contentment at least daily. It may, in fact, be the most vital nutrient for the health of the human spirit. Just as you have allowed yourself to be learning about better food and cooking techniques for weight management, so too allow yourself to explore and grow in your ability to fully value yourself.

Use this recharge of your independent worth as the capstone of your fifth simple step. Control your ability to feel good inside regularly. Otherwise, it is easy to use food as a crutch, or worse, to become dependent on more harmful alternatives to ease the distresses of life. Methods for escaping that trap are contained in the next chapter, in the section on Joy Touch keys for breaking the grip of substance abuses.

Joy Touch Keys for Reducing— Pain, Smoking, Alcohol Consumption and Substance Abuse

Pain, nicotine addiction, and substance abuse are three common enemies to full happiness. The Joy Touch technique can be a potent weapon for reducing their negative effects on life. That is not to imply that the Joy Touch alone is the answer to chronic pain or serious substance abuse. It is not. It is, however, a revolutionary addition to the existing therapies that address these issues.

It may seem strange to group pain control in a chapter containing keys for reducing substance abuse, but it is actually quite logical. Knowing the mental skill of triggering the septal area gives you access to the body's natural remedies for both physical and psychological/emotional pain. Further, our society has truly become a drug culture when it comes to over-the-counter pain medication. The variety of aspirin, ibuprofen, and acetaminophen products available is staggering. We are literally semi-addicted to taking a pill for every little ache. It is time to let the body's endorphin benefits be available to more than just marathon runners.

Pain Control

You *can* learn to use your mind to trigger the body's natural pain-relieving mechanisms. The Joy touch makes the process simple and easy. It can be used to control everything from minor discomfort to postsurgical pain.

Headaches

Students who regularly apply the technique report that they have a lower incidence of headaches. Routinely stimulating the septum pellucidum area keeps them from creating the tensions that cause them. When they do get headaches, the Joy Touch helps to clear them more rapidly. The key is remembering to use the technique as soon as you feel the onset of the headache. Equally important, is triggering the technique from a different direction than the location of the headache. For example, if you have a sinus headache (or severe allergy reaction), attempting to trigger the septal area from the front may actually increase your discomfort. Focus instead on doing the Joy Touch from above or from behind. If you feel your headache (or a loved one's) is being brought on by neck tension, try the neck rub with hand at forehead described in Chapter 3. Let one hand be stimulating the septal area from the front, while the other is relaxing the muscles at the base of the skull.

Migraines and Throbbing Pain

As with regular headaches, one of the keys for migraines is to apply the Joy Touch as soon as possible. One of my instructors, Zale Atley, has suffered from migraines for years and found a way to use the Joy Touch to end a migraine virtually before it starts. Zale's headaches are often preceded by an auric effect (a feeling and a pattern of lights across his vision) very similar to what some epileptics experience before a seizure. He found that if he started the Joy Touch as soon as the sensation began, he could prevent his tension from blossoming into a full blown migraine.

Once a migraine has hit full force, there is often little that can moderate it. The pain can be so intense that it's all consuming. Any other activity is prevented. Sufferers are often confined to the dark for quiet bedrest. Even then, the slightest movement can increase the migraine's intensity. During those times anything that distracts attention from the pain can help, particularly if the distraction is timed to the throbbing of the pain.

It must be mentioned at this point that the primary goal is moderating the pain—handling it rather than specifically trying to eliminate it. First of all, trying to totally stop pain can set up an efforting tension that actually makes the discomfort worse. Second, anything that lessens or reduces the pain is a positive step. Be satisfied with that progress and proceed from there. Many migraine sufferers take on the added burden of guilt that they can't eliminate the pain. They see it as a personal failure when they can't make the headache go away. Don't submit yourself to that additional mental torture. Do what you can and praise yourself for it.

Many migraines have a length that just has to run its course. Use the Joy Touch to help ease your discomfort during that duration. Pulse your stimulations of the septal area to the throb of the headache to mentally distract you at the height of the pain. In particular, doing the Joy Touch from above seems to work best (probably because it shifts your focus toward the Soul and out of your body). That Soul-shift effect (described in Chapter 3) can also help ease you into a light sleep that ends some migraines. Instead of falling asleep out of exhaustion, focus on Joy Touching and Soul-shifting for sliding into a drowsy state of mind. The key is doing something instead of merely being consumed by the pain.

Dental Discomfort

That same principle can be applied in dental situations. Moneca Ryane, another instructor, uses the Joy Touch to ease her discomfort when she has her teeth worked on. Not only does stimulating the septal area make her less anxious, but it blocks the pain during procedures where Novocaine is not usually given. Because of her sensitive teeth and the deep scaling she requires, getting her teeth cleaned is usually an excruciating experience for Moneca. She excitedly called to tell me how she got through it with barely a whimper after she knew the Joy Touch.

Don't get me wrong. I think Novocaine is a marvelous addition to dentistry. I accept it gratefully anytime the dentist recommends its use. There are, however, additional dental uses of the Joy Touch other than pain control. It makes the entire visit less nerve wracking.

There is something particularly unnerving about visiting the dentist, even for simple procedures. First of all, the angle of the chair seems to trigger every possible helpless feeling stored in our genetic memories. Second, having your mouth wedged uncomfortably wide open for what seems like an eternity magnifies even minor discomforts to major annoyances. Then to top it off you get to worry about drowning in your own saliva, and all the while you are incapable of speaking (even though the dentist seems to forget this or maybe is specifically asking you questions just to torture you). It is easy to walk out feeling like a giant bundle of frayed nerves. I use the Joy Touch to counter those effects and feelings.

Something in me rebels against suffering and having to pay for it too. By using the Joy Touch, even before I go in the door, I am able to adopt a more relaxed frame of mind. I literally look at the visit as a chance to lie down during the middle of my day. Triggering the septal area while I am in the chair helps me to be at peace with my thoughts and enjoy the rest. I get more upset at the dentist's questions interfering with my reflections, than his seeming lack of awareness that I can't answer without choking. It might seem unbelievable, but it is almost comforting to know that I can't be disturbed by business phone calls or rushed trying to be a taxi service for the kids. As long as I have to be there, I figure I might as well unwind as best I can. I apply the Joy Touch repeatedly to deepen my inner levels of peacefulness. This is an approach that can help you with even more major medical procedures.

Joy Touch Before, During, and After Surgery

Several years ago, after a freak accident, I required surgery on cartilage and ligaments in my knee. Rather than full anesthesia I chose to have a leg block. I wanted to be fully conscious during the operation so I could use the self-healing techniques contained in my first book *You Are Psychic!* That way I could start the healing and pain-control procedures even while the surgery was taking place. Before the operation, I used the Joy Touch to lessen discomfort as four needles were plunged into nerves in my groin and hip for the leg block.

(**Note**: In many major operations a small amount of curare or other muscle relaxants are used to help the incision be less jagged. Without them the tissue tightens and resists invasion. The rougher the cut the longer it will take to heal and the more post-operative pain there will be. Doing deep versions of the Joy Touch before anesthesia can help your body be even more relaxed and less resistant to the scalpel.)

During the surgery, I stimulated the septum pellucidum regularly to keep my blood pressure low. Doing this made it easier for me to do my mental healing exercises as I watched the video monitor showing the inside of my knee. As a result, I had virtually no pain after the leg block wore off. Not only did I not use the pain medication the doctor prescribed, I didn't even need Tylenol.

I was shocked. I wasn't being macho or merely toughing it out. The pain simply wasn't there. During my high school years I had less extensive surgery on the other knee and remember that pain well. This time, despite having ligaments cut and three cartilage tears (not just one) removed, I had virtually no discomfort. If anything, I needed the Joy Touch more to lessen my postsurgical irritability than to control my pain.

I do not take well to being less than fully mobile. Although my mind/body healing techniques consistently kept me ahead of the normal recovery schedule, I can honestly admit the restrictions made me incredibly grumpy. I learned that I needed to use the Joy Touch more frequently (at least once an hour) to combat the irritability. I also found that it was necessary to vary the direction from which I triggered the septum pellucidum. Often, stimulating it from above (like a ray of light coming in the top of my head) worked best.

[**Note**: Several students have told me that this method (from above) and hourly frequency also gives them the best results **for relieving PMS irritability**. It is absurd for a man to attempt writing about PMS, so I will be brief. Many of the symptoms of PMS are limbic brain related. With the Joy Touch, you can counter the cyclical increase in irritability by boosting your positive sensations.]

At other times, coming up the spine with a pulse of energy and touching the joy center from behind worked best. The key was utilizing enough variety that I didn't get bored and forget to use the technique.

Impaired mobility is a permanent reality for the disabled. It is also a major cause of unhappiness for many senior citizens. While possibly not a concern to you now, we are all faced with aging. Mastering the Joy Touch is a key that can help you feel positive and young at heart, regardless of your age or physical limitations. Think of irritability as an annoying mental pain, the equivalent of a sunburn of the brain. Using the Joy Touch regularly can be like Solarcaine for the mind. It soothes the inner friction that increasing physical impairments, minor arthritis and mobility restrictions can cause. You may be stuck with a body that ages and weakens, but you can counter that deterioration with a maturing and strengthening of your mental abilities.

Back Pain

Recent studies have shown that many treatments for back pain (with the exception of chiropratic manipulation) provide no faster relief than rest and the normal passage of time. To me, this means that the best use of the Joy Touch for back pain is in helping you rest. Yes, you can use the technique at the throb to distract you from the pain. More important, however, use it to induce a mellow feeling when you are lying down. Send the message to the body that you are resting and regenerating.

If you choose chiropratic manipulation, use the Joy Touch before and during your examination to help your muscles relax. That way the doctor will be better able to feel and treat your condition. Using the Joy Touch to stay calm after your treatment can prevent muscle tensions from recurring and aggravating your condition.

Severe and Chronic Pain

Severe pain should never be taken lightly. A physician should always be consulted. In addition, however, here are some suggestions that may prove effective along with your care.. As mentioned earlier, pulsing the Joy Touch to the throb of the pain can help by distracting you from the pain's intensity. The effect can be enhanced by projecting numbing thoughts at the area causing the discomfort. This is the mental equivalent of icing the effected nerve fibers.

The key is to do whatever helps you turn down the intensity of the pain signal or to place it in the background. Increasing the input from your other senses (such as listening to music) can accomplish that. Even physical activity (if it doesn't aggravate the pain) can be an effective distraction. Endeavor to manage the pain and not let it win.

One of my students in Northern California has a different approach that works for handling his chronic pain. Scott suffers from severe knee damage as a result of wounds received in Vietnam. The doctors still feel that at some point he may have to lose his leg. Of all the different approaches to pain control that he has studied, he found that the most effective for him was Free Soul's mind/body healing exercises. He felt the greatest relief when he was sending thoughts to heal the area as opposed to just trying to reduce the pain. Those exercises along with the Joy Touch help him to feel more in command of his situation. **Here is a short version of Free Soul's mind/body healing approach**.

- **First, do the Joy Touch to ease your discomfort and relax.**

- **Second, feel, see, know, or understand that you are a Soul.**
  (You don't necessarily have to do the Soul-shift technique from Chapter 3, just sense yourself as consciousness beyond the body—as the Soul that you are.)

- **Next, imagine all of your Soul energy traveling into your body to the injured/painful area.**
  (Sense yourself moving to the affected area and fully being there within the tissue.)

- **Then, feel the Soul energizing the area, nurturing it to regrow and heal.**
  (Picture healing rays, imagine regeneration taking place, or just think of progress being made. Use whatever visualizations or concepts that represent healing and wholeness to you.)

- **Hold this image for one to two minutes and then seal it in.**
  (Create a mental bubble capturing the energy you have generated and holding it in place.)

- **Finally, Joy Touch to reinforce your increased well-being.**

(For more complete mind/body healing concepts and techniques see chapter 7 of *You Are Psychic!* and the comprehensive *Dynamics of Being a Free Soul* Course.)

This is just one small technique you can use to take greater command of your situation. There are many other mind/body methods that may also be effective. Whatever approach you take, the key is not giving in to the feeling of being a victim. Use the Joy Touch and the esteem-building techniques in Chapters 3 and 4 to reinforce your mental and spiritual well-being. Use each pulse of the technique to reaffirm your worth as a Soul and remind yourself that you are more than the body that is giving you discomfort.

Mind Over Matter

You can always use the power of your mind to rise above the effects of physical matter. First, because the Joy Touch triggers neural pathways, it allows you to use your mind to counter the dominance of other nerve fibers carrying pain messages. Second, because you are consciousness, you can rise above the realm of the mere flesh. That same type of control can also allow your mental abilities to overcome the cellular effects of chemical addictions.

Keys For Reducing Smoking

It is really not too great a leap to go from pain control to reducing smoking. They are linked in several ways. Suppressing the urge for a cigarette is in essence managing the mental pain of withdrawal from nicotine addiction. There is also a link through nuerotransmitters. Nicotine has now been shown to release endorphins in the brain (the same pain relief substance originally discovered in connection with the runner's high experienced by marathoners). It also releases dopamine in the reward centers of the brain, just as cocaine, opium, and alcohol do. Once a smoker is hooked on cigarettes, quitting presents a dual problem. The first is easing the physical discomfort and psychological pain of nicotine withdrawal—which the Joy Touch readily facilitates. The second is replacing the coping mechanism on which many smokers are just as dependent.

Nicotine is a powerfully addictive drug, but it is not the main reason people smoke. The main reason is stress and the need for relief from its negative effects. We have known for decades that cigarette smoking poses a severe health risk. Why then are people still smoking? The answer is that their mental and emotional needs have outweighed their concern for their physical well-being. They are willing to risk an unhealthy habit in exchange for relief from the distress of life's pressures. Also, there hasn't been a quick and natural alternative. Now there is!

Once you know how to stimulate the septal area at will, you have an instant pressure-reducer. Many people are able to use the technique to combat stress buildup so effectively that they don't even feel the desire for a cigarette. For those with more severe addictions, advanced adaptations of the technique make it possible to get as far as putting a cigarette in the mouth yet still not needing to light up and inhale.

Specifics For Joy Touch Substitution

Once the craving for a smoke occurs, the first line of defense is to do the Joy Touch as you take a breath. Because the addiction is associated with inhaling, stimulating the septal area as you breathe in can provide the same relief that is associated with smoking. Most addictions also have strong behavior patterns associated with them. These can be psychologically essential for the comfort that the substance provides. In smoking the whole ritual of taking out and handling the cigarette adds to that sense of relaxation. Being able to "do something" can help smokers feel less helpless about what is making them anxious. The Joy Touch can be that something.

Smokers can even go so far as to put an unlit cigarette in their mouth and stimulate the septal area as they inhale through it. They can get the psychological and physiological relief without lighting up. Those who can't resist lighting up can put the cigarette out after one or two puffs if they effectively use the Joy Touch as they smoke.

It does not work to do the Joy Touch as you inhale a lit cigarette. The dual rush of septal stimulation and the nicotine can create an overload that is actually counter productive. Cindy, a smoker described it as follows, "I know that I frequently smoke out of anxiety, stress, or irritability. When I do the Joy Touch as I inhale, I feel such a zing that it is irritating and actually makes me want to smoke more to calm down. If, however, I do the Joy Touch several times before I take a puff, I find that I inhale less deeply and can put the cigarette out before it is finished."

This option has helped people who were never able to stop cold turkey by letting them phase out of smoking more gradually (an approach that the latest research shows is actually more effective in the long run than an abrupt cessation). Thinking in terms of reducing smoking as opposed to "quitting" is also helpful psychologically. Quitting is always associated with denial and deprivation. This just creates anxiety and a greater urge to smoke to feel better. The concept of reducing can easily be linked with feelings of progress and proven health benefits. Less smoke in the lungs has to be better than more. Anything that keeps you from automatically grabbing a cigarette and smoking it all, will help you to cut down.

Learning Your Triggers

Michael Fiore, M.D., M.P.H., director of the Center for Tobacco Research and Intervention at the University of Wisconsin has been quoted as saying that many smokers who want to quit may relapse five or six times before they learn sufficient skills to overcome nicotine addiction. Key among those skills is identifying the times and places that you are most likely to want a cigarette and eliminating smoking in those situations first. Those circumstances and locations are personal, but there are ones common to most smokers. In each of those cases the Joy Touch can be a significant part of your strategies for at least reducing your cigarette consumption.

The craving for a cigarette first thing in the morning is hard to resist for many smokers, especially during or after that morning cup of coffee (as caffeine increases your sensitivity to nicotine-withdrawal symptoms). Try using the Joy Touch to give you that eye-opening, brain-engaging effect you desire. The mood-boost it gives you can also motivate you to seek other alternatives to that early morning smoke, such as a walk or taking the time to make a healthy breakfast.

Many smokers grab that first cigarette simply to feel better, particularly if they are getting less sleep than they would like. Feeling deprived of that needed relief can make starting the day even more unpleasant. Instead, use the Joy Touch to enhance your mood and follow it with specific thoughts and/or statements that make you feel good about yourself and the day ahead. Emphasize how proud your loved ones will be of you for not smoking. Think of something you are going to love yourself for that day, something for which you can encourage yourself.

Identify your stress points at work. Saul Shiffman, Ph.D., professor of psychology at the University of Pittsburgh has stated that as much as 70% of relapses, strong temptations, and close calls seem to occur during times of high stress or crisis. Rather than reach for a cigarette at those times, take a pause and do the Joy Touch several times. Stimulate your septal area before you go into a meeting that you know will be difficult. Do the Joy Touch after stressful encounters, instead of using a cigarette to help you unwind. Also don't let time pressures keep you from using the Joy Touch throughout the day. It only takes a few seconds and may help you cut your cigarette consumption in half or even more.

Avoid the after-meal smoke. Use the Joy Touch as a relaxing dessert instead of a cigarette. You can also use other things that you enjoy as a substitute, such as listening to music, reading, or taking a nap. Getting out for a digestive stroll can also be a good alternative. Exercise releases the endorphins your brain may be craving and additionally burns calories. That can help with the weight gain that often accompanies quitting smoking.

Have a Joy Touch after sex instead of a cigarette. Let stimulating the septal area increase your feelings of closeness and help your intimacy linger. Use other pleasurable sensations such as hugging and kissing to take the place of needing to smoke.

Know your emotional triggers. Use what you have learned in the preceding chapters to clear the turmoil created by worries, hurts, angers, or fears. Ease your distress with the Joy Touch and the Comforting Connection, rather than using cigarettes as pacifiers. When the urge to smoke out of distress is just too strong to resist, remember the steps outlined in the previous section for using the Joy Touch to put out the cigarette before it is finished.

Never underestimate how powerfully addictive nicotine is. Rather than criticize yourself for perceived failures (which just creates additional emotional distress), praise yourself for your efforts. Even if you did relapse, you have helped your body during the time that you have refrained from smoking. Next time strive to make your efforts last longer. You may want to consider nicotine substitute systems to further support your efforts.

Incorporating Nicotine Gum or Patches

If you are really hooked on nicotine, it may be nearly impossible to quit smoking without the aid of a nicotine replacement system. The Joy Touch can help with mood-elevation and emotional distress control, but it may not be enough to overcome powerful withdrawal symptoms. Don't make it a test of how perfectly you can do the Joy Touch. Let the patch or nicotine gum help in your efforts. Also don't reduce your dose of nicotine too quickly too soon.

Peter Sachs, M.D., director of the Palo Alto Center for Pulmonary Disease Prevention recommends that a hard-core smoker should be cigarette free for 30 days before they start lessening the nicotine replacement dosage they are getting from patches or gum.

Even though the patch may be easier, nicotine gum actually is more adaptable to use with the Joy Touch. Because the patch is put on only once a day, it doesn't really help you increase your frequency of doing the Joy Touch. It also doesn't provide a specific replacement for having the cigarette at times of high stress, as gum can. When a craving is so strong that you have to do something, the oral gratification of chewing gum can help be an effective distraction. It can substitute for the ritual of taking out and lighting up the cigarette. Remember to do one or two Joy Touches for each piece of gum you put in your mouth. You can also use disposing of the gum as a reminder to do the Joy Touch one last time.

The biggest drawback to the Joy Touch technique is that people don't use it regularly enough to get the consistent benefits their levels of emotional stress may require. The whole key is making the technique automatic and almost instinctive. We actually have more training to brush our teeth or blow our noses, than we do too cleanse our minds.

You can use your cigarette cravings to help make doing the Joy Touch more automatic. Whether or not you give in and smoke, use the desire as a trigger to remember to do the Joy Touch. The more you use the technique, the more your overall well-being will increase and the less likely you will be to smoke merely for the anti-depressant effects of the nicotine.

Similar techniques and approaches can be used for helping to reduce alcohol consumption.

Joy Touch Specifics For Reducing Alcohol Consumption

As with smoking, alcohol abuse has many habit patterns and triggers that may be just as psychologically ingrained as the chemical is addictive. The whole ritual of preparing the drink and handling the glass have strong associations with getting relief. As much as possible use the Joy Touch for mood-elevation instead of alcohol, and replace the beverage with juice, a soda, or even refreshing ice-water. Also, specifically trigger the septum pellucidum with each sip.

If your drinking is associated with giving yourself a treat or has become a special end-of-the-workday ritual, keep that same pattern. Just substitute a nonalcoholic beverage you enjoy. Also, do the Joy Touch as part of that celebratory transition to a new part of the day. **Do the Joy Touch at least three times before your take you first sip**. Stimulate your septal area first to release the stress of the day. Do it again to start off the next phase of your day mellow and at peace. Finally, do the Joy Touch a third time as part of the celebratory toast that you are choosing a healthier alternative. Then, and only then, take your first sip of your nonalcoholic beverage.

If, for what ever reason, you do find yourself drinking something with alcohol, use the Joy Touch to get relief from one drink instead of five. Make *yourself* happy, rather than the stockholders of alcoholic beverage companies. As with weight control, one key is to slow down. **Do the Joy touch between each sip**. First, to prevent you from drinking too rapidly. Second, to mood-elevate naturally so that you don't require as many drinks to get the desired effect. With the Joy Touch you have a tool to reduce your alcohol consumption.

You Are the Key

The single most important factor in reducing alcohol abuse is your sincere motivation to cut down and your faith in yourself. The latest studies indicate that the common element among successes is the belief that you can do it. Whether you do it alone or with the help of groups such as Responsible Recovery or Alcoholics Anonymous, maintaining your personal motivation to cut back is the key.

Familiarizing yourself with the full spectrum of harmful effects alcohol has on the body, can give you the incentive to maintain your commitment. Most people are aware of how alcohol damages the liver, but may not know of its other negative side-effects. Alcohol abuse can lead to cardiomyopathy, in which the heart literally wastes away. It also impairs blood flow, which leads to an increased risk of strokes, as well as steady degradation of a variety of mental functions. Because it takes such large quantities to trigger mood-elevation (relative to other substances), alcohol exerts its toxic effects on virtually every organ of the body.

Once you know the Joy Touch, this type of global poisoning is just not worth it. It is even more ridiculous to pay someone else to slowly kill you. Yes, alcohol releases endorphins in the brain and provides relief, but you now know alternate ways of achieving the same effect. Use what you have learned in this book to feel better and start today to reduce your level of alcohol consumption. That does not mean you have to give up alcohol completely (in moderation it has been shown to have some health benefits).

Not Just Cold Turkey or Wild Turkey

According to Dennis Donovan, M.D., a psychiatrist and director of the Alcohol and Drug Abuse Institute at the University of Washington, "Abstinence is no longer the gold standard in the treatment of alcoholism." In other words there are alternatives to the myth that alcoholics must either quit "cold turkey" or stay stuck in their same abusive drinking pattern. Some former alcoholics do require unequivocal abstinence, but others may be able to drink in moderation—an approach to reduction nicknamed "warm turkey."

If you are ready to stop drinking completely, bravo. Your body will definitely thank you in the long run. If, however, you seem unable to, for whatever reason, it is important to know that you have other options that can reduce alcohol's negative effects on your life. Making a commitment to change is your most important first step. Then, you can apply the Joy Touch specifics at the beginning of this section to reduce the amount of alcohol you need to consume.

Up until now, you haven't had a natural alternative to drinking for feeling better and dealing with life's stresses. Now you do. With the Joy Touch, the Comforting Connection, and the esteem-building techniques you have learned, you have specific methods that you can employ. These, combined with the knowledge that drinking in moderation is not failure, can be your gateway to cutting back. You already have the desire and an initial set of defenses. All that is required to complete your Alcohol Reduction Triangle are strategies to ensure your success.

Strategies for Reduction and Relapse Prevention

Planning and common sense are important parts of any approach to decreasing the power of alcohol in your life. Developing a system of strategies that will safeguard you is not only wise, it is imperative. As long as our society is still heavily alcohol dependent, you are going to be surrounded by temptations and outright advertising efforts to get you to drink. In conjunction with the Joy Touch, remembering the sensible steps outlined below can make your desire to cut down a reality.

Avoid situations that you know can lead to excessive drinking. This doesn't necessarily mean that you can't go to parties, weddings, and celebrations. If it is impossible for you to control your drinking in those environments, then by all means don't go. For many, a more common sense approach may be possible. Avoid sitting at the table with the heavy drinkers. Leave at a reasonable hour, before the heavy drinking usually starts. As much as possible, simply do not put yourself in circumstances where you will be tempted beyond your willpower to resist.

Rehearse in advance what you will do in circumstances that can trigger drinking more than you feel is appropriate for you. Have a plan for leaving the party early. Know what nonalcoholic beverage you will enjoy as a treat if you are presented with the question of, "Would you care for a drink?" Have a nonalcoholic beverage in your hand already to prevent someone from forcing a drink on you.

Sometimes people or situations can trigger difficult memories that can lead to drinking. It is foolish to think that you will never encounter those triggers. Rather than avoid them, prepare for them. Picture meeting those people or going back to the places in question. Then identify the ways you will get through them without drinking.

Traditional approaches say that exposing the drinker to environmental cues like this will just increase cravings and lead to relapses. "In fact, the opposite seems true; the data suggests that cue exposure is the very thing we should be doing" according to Steven Liljegren, Ph.D., clinical director of the Child and Adolescent Services at Brookside Hospital in Nashua, New Hampshire. By facing those situations, without reinforcing them with the "pleasure" of drinking, you become less responsive to those triggers over time. It also gives you the opportunity to build up your ability to cope with those challenges when they do occur.

Reduce how much alcohol you drink using the Joy Touch

specifics described at the beginning of this section. Stimulating the septal area as a mental cocktail can decreases your craving for alcohol and assist your willpower to have an nonalcoholic beverage instead. When you do drink, or if you must drink, use the Joy Touch to slow down your drinking by doing it between each sip.

Maintain your emotional balance by stimulating the septal area regularly throughout the day. This natural mood elevation will alleviate the pressure of life's stresses that can lead to the desire to drink. Life *is* incredibly stressful. That is why entertainers are the highest paid people in our society. Everyone needs relief. It is not a crime to be exhausted and to want to feel better. It is a tragedy, however, to be paying someone else for a form of relief that is physically and psychologically toxic. The Joy Touch gives you a method that is natural and healthy (helps keep your blood pressure lower). It is also quicker than alcohol and doesn't cause hangovers. Best of all, it's free. It can help you keep your mood lighter instead of your wallet.

Because you can use it anywhere and anytime, the Joy Touch can be your lifesaver if you face stormy seas in your emotional environment. Use it to keep from getting pushed beyond your limit to cope. The best reminder I have ever heard for how to protect yourself is **H.A.L.T.—never get too Hungry, too Angry, too Lonely, or too Tired**. Each of those conditions can lead to drinking to block out what is bothering you. Stimulating your septal area when you start to feel angry, lonely or stressed will return your emotional balance and help you to act, not just react. Doing the Joy Touch when your blood sugar drops will help you feel less compulsively hungry. It also gives you the impulse control to choose a healthy snack, rather than a drink, to boost your mood and energy level.

If you know your abuse of alcohol is severe, do not hesitate to get additional help. Alcohol addiction is serious. Use the full spectrum of services that are available to you.

Let the Joy Touch Assist Other Professional Treatments and Options

There is no shame in seeking outside help to break the chains of alcohol abuse. Nothing in this book is designed to imply that you must quit entirely on your own. You know yourself best. If your individual efforts have been unsuccessful, get the help you need. The shame is letting a false sense of pride or denial cause the alcohol to win.

Support groups are excellent for helping you realize that you are not alone. All difficult endeavors are made easier when you are part of a group effort. The Joy Touch can help by boosting your energy for going to meetings or easing your guilt and embarrassment. If you are shy or uncomfortable in a group situation, using the technique at the meeting can help you be more relaxed, so that you can get the most out of your time there.

Major progress is also being made with medications that block the reinforcing effects of alcohol. Naltrexzone is starting to replace Antabuse as the pharmacological treatment of choice, because it is easier to take and is more user friendly. Instead of causing nausea the way Antabuse does when alcohol is consumed, Naltrexzone blocks the part of the brain that makes alcohol pleasurable. Without that reinforcement, the cycle of associating drinking with relief is broken. You can use the Joy Touch to enhance the process even further by reinforcing your choice to have a nonalcoholic beverage. By stimulating the septal area as you take each sip, you build the positive association of getting relief without needing the alcohol.

This train of thought may seem severe, but if you are seriously addicted to alcohol, you should not hesitate to use every means available to regain your freedom from chemical dependence. The same is equally true for drug problems.

Dealing with Drug Abuse and Other Chemical Addictions

Whether you know you have a problem, or think you are just a recreational user, all drug abuse should be taken seriously. First of all, the substances are illegal. Second, their addictiveness is proven and will only get worse, not better, with time. And finally, they will kill you, if not now, eventually, or slowly.

The moment you are aware of drug abuse, you have a problem that is serious enough to merit professional help. The good news is that tremendous progress is being made with less expensive outpatient methods called brief intervention. Several studies have shown that, if designed properly, very brief treatment can be effective even against moderately severe addictions.

The Joy Touch is not meant to replace either these shorter approaches or the traditional therapies. It is merely an extra weapon you can use in the battle. In order to kick addictions to powerful narcotics you will need the full resources of the medical and psychological community and you should take advantage of them. Do not delude yourself that the Joy Touch alone will help you beat cocaine, crystal meth, or heroine. If you are serious about wanting to stop, however, it can make the process easier.

Joy Touch Keys to Add to Professional Help

Weave the following uses of the Joy Touch technique into the treatments you are receiving whenever and wherever possible.

Use the Joy Touch to maintain your emotional balance. Instead of using drugs to stay mellow, do the Joy Touch frequently throughout the day. Remember also that acronym H.A.L.T.—never get too Hungry, too Angry, too Lonely, or too Tired. It is a good barometer of your vulnerability to relapse.

By stimulating your septal area frequently throughout the day, you can maintain the highest mood possible given the rigors of withdrawal. The secret is to find some regular reminder to use the technique. Set your watch to beep on the hour or do the Joy Touch at each transition from one activity or location to another. When you find yourself becoming too hungry, angry, lonely or tired, immediately do the Joy Touch three or four times.

Because your stresses are likely to be more severe than the average person's, don't be hesitant to use the beginning method where you actually touch your forehead with your hand. (Further, for reasons outlined in the first chapter, it may be advisable to approach slightly from left of center—so that your thoughts and energy pass though the left prefrontal cortex—an area shown to boost mood and increase the base level of happiness.).

Use the Joy Touch alternatives described in the reducing smoking and drinking sections. If the substance in question is smoked or taken orally, apply the same strategies described earlier for cigarettes and alcohol. When you feel the need for a hit, do the Joy Touch with a substance-free deep breath. If necessary, handle something the size and shape of what you would normally smoke, or chew gum as an oral substitute.

Equally important, is planning strategies to prepare for the circumstances that you know will tempt you. Avoid those situations whenever possible. If you can't, think of effective responses ahead of time. As described earlier in the section on Alcohol, exposing yourself to some of your triggers and then rewarding yourself for not giving in to the drug craving can be an effective reprogramming therapy.

If you do relapse, use the Joy Touch to help identify what you will do differently the next time. Instead of just feeling guilty and thinking it's hopeless, focus on how to do better next time. Relapses will happen. You shouldn't be glad for them, but you shouldn't unduly castigate yourself either. A relapse does not wipe out all of your previous efforts and progress.

Use the Joy Touch to lessen your guilt and prevent a slide into feelings of hopelessness. Channel your emotional reaction into positive motivation, rather than self-destructive put-downs. It is hard to think clearly when you are in emotional turmoil. Stimulating your septal area can give you the clarity and calmness to objectively review what happened and to plan how to avoid a recurrence.

Do the Joy Touch each time you realize you have stayed drug free. Give yourself positive reinforcement for even minor successes. The Joy Touch can be utilized as your reward when you congratulate yourself for your abstinence. A major part of changing your habit patterns is acknowledging yourself for your drug free behavior.

With the Joy Touch you have a healthy, nonfattening method of positive reinforcement that is both quick and free. Use the technique liberally to celebrate your new beginning. You can also take advantage of its spiritual benefits. The more you do the Joy Touch, the easier it is to feel in touch with your full spirituality and inner strength. That added depth can give you the resources to go on, even when your mental and physical conditions are at their worst.

Soul over Substance

Most of all, don't give up. You can beat it. You are better than a mere chemical. Remember, you are a Soul that has a body. The real you is stronger than even the most intense addiction. With the proper support system and treatment there is a way out. Praise yourself for each step that you take on that difficult journey and know that you will make it. It won't be easy and your success carries no automatic guarantee of bliss.

Even after you are drug free, life will still be challenging. Don't delude yourself with fantasies. The trick is to see the obstacles as opportunities for becoming stronger. Don't make your worth dependent on being happy all the time. You are entitled to feel lousy some of the time. The secret is to be able to rebound from those downs with new learning and further progress.

Honestly and Nobly
Bearing Life's Difficulties

We have this notion that we are always supposed to be happy or something is terribly wrong with us and our lives. I think this may be a negative side-effect of the television age. Far too often, the message is that you are only O.K. if you are blissfully happy or have all the material possessions, love, and power that is possible. This probably started with the overly saccharin images of early television shows. It has definitely been exacerbated as Madison Avenue has mastered the art of television advertising. We are bombarded with images of people who "have it all." This generates more than just the desire for that condition. It creates the expectation that life "should" always be that way.

It's important to realize, that for the vast majority of humanity's existence, the issue hasn't been achieving happiness; it has been maintaining survival. Maybe happiness is not always possible or even the ideal condition for humanity. Some of our greatest achievements and discoveries have sprung from discontent or a troubled spirit. I have often wondered if a certain amount of discontent may actually be a positive in the long run. That it may, quite literally, be the Soul's natural preventative against stagnation.

This is not a new or totally unique concept. The famous quote, "The unexamined life is not worth living," reflects Plato's belief that introspective dissatisfaction is a higher purpose than merely surviving or just pursuing hedonistic pleasure. Quite possibly our genetic make-up as a species will always prevent complete happiness. Even if that is true, you are entitled to a greater sense of control over your life—a feeling that you are not helpless.

The techniques you have learned in this book give you that ability. The Joy Touch gives you the skill to no longer be resigned to being or staying down. With the Comforting Connection you can complete the self-examinations needed for clearing your discontents more quickly and effectively. You have the tools for being in greater command of creating your own happiness.

A drawback to this marvelous gift can spring from within you, however—from the unrealistic expectation that just because you know the techniques, you will always be perfectly happy. That condition would be counter to the human spirit's quest to continue learning. Let your disquiets motivate you to explore how to make your life still better. Remember also to enjoy that journey, not just the destination of happiness. On occasion it is only reasonable to be humbled momentarily by a Universe that is mightier than we are.

Everyone has challenges, people and circumstances that can cause us pain, anger, or anxiety. How we face and handle those situations is a measure of our Soulness. It reflects our ability to rise above the animal nature of our biology. No matter what happens to us, no matter how much circumstances seem to imprison us, we are always free to control our attitude. We can be more than just survival reflexes.

One the most inspirational examples of that truth was Victor Frankl, M.D., Ph.D. A psychiatrist and neurologist, Dr. Frankl survived a series of Nazi work and death camps including Dachau and Auschwitz. Rather than succumb to bitterness and self-pity, he used the experience to develop a dynamic new approach to therapy based on the value of finding purpose in life. His book, *Man's Search for Meaning*, chronicles his time in the camps and his insight for how to make even the worst of miseries purposeful.

At one point Dr. Frankl realized that every freedom except one had been stripped from him and his fellow inmates. Their loved ones and every material possession had been taken from them. Their freedom to practice their professions and to create had been denied. Their strength and health had been sapped by years of hard work, sleep-deprivation, and starvation. Every other conceivable freedom had been stripped from them by the brutality of the Nazi death camps. Everything except "the last of the human freedoms—the freedom to choose one's attitude in any given set of circumstances."

For Dr. Frankl, having a sense of purpose was the key to maintaining a positive attitude despite adversity. His revolutionary Logotherapy was based in large part on Nietzsche's philosophy that "He who has a *why* to live can bear with almost any *how*." This is just another way of saying to focus on the "whys" of life, not just the surface "whats."

Dr. Frankl identified three key approaches to feeling that sense of meaning and purpose in life—through achieving, through loving, and through the noble bearing of suffering. It is the third of these that most applies to this chapter.

We all have hardships and dissatisfactions that we must endure. Nobly bearing these challenges can be the mark of our Soulness. Using the Joy Touch and focusing on being purposeful gives us the power to move through our difficulties with dignity rather than despair.

When my troubles seem insurmountable, I remember the suffering borne by such great Souls as Frankl, Ganhdi, and Christ. This reminds me, not only to put my problems in perspective, but also to strive to emulate their dignity and grace in my life and inner attitude.

When events in life do overwhelm you, don't guilt yourself if you slip into angers, worries, hurts, or fears. Rather, use those times as research material for your next breakthrough. Make it a personal challenge to develop an advanced variation of the Joy Touch and/or find the Comforting Connection that eases your distress and gives you new insight. Enlighten your quest with an eye toward the future—illuminate your way with a ray of hope—hope for a better you, for a better way of coping, and for a better tomorrow.

Together we can make a difference. We are the modern day pioneers of humanity's future. We are forging a way of living that reflects inner control rather than being controlled, serenity rather than struggle. Bravo to you, fellow seeker, for your part of making that tomorrow a reality. Until next time, know that you are a unique, beautiful Soul, that you are loved, and that you are never alone.

Sincerely,

Pete A. Sanders Jr.

•8•

Quick Reference Guides

This chapter is designed to provide you with a rapid way to remember key aspects of the techniques and skills taught in the book. In most cases the quick reminders should be adequate to help you recall the concepts or steps necessary to receive the assistance you require. For more in-depth explanations, check the table of contents for where to refer to in the book.

Septal Area Location & Self-Touch Locating

General Location - For simplicity, think of the septal area as being in the middle of the head (measuring both from side to side and front to back). That means all you have to identify is where is it on the up and down axis of the head.

For that final measurement, think mid-forehead (approximately one and one-half inches above the eyebrows).

Locating that area within your head - (1) Place your middle finger at the center of your forehead (one and one-half inches above your eyebrows) and then also touch the middle of the side of your head with your thumb. Then, mentally imagine lines extending from your fingers into your head. Feel for where those two lines would intersect.

(2) Also try placing your middle finger at the center of your forehead (one and one-half inches above your eyebrows) and your thumb at the middle of the top of your head. Then, mentally imagine lines extending from your fingers into your head. Feel for where those two lines would intersect.

(3) Alternate between steps (1) and (2) several times to triangulate the septal area from all three directions.

(Note) - It is recommended that you do this with your left hand, so that the biomagnetic field of your hand is stimulating the left prefrontal cortex (an area shown to suppress negative emotion).

Additional specifics and reminders - (1) If anything, err on the side of being too high on the forehead, rather than too low. Too low and you run the risk of stimulating the negative areas of the limbic brain.

(2) The septal nuclei, the portion of the septum pellucidum that connects with mood elevation centers of the brain, is at the front of the septal area. If you are not getting as strong an effect as you would like, focus on stimulating an area a little foreword of the center of the head.

Ways to Trigger & Types of Sensation

Ways to Trigger Your Septal Area

Imagine caressing these fibers like stroking the fur of a pet.

Picture energy flowing by the septal area and triggering it.

Feel your mind activating the fibers that connect down to the hypothalamus by strumming them as you would a harp.

Know that this area can activate and simply hold your thought there, or picture a light there, triggering the area.

<u>Do Not</u> try to push a button or force concentration.

Types of Sensation You May Feel

An inner "ah"

A mellow energized feeling

The sensation of a weight being lifted off your shoulders

The way you feel when you get good news or a ray of hope

A contented, focused, and centered inner well-being

(Note) Initially the sensation is lighter. The more you do it and the more exactly you find your best spot, you may even get chills and/or more powerful sensations.

Joy Touch from Alternate Directions

Triggering the Septal Area can be done from any direction. The main reason coming in from the forehead area is so heavily stressed is that **coming in from the front is the easiest** to teach to a beginner (because of the greater ease of describing the correct level in relation to the eyebrows). Once you know the location of your best spot for activating that feeling of mood-elevation, you can mentally approach it from any direction.

Coming down from the top of the head has the additional benefit of helping you feel connected to your Soul and dimensions beyond. It is also easier to do than from the front when you have a head cold or sinus irritation.

Coming up from below is best accomplished by visualizing coming up the spine (as in a kundalini meditation) and then touching forward from the back of the head moving back to front through the septal area. For many people this works best for helping to calm angers.

Coming in more from the left side of the forehead may give a stronger effect than directly at the middle. Recent research has shown that the area of the brain behind the left side of the forehead (called the left-prefrontal cortex) is an area that helps to dampen negative emotions. The right prefrontal cortex actually boosts the intensity of negative emotions. Therefore, it may be beneficial to come in more from the left side. This is particularly true if you are using the hand method (as opposed to just using your mind). Using your left hand (even if you are right handed) may give you a stronger sensation, as the hand's biomagnetic field may slightly stimulate the left prefrontal cortex, thus increasing negative emotional dampening (as opposed to the risk of increasing negative emotional levels from the right hand stimulating the right prefrontal cortex).

Doing the Joy Touch in Motion is beneficial when you are so irritable that you don't feel like sitting down or stopping to do something about your mood. Moving actually helps to get you out of the limbic brain and to connect with higher cortical areas. Walking (or rocking in a chair or swing) may make you more receptive to wanting to do the Joy Touch and/or help you to feel it stronger.

Joy Touch for Enhanced Intimacy

Personal foreplay: The first and most vital use the Joy Touch is to clear your irritability and put you more in the mood for intimacy. It can also ease the pressure of performance anxiety.

Caressing each others foreheads (or lightly running the hands through each others hair) can be a mood-setting activity as well as a loving closeness.

Once a minute triggering your septal area mentally, as you engage in intimacies, can heighten the sensation of each part of love-making.

You can prolong and heighten the plateau phase of arousal (just before climax) by particularly remembering to do the Joy Touch during that portion of intimacy.

Triggering the septal area during climax can make the climax last longer and be more easily repeatable.

Post-intimacy closeness is also enhanced by doing the Joy Touch. Triggering the septal area after climax helps to prolong the feeling of oneness that love-making can give.

Prerequisite for all but the foreplay uses: The ability to do the Joy Touch without having to think about it is essential. In order to get the full effect, you must be so proficient at mentally triggering the septal area, that you can do it despite the intense physical distraction of love-making.

Limbic Stress Definition & the Two Questions

Limbic Stress is the pressure and inner distress that comes from out-of-control negative emotions, created by the limbic system of the brain. In particular, it is angers, worries, hurts, or fears that seem to repetitively cycle (like a broken record) and destroy your inner calm and happiness.

Limbic stress is more than just cardiovascular stress. It is the way that negative emotions can degrade your quality of life and create distress long after the actual stressing event is over.

**The distress continues until you comfort
the root cause of the anger, worry, hurt, or fear.**

The key to that soothing is your <u>Comforting Connection</u>.

If you can remember two questions you can self-comfort any worry, hurt, anger, or fear.

The two Questions for getting your Comforting Connections

(1) What would comfort me in this situation? (What is the essence of what would soothe me?)

(2) How can I give that essence or sensation to myself? (What action can I take? What can I mentally focus on?)

Comforting Connections for Hurts

Rejection - Fully accept (don't reject) yourself.
You want to *feel* accepted. How can you give that to yourself? What action or self-praise emphasizes your valuing yourself?

Betrayal - Don't feel helpless.
You want to *feel* less like a victim (helpless). Focus on the positive action you can take. Don't be unfair to yourself by feeling that you allowed the betrayal.

Loneliness - Feel part of a greater whole.
You want to *feel* not alone. Find ways to feel and cherish your connection to the Universe, or joy of being a part of groups in your life.

Loss of Loved One - Soul cherish your memories.
You want to *feel* them in your life. Remember that every event is still happening somewhere in space time. You can travel into your memories and relive them (cherishing rather than missing them).

Loss of Job - Focus on new beginnings and learning.
You want to *feel* in control and of value. Focus on what you have learned from the situation, and/or how it has made you stronger. Emphasize your opportunity for a new beginning.

Not Feeling Fully Loved - Remember to love yourself.
You want to *feel* loved. Remember that your most crucial love is your love of yourself. Focus on doing something loving and/or cherishing for yourself. This can be anything from self-praise to taking yourself on a date (a special movie, giving yourself time off, or a treat, etc.).

Comforting Connections for Angers

Not Feeling Heard - Write or say what you want to be heard about. You want to *feel* heard. Identify exactly what issue you want to be heard about, as well as how and when to communicate it.

Anger at Self - Allow yourself to be learning. You want to *feel* less disappointed in yourself. Focus on perfecting yourself rather than having to be perfect.

Feeling Helpless - Emphasize what you <u>can</u> do. You want to *feel* less helpless. Anything that you can do helps. It focuses you on how to take greater command of your life.

Feeling Controlled - Realize you can always control your attitude. You want to *feel* less controlled. Remember that even in the most restrictive circumstances, you can still be in control of your own happiness. You may not be able to change the situation, but you can control your state of mind.

Not Being Valued - Find a way to value/cherish yourself. You want to *feel* valued. Make sure you are fully valuing yourself. Acknowledge and praise yourself rather than looking to others to give you your worth.

Irritation Anger - Put it in perspective and control your attitude. You want to *feel* less hassled and more at ease. Don't let the little irritations win and control your inner environment. Remember also, to do the Joy Touch to soothe your irritability.

Anger at Getting Angry - Allow a normal duration for your upset. You want to *feel* more in control. Remember that you are entitled to normal, healthy emotions. Focus on identifying how long your upset should last, and what you can do to calm down and get out of it by that time limit.

Comforting Connections for Worries

General - Worry is the brain's way of trying to ensure that you will not be taken off guard, that you will be prepared. For that reason many worries can be cleared by having some sort (any form) of plan. Even if all of the details are not fully worked out, the mere outline of a plan can help disconnect the broken record reflex of limbic worry.

Thus, **your primary Comforting Connection is to have a plan**. You want to *feel* prepared and not vulnerable.

Feeling Responsible - Be response able (choices versus pressure). You want to *feel* that you can handle it. Remember that you can choose how to respond to whatever situation will develop. If necessary make a plan that outlines what your choices could be for any "what if." Then acknowledge that you can choose from that list when the time arises.

Getting It Right - Realize how well you have done with essentials. You want to *feel* that you have done the best possible. Remember that you are always doing the best you know how with the information you have. Also allow yourself to be learning. Be perfecting, rather than perfect. If necessary make a plan for how to keep refining your choices so that you will have the best result possible.

Financial - Make a plan for how to stretch your resources. You want to *feel* more secure. Outline your options and find ways to help you know what is possible and what is not.

Job Security - Plan your options and prepare for them. You want to *feel* less uncertain. By looking into other options, and preparing your resume or taking job trainings,you will feel prepared.

Health - Resolve to study and act in a way that aids your health. You want to *feel* less vulnerable. Plan what you can do to maximize your health. Remember also that you are a Soul, not just a body.

About Family - Remember that they are learning Souls too. You want to *feel* less helpless. Remember that they, as Souls, must live their own life purposes and that there are forces there to help and guide them. Remember to care about them, not worry for them.

Comforting Connections for Fears

General - Fears are worries taken to extreme. The key is to find ways to keep your concerns from getting blown out of proportion.

Your primary Comforting Connection is to put it in perspective. You want to *feel* more in control. Get out of mental catastrophizing and identify the real concerns. Then, address them practically to help you regain your feeling of control and security.

Of the Unknown - Find out more about what you want to know. You want to *feel* less in the dark. Find ways to gather information that will help you, or set up systems that will help to warn you of possible dangers that are troubling you.

Of Being Helpless - Remember, you are never totally helpless. You want to *feel* safer. Identify what you <u>can</u> do to enhance your security, or at least your feeling of security. There is always something that you can do. Also recognize that your fear can actually be a positive first step. The anxiety can help to make you more alert and prepared.

Of Being All Alone - Remember the resources you do have. You want to *feel* that there is someone who can be there for you. Look into what friends, family, or governmental resources are available to you. Remember also to focus on any beliefs you have in a higher power (that you are never all alone).

Phobias - Expose yourself to small portions of what you fear. You want to *feel* less anxious about what causes the phobia. Realize that the actual situation, or thing, is less scary than the fear of it.

Panic Attacks - Joy Touch each time you have a panic sensation. You want to *feel* calmer. Finding a trigger for doing the Joy Touch more regularly will help you stay mellower and more relaxed.

Obsessive-Compulsive - Joy Touch instead of the compulsion. You want to *feel* good from something other than reinforcing the compulsion. Use the Joy Touch to give yourself a positive sensation without following the pattern of the compulsion.

Keys for Clearing Secret Pain

Secret Pain is a Hurt, Worry, Anger, or Fear that is more rooted in your past (Inner Child issues and/or past-life Soul bruises), as opposed to being totally caused by a current event or situation. Frequently this deeper form of limbic stress is triggered by something in the present, but the true core of the distress lies in an earlier time.

The result is a reaction that is out of proportion (greater) to what the current circumstance warrants. Another sign, that a limbic stress is a Secret Pain, is that the Comforting Connection you develop doesn't seem to fully work.

Secret Pain is secret because we hide it from ourselves. We hide it, not because we are dishonest, but rather we don't know how to heal it yet. Consequently, we bury the issue where its sharp edges can't harm us as often. It lies dormant like preexisting scar tissue, ready to magnify the distress when we are exposed to similar situations.

The key for clearing Secret Pain is to develop a Comforting Connection that also addresses the original issue, as well as the current situation stimulating it. Self-examination and/or therapy are also essential for getting clear insight into the core issue and its roots in your past.

Four Steps of the Peaks and Valleys Concept

We all have Peaks and Valleys in life. Life seems to go in cycles for all people. This is a pattern that is repeated over and over again in nature. All mountain peaks have valleys associated with them. All waves on the ocean have both a crest and a trough.

Only being happy during the peaks is limiting. It restricts you to feeling good only when things are going well. It also reduces the joy you may feel during peak times (by adding the dread of losing the high). Further, without being fully valued, the valleys frequently last longer.

The key is to see the valleys as Prepeaks. They are the harbingers of your next breakthrough and rise to new insight. The best way to convert the downs of your life into positive prepeaks is to use the Joy Touch and Comforting Connection in the four stage process below.

Joy Touch (to mood elevate and get out of just being down),

Comfort (identify the core issue that wants resolution),

Grow (learn a new perspective and/or insight for life mastery),

and Go On (apply it in your life and enjoy your next peak).

Lifeskills & Countering Put-Downs

Lifeskills - Any quality you can focus on for valuing yourself.

<u>Examples of Lifeskills</u>

Effort
Caring
Courage
Initiative
Creativity
Sensitivity
Teamwork
Motivation
Confidence
Perseverance
Responsibility
Determination
Common Sense
Problem Solving

Regardless of your results you can always value yourself for your effort, your initiative, or your perseverance, etc.

Countering Put-Downs with Put-ups based on lifeskills

Give yourself a put-up when you yourself, or someone else, criticizes you. Let the put-up (based on lifeskills) neutralize the acid of the critical put-down.

Example - Criticism: You never do it well enough.

Put-Up: I'm proud of myself for my effort (or initiative, perseverance, caring, courage, or sensitivity, etc) in trying.

Look to give Put-ups to your significant others

Even if you have different styles or values, you can always give others a put-up for some lifeskill and help them to feel valued.

Approaches for Countering Depression

For Mild Depression the key is to **do the Joy Touch regularly** throughout the day. Identify specific times (before, during, and/or after stressful and/or disappointing situations) when you need mood-elevation to prevent a slow slide into malaise.

Also important is using the Comforting Connection to clear repetitive cycles of negativity, by identifying what you need and how to give it to yourself.

For Prolonged Despondency, a more **comprehensive approach** is required. Use any or all of the options below.

Joy Touch regularly **and often.**

Joy Touch in Motion to get you moving and prevent staying down.

Joy Touch more from the left side to magnify the effect.

Joy Touch from above to connect with Soul and greater hope.

Immediately counter negative thoughts with Put-Ups.

Get rest and sleep.

Never get too hungry, too angry, too lonely, or too tired (H.A.L.T.)

Use creative imagery to recharge your brain chemistry.

For Severe Clinical Depression, it is best to **get professional help.** Don't try to do it all on your own. You can use the Joy Touch and the steps listed above to enhance and assist whatever treatment the appropriate professionals recommend.

Gender Strengths for Relationship Issues

Both gender principles have strengths. Identify what aspects of the masculine and the feminine principles you value and admire.

Each of us has the ability to reflect the best of both principles. We each have a masculine and feminine side. Regardless of the gender of your body, you are a Soul and can tap the best of both the masculine and the feminine perspectives.

The medicine wheel concept helps you integrate all your strengths. It provides a way to think from each of the different perspectives (masculine, feminine, and Soul).

For solving relationship issues a rounded perspective is crucial. It helps you to see all sides and to better work as a team to meet each person's needs.

The technique of four chairs gives you a method for self-channeling insight, by speaking from each of the different perspectives. Chair 1 - State the problem. Chair 2 - Speak from the perspective of your gender's strengths. Chair 3 - Speak from the perspective of the opposite gender's strengths. Chair 4 - What is the Soul perspective or that of a higher power on the issue? Chair 1 again, if you want to restate the issue and repeat the process, or pursue a deeper level of the issue.

Basics of the Soul Shift

With eyes closed, focus on your lower legs (feet, ankles, calves).

Shift your focus up through the body (knees, hips, waist, chest).

When you get to the head area, shift up one more level.

Let your awareness be in the space above the head.

Focus your attention there, don't force concentration.

Feel how that part of you feels more extensive, more peaceful.

Notice how you can sense in all directions.

Stretch your awareness to the corner of the room.

See if you can stretch even beyond the room.

When ready to come back, focus your awareness above the head.

Shift your focus down into the head area.

Feel your eyes, then your arms, legs, hands, and feet.

Move your fingers or wiggle your toes to fully ground yourself.

When you feel comfortable, open your eyes.

Soul-Blending Options

Blending with Matter
Helps you to feel more a part of your environment and at peace.

Focus on sinking into the chair and it coming up to join you.

Blending with Energy (Light)
Helps you to extend beyond the limits of matter.

Feel the light's gentle pressure and warmth. Sense the energy as it passes around you, and even through you. Then ride the rays of light, blending with everything they touch.

Blending with the Universe
Creates a feeling of greater oneness with all things.
Puts you more closely in touch with the infinite.

Blend outward in stages. First blend with the chair you are sitting in, next the light and the room, then finally, beyond the room extending step by step to the planet, the solar system, the galaxy and eventually the Universe (and beyond).

Blending with the Dimension of Love Energy
Puts you in touch with the essence and energy of love.
Fills your being with love.

Hold in mind your associations with love energy, the feelings, the colors you think of, the words and thoughts that represent love to you. Let those associations draw you into the dimension of love energy, blending you with its specific frequency and harmony.

Secrets for Feeling Successful All the Time

Identify your periodicity of need for perceived success.
How often do you need to *feel* successful to be happy (monthly, weekly, daily, hourly). Give yourself a feeling of success at least that often (put-up, self-praise, recognition of what you have done, etc.), whether or not you have completed an actual accomplishment.

Identify what your true values are.
Don't let lack of full success, in an area that is not your personal life choice, dominate your happiness. Out of the 100 energy points in the Value Analysis, what were your priorities? Focus on being and feeling successful there.

Focus on the "Why", not the "What" of your want.
Identify the reasons behind your want and address those needs, not just the surface thing or accomplishment. You want to do well at something because you want to feel proud of yourself. Focus on feeling proud of yourself, etc.

Be a "Good Boss" to yourself.
Treat yourself as you would like to be treated (praised, encouraged, allowed to be flexible instead of judged, criticized, rigidly limited, etc).

Play at it, don't work at it.
Strive to have things "work out," not to make them work (turn them into struggle pressure). Find ways to be creative with the way you work, so that it is enjoyable (has variety, challenge, and fun).

Cherish your uniqueness as a Soul.
Remember you are the best you there is, and that you are always doing the best you know how. Cherish the beauty and value you have as a unique, one-of-a-kind Soul.

Five Simple Steps for Weight Control

Step 1: Feel Good About What You Eat

Enjoy the preparation time for meals.

Savor the aroma of your meals.

Cherish each bite of your food.

Step 2: Wait Control (Eat Slower & Avoid Bingeing)

Say a heartfelt blessing before each meal.

Joy Touch between bites.

Joy Touch 3 times before going to a snack bar or into temptation.

Step 3: Care About Your Diet, Not Worry About Your Weight

Invest your energy in picking nutritional low-fat foods.

Drink plenty of fluids.

Focus on your health and fitness - (exercise, exercise, exercise).

Step 4: Value Yourself, Not Your Size

Praise yourself for your efforts, not just the speed of your results.

Counter appearance criticism with appreciation of the real you.

Step 5: You Control Your Weight, Don't Let It Control You

Joy Touch to manage your moods and your waistline will follow.

Get plenty of food for the Soul and create your own happiness.

Joy Touch Variations for Pain Control

In General - Doing the Joy Touch not only can counter pain through its mood-elevation effect, but also through its distraction factor. The mental process of triggering the septal area forces you to focus on something other than the pain.

For Headaches - Trigger the septal area from a direction that is different than the area of the headache.

For Throbbing Pain - Trigger the septal area to the rhythm of the throb. Do the Joy Touch in pulses and time each pulse to the throb of the pain.

For Migraines - Use the Joy Touch as a distraction from the pain, something that takes your mind off of it. For throbbing migraines also use the techniques described for throbbing pain. If you get an "aura" before the onset of a migraine, do the Joy Touch immediately to lessen your tension and stop the migraine before it starts. In general doing the Joy Touch from above works best for migraines (unless that is the location of the migraine).

For Dental Work and/or Pain - Do the Joy Touch to start off relaxed and less on edge. Use it also to lessen the discomfort from having your mouth stretched and prodded. For actual pain, use triggering the septal area as a distraction and/or pulse the Joy Touch to the throbbing of the pain.

For Back Pain - Do the Joy Touch before moving to relax your muscles so that tension doesn't magnify the intensity of your pain. Trigger the septal area during pain to counter it. If the pain is throbbing do the Joy Touch in pulses to the rhythm of the throb.

For Severe or Chronic Pain - Send healing thoughts and energies along with the Joy Touch. Focus on doing something other than just surviving the pain.

Joy Touch Specifics for Reducing Smoking

When You Get a Craving:

Joy Touch several times to lessen your emotional anxiety.

Do the Joy Touch as you breath in, instead of lighting up.

Try not to feel deprived (that will just make you want to smoke).

Know that you can choose not to smoke for the time being.

Go thru all the cigarette rituals, but Joy Touch instead of smoking.

If You Must Light Up:

Do the Joy Touch first to lessen the deep puff urge.

Joy Touch between puffs, so each puff can be shorter.

Use the Joy Touch to put out the cigarette before it is done.

With Nicotine Gum:

Use the gum when you get a nicotine craving.

Do the Joy Touch to soothe emotional anxieties.

Plan Ahead For Countering Trigger Times:

Identify them: at work, after meals, first thing in morning, etc.

Do the Joy Touch before them to lessen their triggering effect.

Joy Touch Keys for Lessening Alcohol Abuse

Pick a nonalcoholic beverage and Joy Touch as you drink it.

Joy Touch before leaving work to clear the day's stress.

Do the Joy Touch before going into the drinking environment.

Enjoy the celebration, but use the Joy Touch for feeling better.

If you must have an alcoholic beverage, drink slower.

Joy Touch three times before your first sip to prevent gulping.

Do the Joy Touch between sips.

Allow yourself to not finish the whole drink.

Don't feel deprived (it will just make you want to drink more).

Know that you can choose to feel good, without as much alcohol.

Resolve to resist fattening the wallets of the alcohol industry.

Joy Touch and celebrate your new level of control / moderation.

Maintain your emotional balance. Remember H.A.L.T.

Never get too Hungry, too Angry, too Lonely, or too Tired.

Joy Touch regularly throughout the day and during stresses.

Don't use relapses as an excuse to binge drink.

Joy Touch to stop and feel good about the progress you have made.

Joy Touch Assistance for Drug Abuse

Seek Professional Help.

Serious drug or alcohol abuse requires all the resources available.

Joy Touch to help motivate yourself to get full treatment.

Weave the Joy Touch into your treatment and/or therapy.

Use the Joy Touch to feel better and counter cravings to "get high".

Joy Touch to positively reinforce yourself for your abstinence.

Maintain your emotional balance. Remember H.A.L.T.

Never get too Hungry, too Angry, too Lonely, or too Tired.

Joy Touch regularly throughout the day and during stresses.

Use the hand-touch version during strong pressures.

If a drug craving starts to overwhelm you (Joy Touch instead).

Joy Touch as you take a substance-free deep breath.

Joy Touch as you treat yourself to a special nonalcoholic drink.

If you do relapse, Joy Touch to reduce guilt and try again.

Joy Touch to stop and feel good about the progress you have made.

Joy Touch and identify what you want to do differently next time.

Keys for Nobly Bearing Life's Difficulties

Remember that everyone has challenges.

Don't let the scenery of your problems win.

Never surrender your freedom to control your attitude.

Resolve to rise above the "animal" reaction to difficulties.

Handle your stresses from a Soul perspective.

Deal with your troubles with Honor and a Noble Spirit.

Model what you want your children to emulate.

How to Reach Free Soul

Contact Free Soul National Headquarters to:

1.) Receive information about other self-study materials.

2.) Get the phone numbers of Instructors near you.

3.) Find out about Pete Sanders' traveling schedule.

4.) Learn about the next National Retreat in Sedona, Arizona.

5.) Be on Free Soul's mailing list.

For any or all of the above, write to:

Free Soul
P.O. Box 1762
Sedona, AZ 86339

You can also find us on the internet at:

http://freesoul.net

(See next page for additional training options.)

Additional Free Soul Training Options

The Dynamics of Being a Free Soul Comprehensive Course

A 10-Lesson, 80 technique integrated course that step-by-step helps you develop your unlimited potentials for mind/body healing, Soul awareness, self-understanding, practical psychic sensitivity, and clearing limiting conditioning and programming.

Available as:

1.) a self-study 200+ page Textbook.

2.) audio version [12 X 90 min. cassettes].

3.) an Instructor-led course (10 X 3-hour lessons).

Access Your Brain's Joy Center Workshops

Beginning and Advanced programs on the Joy Touch and Comforting Connection techniques led by Pete Sanders and/or local instructors. [Options available tailored for specific needs, i.e. weight control, reducing smoking, etc.]

Also available as Business Training for:

1.) employee stress reduction.

2.) making the workplace more enjoyable.

3.) improved job performance and reduced absenses.

Discover *"Inner Technology"* ® Workshops

Beginning and Advanced programs by Pete Sanders and/or local instructors on mind/body healing, higher mental potentials, enhanced intuition, and exploring dimensions beyond.

Also available as Business Training for:

1.) maximizing mind/body potential.

2.) enhanced creativity and decision making.

3.) understanding/managing the various perceptual types.

Scientific Vortex Information **Booklet or Book and Tape**
Advanced Workshop Tapes (Various Topics)
Free Soul Reflections (Weekly Meditations & Self-Journal)

(See preceding page for how to reach Free Soul.)